IN 1918 the Volunteers were in a sta[ ] were very few people who could or [ ] whole time to helping the army – no[ ] think. I was attached to Organisation Staff under Michael Collins. I never received instructions, memos, or help. I was told to organise a county, given the address of someone on the Brigade Staff who might not be at home when I called – then I was left to myself utterly.

The idea of working for another Rising such as '16 obsessed us; we did not think in terms of a guerrilla fight but gradually, through GHQ – and the RIC who also helped us to make up our minds – we began to recognise that a stand-up fight would not suit our country.

The RIC were the eyes of the British Army ... and often I wished our people were as loyal to the Republic as the RIC were to their masters. We had from centuries of oppression the faults of slaves, seldom their vices, and when one met men who were born free one thanked God for it. The girls too developed and broke away from strict parental discipline. This to my mind was the greatest innovation. The people were gradually drawn into the movement. One cannot write about the older women; they understood us so well and their great hearts reached out to us lonely and tired.

It was a people's war, that is why we fought so well as from November 1920. The people understood, they made allowances, and there was need for that.

Unpublished notes by Ernie O'Malley

ERNIE O'MALLEY

RAIDS AND RALLIES

ANVIL BOOKS LIMITED

First published in hardback in 1982 by
Anvil Books Limited
45 Palmerston Road, Dublin 6
Paperback edition 1985
This edition 2001

2 4 6 5 3

© Cormac K. H. O'Malley 1982

All rights reserved. No part of this publication may
be reproduced, stored in a retrieval system or
transmitted, in any form or by any means, electronic,
mechanical, photocopying, recording or otherwise,
without the prior permission of Anvil Books.

ISBN 1 901737 28 4

Typesetting by Computertype Limited
Printed by Colour Books Limited

CONTENTS

	Introduction	7
1	The Sack of Hollyford Barracks May 1920	11
2	Drangan Barracks June 1920	27
3	Rearcross Barracks July 1920	41
4	Rineen and Reprisals September 1920	67
5	The British Enforce Martial Law December 1920–January 1921	91
6	Ambush at Scramogue March 1921	100
7	Ambush at Tourmakeady May 1921	117
8	Modreeny May–June 1921	134
9	The Hard Road to Carrowkennedy May–June 1921	156
	Afterword April 1952	203
	Author	204
	Index	205

Maps: Ireland *(page 2)*, Rineen *(page 66)*, Scramogue *(105)*, South Mayo *(116)*, Tourmakeady *(133)*, Modreeny *(140)*, North Mayo *(157)*, Kilmeena *(164)*, Carrowkennedy *(187)*.

INTRODUCTION

There are the general histories of the 1919-21 war in Ireland, usually incorporated within political histories of the period, and there are the long memories of its guerrilla fighters with their own accounts of localised actions against the British Crown. One of those veterans of the Irish Republican Army was Ernie O'Malley, whose determined part in the fight for Irish freedom from 1916 to 1924 has already been told in his published two-volume coverage of those years.

In *Raids and Rallies* are descriptions of some eight important offensives by the Republican Army against the British power in Ireland at that time, and in its detailed accounts of IRA actions, strategy and motivations is explanation for that Army's success until 1921. It may be said to have been written on behalf of the local rank-and-file fighting men.

Ernie O'Malley was well qualified to write of the two climatic years of the War of Independence — or the Tan War as he together with others would name it. At his death in 1957 it was said that 'he had made himself in the last twenty years and more the historian of the Resistance.' He first became a young Irish Volunteer in 1916 following the heroic failure of the Easter Rising in Dublin, abandoning his medical studies at University to enlist as an HQ field officer who travelled the country areas and took part in any military operations that could be generated.

The British Government's executions in 1916 of the leaders of the Rising, followed by the impact of the prisoners issue, had led to a further resurgence of Irish nationalism. Wholesale political arrests, the violence of British troops and armed Royal Irish Constabulary in the suppression of separatist and cultural organisations — Sinn Féin, the Irish Volunteers, the Gaelic

League and Cumann na mBan, the women's organisation — the deportation of separatist leaders, and then undoubtedly the threat of conscription at a time of crisis in the Great War had helped to win a decisive all-Ireland 73-seat victory for Sinn Fein, the separatist party, in the general election of December 1918.

Since the Rising, disorder and bloodshed in the country had been the work of Crown forces. John Dillon, the Irish Parliamentary Party leader and inveterate enemy of Sinn Fein, declared that Ireland was 'lying under the unfettered tyranny of a military government'. Yet no policeman, no British soldier had been killed, but a majority of the Irish people had grown to put their trust in Sinn Féin. On January 21, 1919, the twenty-six available Sinn Féin Deputies (forty-five were in British gaols) met in Dublin and proclaimed the first Dáil Government of a free Ireland. On the same day at Soloheadbeg in Co. Tipperary, Irish Republican volunteers seized a cart load of gelignite, and the armed escort of two Royal Irish constables were killed in the attack. Three of those at Soloheadbeg, Seán Treacy, Dan Breen and Séamus Robinson, take part in the first chapter of *Raids and Rallies* when they join Ernie O'Malley in the attack on the police barracks at Hollyford, Co. Tipperary. The first three chapters of the book enlarge and supplement the three attacks on RIC country barracks already recounted in his own story of the Tan War where he, as a Staff Captain accountable only to HQ in Dublin, had overall command. In subsequent chapters O'Malley writes of actions where he did not himself take part and was therefore dependent on the information supplied to him by those who had been involved in operations. However, his first-hand knowledge of similar events, his comradeship with some of those most actively involved, together with judgements formed from the hundreds of interviews he had conducted with so many former IRA men in the years after his return to Ireland in 1935, allowed him to check and assess from particular experience.

This book is unlike his previous Irish war memoirs in that it does not wholly deal directly with his own part in it. His first book was acclaimed by a noted American critic as 'the outstanding literary achievement of the Anglo-Irish war' (*On Another Man's Wound*, first published 1936; latest publication 1979). His second was *The Singing Flame* (1978 and 1979) described amongst many other tributes as 'destined to become the classic of the great tragedy that was the civil war'. After the first three chapters of *Raids and Rallies* it is not his own story, though much of the author of the 1916-24 memoirs remains throughout, with his thoughts and opinions, his reactions to the reprisals by both sides, his decided expectation for courses of action.

Some parts of this book appeared in the *Sunday Press* (Dublin) newspaper in a weekly series of well-publicised articles lasting from September 1955 to May 1956. For the purposes of present publication the episodes have been rearranged into a chronological order and additional material included from the parallel versions that O'Malley wrote or drafted during the last years of his life.

1920-21 were the years when it was Lloyd George's declared policy for Ireland to 'fight murder with murder', and to do so the British Government recruited in England the Black-and-Tans and the Auxiliaries. Because of the policy of criminalisation, the British were obliged to claim that only police measures were needed in Ireland, with all their additional military forces proclaimed as official off-shoots of the Irish police and in Ireland only to assist in maintaining law and order. Accordingly the British Government made maximum use of its powerful forces in attempts to defeat the IRA. There were the Black and Tans, so called because of the mixture of English khaki and RIC black (or bottle green) in their uniforms and equipment, and the superior ranks of the Auxiliary 'cadets' formed by ex-officers from Army, Navy and Air Force; together with undercover agents and military intelligence, but all of them having to rely on almost total support from the regular Royal Irish Constabulary police force. Also significant was the assistance of those in the population who either by impulse or design have always acted as the disparate pro-British elements in Ireland.

In turn the IRA depended first on their own determination

and resiliance, and then on active support or passive allegiance from those in whose community they operated, especially in the rural areas. There was indeed a much greater and more widespread surge of popular feeling throughout Ireland for the IRA men of 1919-21 than for any other armed combat in the 'six times during the last three hundred years', based as it was on resentment of the British presence and commensurate sympathy for 'the boys'. And yet it was still as Ernie O'Malley was to state bluntly to Cathal Brugha, Republican Minister for Defense of the second Dáil Government in the days before impending civil war, and was called to order for it: 'If we had consulted the wishes of the people we would never have fired a shot.'

While *Raids and Rallies* stresses the common cause of a people against an alien government and its alien law-and-order forces, it also underlines what condemnation there was of the 'war of independence' at the time. Much of it is familiar. There were the thunderous editorials of the daily press, the pronouncements of the Catholic Church Hierarchy, and the pressures of establishment propaganda. A valid account of an Irish freedom struggle can hardly be disclosed in contemporary reports. It needs must wait for a further stage of the resistance. These accounts of warfare in several Irish counties of the West and Midlands by Ernie O'Malley, who was to die an unrepentant Republican, collected by him so many years later, in different times, in a different national climate and therefore acceptable, contain the vital resistance of yesterday and possible interpretations for today.

FRANCES-MARY BLAKE 1982

CHAPTER ONE

THE SACK OF HOLLYFORD BARRACKS

MAY 1920

At the end of the first week in May, 1920, Séamus Robinson, Seán Treacy and I were in the 2nd battalion of the South Tipperary Brigade. Robinson was Brigade Commandant and Treacy was his Vice-Commandant. They had come around with me as I went from one battalion to another, inspecting companies, holding officers' classes or ordering sudden night mobilisations of half-battalions under arms. I had been attempting as well to establish an organised intelligence service, but reports even of the enemy strengths in each company area, or the plans of barracks, had been difficult to obtain from officers. We could and did sketch barracks by ourselves, but the first need was for the company officers to view and appreciate the strength and weakness of the British posts in their area. Not since I was in the two most northerly battalions of North Clare over a year ago had I two brigade officers who would spend their whole time with me as each battalion was thoroughly investigated and recorded. We stayed in Glenough among the hills where there was a number of good men.

One evening Ned Reilly and Jack the Master came to see me. They were really trying to sum me up according to their standard, as I afterwards found out, for they had been instructed by an assistant member of the Brigade staff to keep things quiet in the area whilst I was working in it. They intended to attack a police patrol on the following morning and they had come to tell me about their project. I offered at once, to their surprise, to go with them. They left somewhat mollified at this unexpected eagerness from a Staff officer and they agreed to call me early the next morning, but they did not do so. Nor did I mention their proposal to the two Brigade officers until the men returned with their story. The attack had duly taken place near

Clonoulty and the sergeant of the patrol was killed, but a constable who had escaped was able to recognise the men who had been present. Their descriptions were soon to appear in *The Hue-and-Cry*, the Police Gazette. As a result of these events we expected that the police or military would soon raid the entire district for the wanted men, and all of us kept ourselves in readiness for possible developments, that day, May 9th. We were armed and we could fight, but the routine staff investigation work in the area had to go on, no matter what threat lay outside the approaches to the hills.

We had discussed barrack attacks as we visited the battalions, but it was thought advisable to first reorganise each area thoroughly, making it especially aware of British military and police movements by train, lorry and on foot, so that each battalion would be better able to combat enemy aggression when it began its own activities, and its organisation could be maintained in spite of losses in officers and men through raids. The company areas bordering on Rossmore had now five or six men under arms. Some had rifles, and this number added to those of Brigade officers made up a small column. The foundation of what was called an Active Service Reserve had been discussed by us and I had taken men for a few day's training course. It was thought that in each battalion a similar small group could be organised and trained at regular intervals. It could form a basis for united action with men from border areas, and it would concentrate the energy of men who might otherwise become aimless. This group was, in effect, the genesis of a column, but the idea was not developed in the Brigade. Men now carried their rifles openly and that in itself was an innovation and a welcome change. The hill country people had learned not to talk save among themselves, and this reticence was an additional protection. They watched in amazed wonder the armed men who cycled towards Hollyford.

Hollyford lies snugly amid hills in the valley of the Multeen river, on an old road from Nenagh to Tipperary town. To the north the way leads through the mountains for more than twelve miles, but southward the narrow valley which confines the road and river opens out within a few miles.

THE SACK OF HOLLYFORD BARRACKS 13

That evening, Robinson, Treacy and I discussed Hollyford barracks with the company captain and the local battalion commandant in Shanahan's house which was on the roadside beyond Glenough and close to the village. Phil Shanahan kept a public house and it had been a refuge to South Tipp men despite the risk to them and its owner. His pub was one of three famous haunts of men who met each other in a casual way among strangers, but whose special rooms were always at the service of the Irish Republican Army. Phil had always been generous as a host and he parted easily with his money.

The barracks, we were told, was a well-built, isolated house. Its defences had been prepared by British sappers who had been moving from post to post during the spring. They had cut out loopholes at gable-ends and on communicating inside walls. They had added steel shutters to the windows and had strengthened doors with steel. The barracks was built on rising ground and was of considerable height. There were low walls some distance away which gave cover, and the one gable-end had an open space near it.

I saw the barracks at dusk, but darkness seemed to increase its height as it looked down on the river and the houses below, as a symbol of armed authority. There was a lean-to structure in the rear, attached to it. The gable-end to the south had whitethorn bushes and a fence a short distance away from it. In front a porch stuck out and it was said to be loopholed. There was a small walled enclosure beyond the porch, which could be reached by police hand grenades. The northern gable looked out on to sloping ground, and there was a gully fifteen feet away beyond the roadway which led uphill towards Glenough.

The three of us discussed an attack on this post, and although there were other barracks easier to attempt, yet it was time to make a start. Robinson and Treacy had been already tested in many ways, but they had never taken part in an attempt on a post. I had worked out attacks in North Clare and in Finglas in North County Dublin in 1920, but I had to leave the areas before any plans were put into action. Proposed methods had then varied between heavy bombs, incendiary mixtures and the use of explosives. In Monaghan in February I had taken part in an attempt on the barracks at Ballytrain. On that occasion I had incendiary material which included jars of phosphorus ready to use on the roof in case the heavy explosives failed to detonate. The one end-wall of the post had abutted on a large store and the partition wall on the top storey had been cut and then mined. The explosion blew in the wall, the barracks was rushed and its rifles and equipment were captured.

It was decided to begin the attack on Hollyford by blowing in the northern gable. Already we had ordered all explosives in the battalion and all arms and ammunition in the surrounding companies to be sent in to us for inspection. When the gelignite arrived, it was found that most of the sticks, which resembled the 'Peggy's leg' that was sold at patterns, were frozen. The main bulk of it had been captured at Soloheadbeg in January of 1919 and it was then hidden in a hurry. The countryside had been carefully searched for the men who killed the escort on the quarry supplies, and it had been difficult to look after the booty. Often enough an open bank might contain a wooden box; a loose board in an outhouse might serve as the entrance to a hideout, and cold-wall contact would not only shelter the gelignite but also keep it frozen. There were, however, some sticks which had been taken in a raid on Thurles in 1917 and these, although small in quantity, were good enough for immediate use.

The frozen gelignite was placed in tin cans in boiling water inside iron pots close to the fire in Shanahan's kitchen, while detonators and fuse were examined. As I watched the softening of the beige sticks I was careful. I had learned enough about the process to avoid the headsplitting pain that would result from too close a contact with the gas given off by thawing explosives, which could render a man incapable of active work for five or six hours. If the explosive was well tamped, demolition force would be directed against the gable, and from my calculations we had sufficient gelignite to blow in a fairly decent hole. Tamping meant sandbags, which would have to be carried on the backs of men and then quietly placed against and around the explosive close to the butt of the wall. Tamping would need time and very silent movement so as not to disturb the policeman who was expected to be on night duty inside the room close to the gable.

Jim Gorman, who had once served in the Australian Army, came to see us. He had deserted when he came home on leave, and since he had been posted as a deserter he was liable to arrest, but friends and neighbours helped him to keep a wary watch for peelers. He had worked for farmers below the slopes of Slievecamalta and had taught hill companies a rigorous training in the use of ground to conceal a slow advance while he watched and made the men repeat what had often seemed to them a welldone movement. He was now a lieutenant in the Hollyford company, tolerant of untrained men, in the easy freedom of the hills. He was a fine shot, more inclined to do a thing than ask his men to do it; assured, yet reserved. There was a laconic sense in the hills which was chary of talk; it entered into humour and it surrounded the good men like a mountain wall. Though not a regular ballad-maker, yet he strung rhymes together on occasions. This use of ballad was a hill tradition which fostered and spread song.

Below Mauherslieve, *An Fánuidhe Aerac*, as Paddy Walsh was called, had taught Irish classes, for years. Relying, as had Jim Gorman, on the kindness of the people and the safety of the mountains, when some other areas between 1917 and 1919 had made ample use of their tongues, I had spent many an hour with him as he puzzled out the derivations of surrounding placenames, for that was his delight. He it was who had instructed some of the Upperchurch men in the use of a rifle which they had captured in Kilcommon. He had been conscripted in England, but had deserted from a garrison in Cahirciveen in 1917 and had brought his rifle with him. He was a good balladmaker and his verses gave an additional incentive to the singing word.

Gorman's blue eyes shafted out of his brown-textured skin as he listened to our plans. Abruptly he said: 'You might as well try to shift the Rock of Cashel with that gelignite, for the inside of the barracks is six feet above the outside level.' That information made nonsense of our plans. Props could have been used to raise the explosives on a small platform, but it would mean a Heath Robinson contrivance, with the odds of success in favour of the garrison. The alternative was to set fire to the barracks by the use of petrol and paraffin. As supplies of both were short, they had to be sent on from Tipperary to Hollyford creamery where they could be convenient for use next day.

We were in a hurry to attack because the round-up, which we expected as a result of the killing of the sergeant, might come suddenly, and anyhow it was as well to have a plan quickly carried out.

Jack Ryan the Master, Ned Reilly and Jim Gorman had already been with a few men from the hill companies at attacks in Mid Tipp areas, but none of these ventures was successful. It was the habit in the hill country, which touched on four brigades, East Limerick, North Tipp, Mid and South Tipp, to help one another. The men of the hills had confidence in each other, a tendency to roam the mountains and a reluctance to remain on the plains. Hollyford company itself touched at three brigade boundaries, but the speed with which the attack was launched obviated the presence of friendly groups, save a few men from Doon battalion in East Limerick.

May 11th was the date fixed for the attack and all during that day Shanahan's house became a busy workshop where rifles, shotguns and revolvers were carefully examined and cleaned. Hand grenades were stripped and put together again; refilled shotgun cartridges were dried and rifle cartridges examined for mould and dirt. Soon weapons were burnished brightly. Houses had already been ransacked for empty mustard, cocoa and snuff tins to be used in the making of improvised grenades.

I made bursting charges by packing gelignite into tin cans. When the charge was exploded against the barracks roof, areas of slate would be blown away, and in addition there would be the sudden concussion in the darkness which would help to disconcert the police. There were long light sticks which were cut into lengths, to be attached to these tins to enable them to be moved along the roof. When dropped through gaping holes they could keep the police at a distance as their blast would affect bone as well as nerve. Seán Treacy made improvised grenades by using tin cans packed with scraps of broken iron pots which when detonated would spread around as shrapnel. Bolts and screws at either end had to add sufficient holding power to keep the tins taut, as we had no time to make them more thoroughly resistant by the addition of solder. The people of the house were full of wonderment at our doings. They watched us eagerly as we cut up fuse, crimped it into detonators, and added to our pile of tin cans.

The barracks chimney was about forty feet from the ground, but the southern gable, which was lower, could not be made use of simultaneously, as the whitethorn hedge and a fence interfered with the moving of a ladder into position there. We had thought that incendiary liquid could be carried up at either gable. The forty-foot height was an obstacle as there was no ladder of sufficient length to top that distance. Luckily there was a mason in the Hollyford company who had been a sailor and who had also worked as a slater. He inspected the local ladders which were all in good condition, and from them jointed four ladders with ropes in intricate knots learned on land and at sea. They were difficult to lift upright on high as they seemed to have a tenuous life of their own, and they were hard to carry forward when they were upright, to be placed against a high wall.

I supervised this ladder drill with a section of the men until with patient practice their number was reduced to the safety limit of the few who were to manipulate the ladders later in the night. The ladders' top portions waved irresolutely like lobster antennae, and their weight was difficult to control and to move forward side by side in trial assaults on Shanahan's gable. The rehearsals looked like a circus troop stealthily preparing for an opening night in an important town.

In the interval of rest in the long May twilight, the ladders lay side by side on the ground in a narrow bohereen. Two men, one of whom was from an outlying company, were on the road looking down from a rise. They saw the ladders glistening in the half-light. Their reported conversation may have been apocryphal in the laconic humour of the hills, but it gave us an additional laugh.

'What are they doing down below there?' asked one of the men, as he saw a group spread out to lift an object below him.

'They're taking up the railway — can't you see?'

'What railway, are you codding?'

'Faith, I'm not. It's the main line to Kilcommon they're at.'

Séamus Robinson and I decided to mount the ladders. Seán Treacy was to supervise the men on the ground around the barracks and he was to receive regular reports from the outposts at a pre-arranged centre near the village.

We two would have to be as self-contained as possible, as it might be difficult when we got beyond the lower loopholes to get down again by the ladders. The upper loopholes could be quickly dealt with if the police did not hear our preparations, for they could be eliminated when the inside floor was set on fire. We strapped and unstrapped loads on our backs and sides until we looked like prospectors in the Alaskan gold rush.

Jim Gorman was to take charge of men near our gable-end, and he could fire at the loophole flashes. Treacy, at the beginning, was to keep in front of the building, under cover of the low wall. There were a few men to the rear and to the flank beyond the other gable. After the initial volleys to disconcert the police, Treacy was to see that ammunition was very sparingly used and that the supplies of combustible material and explosives were brought up towards our gable. Ned Reilly and Jack Ryan had a roving freedom which suited their temperaments.

At last we were content enough with arrangements. Sufficient petrol had not been sent on, but there was a good store of paraffin. There was an ample supply of bursting charges and improvised grenades, with a useful reserve of gelignite for emergencies. Weapons now shone in the lamplight. We washed and shaved before we left the house with a warm feeling of fitness and grateful remembrance of the hospitality of the people who had given their house to be used as an improvised and dangerous workshop.

Before we moved against the barracks I visited the different outpost positions and spoke to the company officers in charge of them. I wanted to satisfy myself about the dispositions and that orders had been thoroughly understood. Jim Gorman was with me on the road to Milestone. There did not seem to be much material available there for roadblocks, except old boulders, stones and banks of earth. 'It'll be all right, don't worry. They'll throw the road over the ditch', said Gorman, pointing to a pile of picks, crowbars and shovels by the roadside. Telegraph wires would be cut at a specified time. Hollyford police post would then be cut off from outside support. Quickly we moved down towards the barracks. Some distance away, the ladder party took off their boots, and the covering party for flank and front went on ahead in the darkness.

Séamus Robinson and I tested our swinging weights and adjusted our network of ropes, but I felt like a Christmas tree loaded down with unwelcome presents and prickled with the rough edges of determination. We went in front to cover the lower loopholes with revolvers, while picked men from the Rossmore company hoisted the ladders in the air and moved them forward until they seemed to close together. There were stray whispers and straining breaths which seemed to beat through the barracks wall as we waited. I climbed my ladder as Séamus began to mount his rungs, but I had to come down again. It had to be shifted to lie against the top of the chimney and yet be close enough to the other ladder so that we could help each other in case we were either wounded or severely burned. I whispered to the men to get away behind cover but they would not move from the base of the ladder until I had reached the roof edge where I found Séamus had begun to burst in the slates. We each had a two-gallon petrol tin tied on our backs, and five or six sods of turf which had been well soaked in paraffin. There were five bursting charges in my haversack, two Mills grenades, a few of the improvised grenade tins, lengths of fuse, detonators and a pliers. We carried two revolvers each, a pouch of ammunition and a strong hammer tied to our left wrists. We crawled across the roof; then, as we smashed hard with our hammers on the slates, we heard our riflemen open up below.

I threw in a hand grenade through a gap and I heard the crash of Séamus's missile almost at the same time. Petrol was poured in through the rough-edged holes. Lighted matches were held against our sods of turf which flamed up noisily and quickly caught the dripping petrol in a roar of leaping light. With a sudden blast, fire thrust back and forward on the roof in a growing wind.

We made as much use as we could of hammers as we moved on along the slates. Splinters and wedges of slates chipped up at us and we could not be sure whether this was due to our hammers or to the rifles of the police beneath us. I lighted the fuse of a bursting charge which I slid on its flat side along in front of me. Then I kept my head between my arms so as to avoid the sharp edges of slate that would be sent flying by the blast of the explosion. Nothing happened, so I raised my head just in time to stop a flying splinter with my forehead, for I thought the glowing fuse must have been wrongly cut. I had timed it to burn for two seconds, and when I had slung it forward I counted up to three, but I had evidently counted too fast. We poured in more petrol, but the slates burnt to the touch and flames jumped up quickly out of the darkness. Very lights shot up in a mounting curve as signals for police reinforcements lighted up the surrounding hills in a prolonged flash of lightning. Police were firing in our direction from the lean-to building, and seemingly from the rooms further back in the main building.

I moved up to the chimney and as I reached the top I found that it was covered with cement. Here was a convenient platform from which to fire downwards through the roof with a revolver, but a very inconvenient seat if the police replied by using their rifles up through the flue. I lay flat to steady my aim as I fired, or sat dangling my legs on the edge. Afterwards I was told that when I fired rapidly my hand could be seen against the blaze which mounted higher.

Below us, Jim Gorman watched the lower loopholes as he fired at rifle flashes. Then he carried across buckets of petrol which Séamus brought up on his ladder. We splashed the liquid across the roof, and by this time we were both soaked with incendiary fluid. Our hands had been burned by the flames which had been blown to and fro by the wind and the vacuum eddies. My face was blistered and sore and I could smell my burning hair. When I looked at Séamus I could not help laughing, for he had a halo of fire on his tufted head and shadow lights played on his face which was a cross between the face of a bruised prizefighter and that of a chimney sweep. When he heard my laughter he turned his startled, black-minstrel eyes upwards. Then he laughed himself at our increasing masquerade.

The chimney platform was about eight feet above Séamus' ladder-top. As I flung a grenade it caught in the eaves just at the moment when he was coming up the ladder with more petrol and was close to the roof edge. I shouted to him and he must have heard me. Luckily he was below the roof when the explosion came. It deafened him for a while.

If I had a rifle, I thought, I could send bullets into the lean-to down through the barracks roof and through the floor of the top storey. I went down for a Lee-Enfield and when I got back with it to the chimney I lay down with the sling to steady my shot and distributed impartial clips into the low building and, when I reversed my position, into the main building. Meanwhile, Séamus brought up further splashing buckets, and Jim Gorman carried some up as well. I was able to slosh their contents forwards for a considerable distance from my eyrie.

Seán Treacy watched the paraffin supply which was brought from the creamery to a house close to the barracks and then to the wall fronting the gable. That meant numerous journeys, as over fifty gallons of paraffin were used to keep the bonfire working. Once the fire had taken hold an odd shot was all that was necessary from the seven riflemen and the shotguns around the building. The police fired away at intervals as if the noise relieved their minds. They were hoping for reinforcements. We hoped that flames would leap towards the other gable, but the fire, as we found later, did not cross the partition wall. There was a coloured door on the second storey and although the floor close to it was burned away and the walls scorched, the emerald-green portal remained uninjured. Country people for weeks afterwards came to look at this national symbol in wonder.

Enemy reinforcements were a dangerous possibility, yet darkness formed a surrounding wall. Around us in a ring were Rearcross, Kilcommon and Shevry barracks to the north; Cappamore, Doon, Cappagh White, Annacarty to the west; Clonoulty, Dundrum, Roskeen to the south-east. The nearest strong barracks, Dundrum, which often held military, was somewhat over eight miles distant, and the military barracks at Tipperary and Templemore, which held battalion strengths, were fifteen and seventeen miles away. Nenagh, a smaller barracks, was nineteen miles from us. Police from smaller posts might hardly be inclined to move out into the countryside before dawn, yet during attacks elsewhere they had sent out patrols. Their principal difficulty was that they were seldom sure before morning what had been the decoy threat and where had been the real attempt. Long practice of night patrolling had made the constabulary men thoroughly familiar with local landmarks in darkness and they had already travelled every bohereen and lane which led up to a house. They could then cross the hills, guide military or lie in wait for Volunteers who might have entered the area from an outskirt company. In the darkness the effectiveness of weapons changed their values. A shotgun, with its unaimed and scattering fire, was the most important weapon, and even the amateur grenade had advantages which it could not prove in daylight. The rifle deprived of its sights lost accuracy, and the revolver was now more than ever for hand-to-hand fighting. The bayonet lost its threat because it should be seen before experienced and it required a sound knowledge to steady its advance. Rifle grenades and hand grenades would well serve a British approach in the darkness, as would controlled volley firing at close quarters. Noise, indeed from any weapon, had now a special psychological importance. The defensive ring could, however, move from one prepared position to another, and the well-armed attackers would have to rely on reconnaissance before they pushed onwards, and if even three shotgun men used their cartridges at the first onset a further advance would be slowed down. Transport would have to be parked a considerable distance away before infantry or cyclists made what might purport to be a noiseless advance. The countryside at night was no longer passive but was a real threat to the British. Any small obstruction such as a few strands of barbed wire, a collection of prickly whin bushes or a thick clump of whitethorn brambles became a considerable obstacle. The narrow valleys up and down towards Hollyford were an additional safeguard to our outer protective ring. Small heaps of stones scattered over a large stretch of road, tacks or slating nails for cyclists, and taut low wire could hold up reinforcements at a distance from defensive positions. Barricades of stones and felled trees close in to the posts attacked were now formidable obstacles, but the assurance of waiting country men who knew their ground well was the moving element which turned all these threats to enemy advance into an active menace. Police, when they were surrounded, had a trying time, as the initiative in all these attempts on posts was with the Volunteers on the outside, at least until the coming of dawn. The RIC would be kept in suspense about the next move which might come through a sudden explosion or by means of an unforeseen aspect of that disconcerting element, fire. Silence also could affect morale as it would surround them with an added uncertainty.

Prior to the Hollyford attack I had emphasized that there should be no shouting and, especially, no threats to the defenders during the action. As I sat on the chimney I heard a man shout at the police and then the refrain of the taunt was taken up as an echo: 'We'll have roast peeler for breakfast'. The next variation of the threat had an accompaniment of yells. Whatever inclination to surrender might have been wedging its way among the garrison, it was unlikely to gather impetus from this behaviour. Preparation for a meal at their expense would only make a reality of their carefully nurtured fears as to what their fate would be, should they fall into our hands. The only threat which I thought was of any use was our determination to capture the post.

Dawn came shortly after four o'clock and by this time there were great holes in the roof and a cavern of thick smoke beneath. What remained of the slates retained a fierce heat because of the smouldering rafters that supported them. We tried hard to get further along the roof but warm-edged gaps kept us at a distance. We tossed a small barrel of tar into the glow beneath, but instead of flame now came a dense black cloud which furled upwards. Our last three buckets of paraffin followed the tar through the roof. I slung mine forward from the chimney platform in spurts, and Séamus tried to make jets of his liquid supply. For a few moments, while we watched the roof, there was a quiet interval, then flames sprang violently to life again, yellow-red in licking spray. The wind drove them against the chimney and around the top of my ladder. They swirled about Séamus as well. I was cut off before I realised what was happening, and found myself unable to get down. My clothes took fire, and my hands, which were holding on to the cemented edge, had been frequently burned already so that the skin had contracted and I had little grip left in them. I felt that I might soon drop into the flames below me.

It is said that our subconscious mind takes control in moments of dire mental and physical stress, and that impressions are formed upon the screen of memory all unknown to us. These impressions seem, for some reason, to remain more indelibly etched upon our souls than those we gain in our more normal moments. So it was with me on that morning. I was about to die, I believed, and yet with no conscious effort on my own part my mind seemed to be busily noting the little inconsequential details that were taking place around me. I seemed to be a disinterested spectator of my own fate, a casual onlooker more concerned with observing the evolution of things about me than with facing the fact that my end was upon me. The many and complicated details of that scene remained stamped vividly upon my memory by an act of will entirely outside my control.

When I looked down, the small village was splintered with orange light which climbed up the sides of the houses and showed up the darkened hills which seemed to move as flames wavered. Light was reflected off windows while shadows edged the spattered illumination. It was a Caravaggio canvas, that scene which I firmly thought would be my last.

Séamus looked as if he had mounted his funeral pyre above this strange landscape. I knew suddenly that I could neither hold on to my ledge nor to the tattered edges of my will. 'Goodbye, Séamus', I shouted. He turned his face upwards. '*Slán leat, agus* —' but the remainder of his words were wrapped in fire.

Flames swayed and drifted as both of us held on to our

insecurity. Then with dramatic suddenness that matched the manner in which they had unleashed themselves at our positions, the flames darted off towards other points, leaving us with a clear way down. As I went down the ladder the rungs were suddenly free from the bright menace which had eddied away from both of us.

I met Séamus opposite to me as I went slowly down. His hair was crimped into short spirals, his face and hands were blackened and blotched with blisters, and small spots of light like burning furze smouldered through his hair. His clothes were a flight of fireflies. He, too, found it difficult to grasp the edge of the ladder.

The wind blew a raucous searing into my face as if I had been skinned. I laughed as I looked across at Séamus, and his eyes turned up seriously out of his mottled face. Then he, too, broke into chuckles for I was a reflection of his ridiculous self. When we got behind a wall we wrung our hands to ease them but that only added to the discomfort. We laughed at each other. Séamus had no eyebrows now and his lips were also burnt, so that neither of us could articulate properly. He pointed to my face. 'You wouldn't bother much about mine if you could see your own,' he managed to mutter. Seán Treacy's quiet grin changed to a long drawn-out chuckle as he looked from one of us to the other. 'You're not very inflammable, either of you,' he said, as he tied a bandage around my blistered neck.

Suddenly I heard rifle shots to one side. I crawled to the back of the barracks. There I found one of our men flat on the ground and with his rifle trained on a slender loophole in one of the steel-protected windows. By his side was a pile of empty cartridge cases. He turned his head and smiled gaily when he heard my approach. He was having good sport. In his hands were a rifle and ammunition and thirty yards away was a metal slit. I stuttered with the burden of what I was unable to say, for the state of my lips made normal vocal effort impossible, and his smile had an expectant quality as if he waited to be patted on the head, as if he had been making a special collection of these empty cases. He knew, however, what I meant to say.

'Will you count your empty cartridges?' I asked. He counted

them. 'Some day, maybe, a man or two from the company will lose their lives because you wasted this stuff in hitting a steel plate. Don't fire again except you see a peeler between you and the wall.'

Seán Treacy and I wanted to remain on close to the barracks for a while longer, though it was then broad daylight. A portion of roof might collapse or a smouldering floor spread the flames, and we might be able to cross by the roof ridge when the building cooled down. Séamus was eager to withdraw the outposts and as he was the Brigadier he had the last word in a long controversy. Outposts were in danger as troops could now outflank them from on high, since there were few riflemen to hold the valley positions. An order was sent for the companies to withdraw to their areas. We waited until a despatch rider told us that the outer ring of men, who had patiently kept their monotonous watch, had gone to their homes.

We had failed in our undertaking, we told each other as we went uphill, and we had used a fair amount of ammunition and explosives. We had learned that some kind of force pump was necessary to spray incendiary material forward across gaps and as far as distant gables. Bottles filled with paraffin or petrol might be hurled to smash against the slates and spill out their contents to aid in the spread of flame. At least we had the memory of an attempt and the example of the Roskeen men who had waited patiently under the loopholes. Jim Gorman had added his courage in bringing forward petrol and paraffin and by helping Séamus to carry the heavy buckets up the ladders. His clothing dripped paraffin and was nose-irritant with petrol, but he had not been burnt.

Below us, as we turned to watch, smoke eddied and was wafted slowly above the roof, while odd shots proved that the police were still busy repulsing attackers in the otherwise peaceful-looking valley.

CHAPTER TWO

DRANGAN BARRACKS

JUNE 1920

The last week in June of 1920 found Séamus Robinson, Seán Treacy and I in the Comeragh mountains, to the south of the Suir in the county of Waterford. We were strengthening small sections which were known as outposts, endeavouring to bring them up to company strength, and I was training the officers and outpost leaders. The people on either side of the watershed were good, especially in the Nier valley, and there was a bare, mountainous core untouched by roads. The mountains were steep and well wooded in spots, roads were narrow and precipitous, and there were deer to kill if food was urgently needed. This area was often used by South Tipperary columns in later times when they needed a secure refuge, or when they hastily left the plains to outwit converging military.

We examined the constabulary posts in this portion of County Waterford. We thought some of them could be attacked when the men in the outpost areas had experience. At the moment they were unable to undertake such operations without help from another battalion. The fact that a Volunteer company had been in existence for several years meant that its men had been tested in many subtle ways. There was less talk and no belief in RIC prestige. Strangers could put up in, or move through, the area without their presence being known to the police; a more careful watch was kept on actual and potential enemies, and minor operations were sifting men and testing organisation. We thought it best to carry out the next attack in an area which would be able to deal with a post and the surrounding complications by itself.

We had spent a night with Dr. Murphy of Carrick, a staunch host always. We had been discussing forays on a series of barracks in the Brigade area, using a variety of means of assault.

We had intended during one of the proposed attacks to lie in wait for reinforcements, whether the post was captured or not. A set-back to the British in the help sent to a hemmed-in post might make them wary or dilatory about the sending of a relief force in future.

Up to this time I had been busy on a round of battalions, organising, training, building up staff work and attempting to concentrate the energy of the officers on the problems of their commands. I was anxious, therefore, before I was suddenly moved by GHQ to another brigade, to test successive battalions in action. We had already wandered through the 7th battalion area, whose headquarters was at Mullinahone. Tommy Donovan, the commandant, was eager and willing to fight. He was wild and wildness counted. He would help to the utmost in any attack which would be made in his command. We had talked particularly about Drangan RIC barracks which we had already seen, and as we knew the district and its resources it was easier to concentrate on the problem. The village was narrowly circled by plain, surrounded by rising ground at the southern limit of the Slieveardagh hills. Close into it were RIC barracks, and Callan to the east was strongly held. Fethard, an artillery barracks to the west, had a garrison of about a hundred and fifty men. Some of the smaller police barracks or houses in the villages were sometimes taken over to house soldiers for a brief stay, but we would have warning of their sudden presence.

Four crossroads, we found as we looked at our maps, if thoroughly held by barricades would command all the enemy approaches to the village during the hours of darkness. The blockades on the roads leading in to the post would have to be strongly built and firmly held, as reinforcements could come quickly from low-lying areas outside of the immediate hills.

We decided to go on to the 7th battalion on the following evening to begin preparations for an attack. From our experience in the Hollyford attempt we realised that a good force-pump which could throw petrol or paraffin to a distance was essential. A pump had been borrowed from a creamery in the Mullinahone area, and it was thought to throw inflammatory liquid a considerable distance. Bursting charges had worked very satisfactorily at Hollyford the previous month, but there was always a danger that they would slide from off the sloping roof.

We had already experimented at Davins' in Rosegreen with a dauby yellow clay which would adhere to a sloping, or even to an upright surface when hurled. Then we had tried this clay by wrapping it around a half-stick of gelignite with a detonator and fuse attached. When the fuse was ignited and the clay thrown, the attached glutinous material adhered to the roofs of deserted outhouses on which we had tried its force. As a result of the explosions, slates were blown from a large portion of roof. This solved one problem, that of making holes in a roof at a distance from the thrower. Through the holes, grenades could be lobbed and liquid or flaming paraffin thrust directly downwards into a room. In addition the mud bombs could be used against lorries or armoured cars, for with the use of a short fuse they could be exploded quickly. They could, therefore, be employed against the reinforcements in the early morning after an attack.

As we talked on into the early hours a despatch rider came to the back of our house. He brought us news from Michael Brennan who was Brigadier of East Clare. With him, Breen, Treacy and Robinson had stayed for a while the previous year when they were being carefully sought by the British. There was to be an attack on Six Mile Bridge barracks, but Brennan needed a few men who had experience in the use of explosives, to help him. Séamus Robinson and I decided that we would go on to County Clare, and that Seán Treacy would make the necessary preliminary arrangements for the attack on Drangan with Tom Donovan. We fixed a tentative date for Drangan, as we felt we would be back again within four days' time. We were anxious to gain what experience was available in the meantime, as Brennan mentioned that he had more than an ample quantity of explosives.

Séamus and I set off together, well-armed for any sudden mishap on the road. The nearest approach to an encounter was in Limerick city, but we had our work to do in Clare and had no immediate time for the police who tried to stop us.

The attack began and ended with the thawing of gelignite.

There was a large quantity of it, more than twice what we needed, but it was frozen. The officers who thawed it out were more eager than they were careful, and the result was a succession of prostrate officers sickened from the fumes of the nitroglycerine and capable only of crawling away to bed. We, however, as visitors, saw the attack without much responsibility. We lay out on the long lush grass of the dykes, watching the yellow river and the islands in the distance, talking with the Claremen and West Limerick men, some of whom were soon to be wrapped in the earth.

In the end I became responsible for the attack as the local senior officers were dizzy from the nitroglycerine fumes. Gelignite had been thawed out in sufficient amounts, but there was now too little day left to cover our possible initial mistakes. Countermanding orders were rushed to the outposts, but some feint attacks on posts in other remote battalions, which were to entice enemy strength in their direction, could not be called off in time. Fire and explosives were to have been simultaneously used from a nearby public house and I thought the resultant explosion, with its incongruous blend, would have been as serious for those of us who worked in the pub as it would have been for the police.

Séamus and I hurried back from Clare, through the lands of the Shannon towards the Kilkenny border to be in time for the Drangan attack. Our career was nearly interrupted when we were on the main road east of Limerick. A convoy of RIC in open tenders suddenly came around a corner from the Kilmallock direction. They carried red flags attached to small sticks as a sign of freedom from routine, and as they came close to us they fired their rifles to relieve their spirits. We looked at each other and we rode onwards, determined to fight if we were stopped by this crowd of swashbucklers. One lorry, the second in the line, halted in front of us. There was no chance of escape now. The country was bare, with no immediate cover.

Séamus was ahead of me. 'I'll take the front of the lorry if you'll tackle the end of it,' I called to him, and he nodded. We had each a revolver, an automatic and a hand grenade, and we could grip a weapon as soon as we were halted. The tender, however, started up again before we came up to it, and that movement released the tension of imminent death. The Tans and RIC who shouted and cheered as they swept forward were lightened in mood through whiskey and stout, as we were through relief.

In the late evening, picking up odds and ends of information in the neighbouring companies, we reached the house of George Hayden who was the engineer for the Mullinahone area. His home now resembled Shanahan's near Hollyford before the attack on the RIC there, in its variegated collections of weapons and explosives. Seán Treacy had made all arrangements for the attack with Tommy Donovan and there were also men to come in from the Callan battalion in County Kilkenny. Blockaded roads would be well held and patrolled between the obstructions and the village. There was no shortage of petrol or explosives, but the prize exhibit was the pump borrowed from the creamery. It had a good length of hose attached to it and liquid could be pumped almost fifteen yards away. On that pump the success of the attack would really depend, so we looked on it with affectionate awe.

Some men had come with Seán Treacy from the Tipperary battalion and five or six from the hills in the Rossmore direction, including Ned Reilly with the Hanlys and Jack Ryan, the Master. They had cycled on towards Drangan to George Hayden's house west of the village, a few days before the attack was due. They found that Tommy Donovan had brought up a plentiful supply of petrol and paraffin to Drangan and that the engineer had explosive material in his house. Next day they searched through the field for a good soft yellow clay. After a long trial of soils they found a suitable variety. They brought a number of buckets of the material with them. The clay had to be thoroughly mixed first to reduce it to the proper consistency, and then when it had been well kneaded it was ready for use.

Jack the Master had a 'Peter-the-Painter' and his rifle. The Peter had been added to his armament some time previously. He, with Ned Reilly and other Rossmore men, had been on his way to inspect Drumbane Hall which they had once attacked and which had then been evacuated by the RIC but was again to be occupied, by military this time. A British officer on a motor-bicycle had passed them by on a hill and while they awaited his return he came down suddenly against them, free-wheeling. Jack Ryan used his revolver at close range but, to his amazement, the officer continued on his way down hill as if a pea-shooter was rattling at him. Then he stopped, placed both feet on the ground to steady himself, fired his automatic carefully, and passed out of sight. Paddy Britt was badly wounded by his fire and died some days later. Jack was so entranced at this magical protection given to their opponent that he looked on helplessly, a bewitched spectator of the action. There was no doubt that his bullets had hit the officer, but Ned Reilly alone surmised that he must have been wearing body armour, which was carried by some RIC and army officers. The British officer has been wounded, however, though the Tipp men were not aware of it.

Ned Reilly and Ryan had now very little trust in their revolvers, but Treacy, who had influence with the Quartermaster General's Staff in Dublin, was able to get automatics from them. The Mauser, due to its high initial muzzle velocity, was used to pierce body armour. It had a sharp lashing crack when in use and, with its adjustable stock, was accurate up to four hundred yards.

Ryan's flaming red hair matched his willingness to act spontaneously. He was inclined to rush into danger and to decide on a project from a sudden prompting of his eager will. He was low sized and stocky, spattered with freckles, and his long rifle stuck up in extra height behind him.

A hole was to be burst with hammers through the roof of a small one-storey house which adjoined Drangan barracks. The hosepipe would serpent upwards and curve above the barracks roof, and the pump, it was hoped, would squirt forward a mixture of petrol and paraffin. There were ample men available for any emergency or for any additional project.

Patrols on foot and on bicycles moved in and out between obstructions on the roads and the village; and then beyond the barricades, cyclists kept in contact with the outposts on either flank and with a central point in Drangan. Road blocks had been well prepared, I found when I inspected them, and they would take a good deal of opposition. Seán Treacy had made good use of the local battalion. The ring of RIC posts — Killenaule, Ballingarry, Mullinahone, Fethard — were none of them more than seven miles away. They were a potential danger as long as an attack lasted. Their garrisons had been increased by Black and Tans who were expected to stiffen police resistance as they had been hardened by fighting during the first world war. Actually they were a terrorist force for implementing a British Cabinet policy and were not responsible to local police control. Killenaule and Callan, where there were District Inspectors, would have the added strength of these 'bold invaders', as would Cashel in the outer ring. Fethard, less than seven miles to the south-west, held an artillery barracks, and although gunners were more aloof than infantry in raiding strength, yet their garrison was sufficient to send out strong reinforcements. Mullinahone was, however, kept in check by armed Volunteers who controlled the immediate neighbourhood. The main danger was Clonmel, twelve miles away, which contained a strong infantry garrison and ample Royal Irish.

I went with Ned Reilly, Bill Dwyer and some of the Rossmore men to find a position in front of the barracks so that we could use covering fire to protect the men who were ready to use the small house beside the barracks as a supply base. We wandered around until we reached a haggard behind a high wall which fronted the barracks. We had no local guide. We carried a bucket of yellow clay which would help us to sling mud bombs on to the front of the barracks roof, and we had jumpers and picks to loophole the wall. As quietly as they could, men worked on the wall. I told them to take off their boots and not to talk when they were working. At either end of the wall there were low houses, but when I got in quietly through backdoors I found the windows were level with the street and as they seemed to be large they would not be of any use to us.

Ned Reilly had gone as far as the house at the far end of the wall. When he stuck his head out of a window he found that the high wall was cemented in front and that could add difficulty to our boring. In the meantime jumpers had found resistance when they probed their strength half-way through the wall. By this time, too, village dogs had begun an acrimonious concert which was joined in by the irritated informing of crows from the old graveyard near the barracks. If I had hoped to disturb the constabulary by my attempt at boring, I could not have succeeded more noisily. As I left a house by the back door I heard a murmur of talk. Our patrol was evidently discussing some problem, but when I had moved a few steps I heard shouts, then shots from behind their position. I ran towards the flashes, presuming that they came from police, and I collided with a man in the darkness as I began to fire my revolver. I kept going until I was held up by barbed wire which tore my ear and my left cheek. Bill Dwyer was on the ground, some distance from the wall, wounded. I gave him a tablet of morphia which I carried with me in a glass bottle, and I bandaged his wrist.

Our supposedly silent advance had now developed into a noisy engagement. Evidently the police, disturbed by dogs, by movement or by talk, had sent out a patrol of three RIC. They had come up by a small lane beside the haggard and opened fire on the men close to the wall. But even as they retired hastily, a sergeant was captured by one of our outposts.

Ned Reilly and I brought Dwyer away to be looked after by Dr. Conlon who was ready at a first-aid post in Boland's cottage outside the village. He had come across from Mullinahone on a pre-arranged sick-call and he had hired a motor car which he kept ready in case it was urgently needed to remove arms or wounded.

We went around towards the parish priest's house until we met Seán Treacy, and I told him what had happened. Hanly was missing from our group. Reilly and I went back to search for him but now our way was well illuminated by Very lights which showed up the haggard in a blinding clearness, but also bared ourselves to the top storey of the barracks. We could not find Hanly. Some of the Very lights had a disconcerting series of loud explosions which tore their luminous way into the night sky. The sergeant in charge of the post was not anxious to use the front loophole as the first few Very lights expended had brought in a bullet which parted the hair of one of the constables who was ready at the steel slit. He now fired up through an opening in the roof.

Séamus Robinson was on the roof of the one-storey house when I came out on to the street close by the barracks. A rapid *tat-tat* from the Peter and the long Parabellum used by Jack the Master and Treacy kept the loophole incapable of return fire while the barracks roof was being smashed in with fast sledge blows. The snaky end of a long tube was pulled upwards through the slate holes and its squirming length was confined by a long wooden lath. From behind the cover of the upper half of the barracks gable Seán Treacy flung his mud bombs. Their sharp cracks were followed by whistling slate fragments. The hose was pushed forward and as it was controlled by its lath, fluid could be scattered over a large surface; then flaming turf and oily waste were thrown upwards. The dripping paraffin blazed up suddenly in a loud burst of rising flame. A few grenades lobbed into roof holes made the garrison retire further and rendered movement insecure even beyond the radius of the burning interior. The loophole had been nullified at once and as that was the greatest danger, our men felt secure. The only threat the police had now was to throw grenades from the remote part of the upper storey, or from the ground floor, so that they burst outside of the small house. Fragments would then endanger the men on the roof.

The pump had failed while I was on the roof, but after it was reconnected it began to beat out oil in long spurts. The real danger to the men in the small house was the collection of paraffin, petrol and improvised grenades. The floor was wet with fluid which was being poured into wooden barrels and which dripped down as well from the roof hole. Small electric lamps had a habit of suddenly dimming while men continued to work in the darkness. An ember from the burning roof or a spark from a match igniting a fuse on the roof overhead would have created an immediate explosive blaze.

While I was helping inside the house I heard a shout from the roof: 'Look out below — a bomb!' Then came two crashes, increased by our apprehension, as clanging metal hit off the roof and came down with a crash on the pavement outside.

I was close to the door, and on an order, 'Throw yourselves down', we flattened ourselves close to, and upon each other. I counted aloud: one ... two ... three ... in seconds intervals, as I thought; then I continued to add until I reached the mystic number seven — yet no explosion came. We rushed out to search for the heavy tin can in the darkness and when we found it, it was hurled out into the street.

Ned Reilly and I, with the help of other men, made a barricade of tree trunks across the wide street as a flank protection to the men in the small house. The trees had been lying on the opposite side of the street. They belonged possibly to a wheelwright or a carpenter. We carried them into position and from behind a double line of holes we fired a few shots at barracks loopholes.

With the pump out of control a number of times, the burning had taken longer than expected and we feared relief would come with the dawn to the besieged RIC garrison. Morning light would help relief forces which could make use of the level ground for easy transport, except to the northwards, and the IRA would find it difficult to hold any one blockade in daylight as they would have but a few supporting rifles on that spot.

Ned Reilly had gone around to the rear of the barracks and I met him when he returned. The ground there was as high as the top storey of the post. Flames which lighted up windows in rear and front simultaneously showed no movement within, nor was there any reply when a few bullets were rattled off the steel on the upper windows. The police must have been driven down to the ground floor. When I heard this information I returned to the working beehive beside the barracks, which seemed to buzz with men. The pump had again failed a few times, but it was now throwing jets of liquid. There was a danger that a change of wind or the dripping trail of fluid could lead a trail of fire on to the small house which had sufficient loose inflammatory liquid and saturated air inside to blow up quickly.

Dawn had crawled to the sky, leaving a radiant brightness in its path. I could see roofholes in the barracks outlined by smoke with out-thrusts of flame. We discussed whether the police should be asked to surrender as the roof collapse might take some time, but I was opposed to this proposal. Not until we had an alternative method of attack which we could quickly use, should a surrender be demanded. Tools for breaking the wall which abutted on the small house were brought inside. Men began to use picks and jumpers to strip off plaster until they could reach joints in the stonework. Grenades could be used through an enlargement of this opening to drive out whatever police might be in the adjoining room, then with rifle cover the building could be rushed.

I went to the Mullinahone side of the village where I saw the police sergeant who had been captured when they sent out a patrol before our attack began. Dr. Conlon, who waited in his dressing station, had attended to Jack Foley, company captain of Drangan. Foley had been wounded in the back when he went to guide the Callan men from County Kilkenny into position. As I walked down the street I could see Slieve na mBan which was an aeroplane flight of six miles away; it raised its dark-storied head to the southward and its clear sloping ridge shone in the soft morning light. There was something about a mountain of tradition which made its outlines familiar even without a close look. It might yet be our shelter this morning, I thought, as its flanks protruded sufficiently through the otherwise narrow road network. To the north and to the north-east towards the Kilkenny-Leix border was the long undulating ridge of the Slieveardagh hills, but our line of retreat lay over the hills to the north-west, and then across the twisting Suir.

Ned Reilly and Hanly had gone up the street under cover of houses towards the barracks. I was on their heels and when I reached them I found they were readying themselves to fire at the ground floor of the barracks, which was under their rifle-sights. Soon I saw a rifle with an attached shirt, waving from a window. That was a token of surrender, but a token was one thing and surrender, as we had now learned, was an unrelated problem.

'What do you mean by that rag?' I shouted. 'Do you want to surrender?'

'Yes, we want to surrender.'

I walked across by the front to a slit in the steel shutter.

'Throw out your rifles and small arms at once.'

'But what are you going to do to us?' Will you shoot us?'

'No, your lives are safe; throw out your arms at once and bring out your ammunition, but hurry up.'

Fire was now spreading fast. The pump and its supply train under Séamus Robinson was making a certainty of the experiment. I had heard odd explosions from rooms exposed to the flames which meant that their ammunition was being detonated. It also meant that there would be less ammunition for us to capture and good rifle food was badly needed.

The police hesitated for a brief while, but it seemed a long time as I stood in front, thinking of the ammunition and of my meagre hope if they changed their minds and misused their flag of truce. They, themselves, were naturally more concerned about the chances of their immediate futures when they came under what they considered our dubious protection. 'Hurry up now, throw out your arms,' I called in through the slit.

With a heavy clatter, rifles and revolvers were tumbled out in a heap. The constabulary formed up outside on the street, under a recent recruit, King, who had served in the Horse Artillery. He had a wound across his forehead which reddened a handkerchief, but he made light of it when I offered to help him. He had marched out under a tricolour flag which showed white at first, then green and orange were added as it was unfolded by the wind. The flag had been captured during a raid and had been kept by the RIC as a trophy in the barracks. The names of the prisoners were taken down by the Brigade officers, and they were warned that the next time they were captured in arms there would not be the same security about their lives. They formed up again on the street, I gave them a right turn, told them to keep five paces apart and not to look back. They walked away erect with a swing on the road to Mullinahone, but they were halted again and held until all of the IRA had left the vicinity.

I ran towards the barracks as I was thinking of the ammunition inside. The doorway was deep in sandbag protection, but the larger room to the left of the entrance, into which the police had finally retired, was narrowed by a double row of sandbags, and loose sand, thickly scattered, had been made use of to quieten small blazes. The constabulary had made a stout resistance.

Ned Reilly was with me and we had a few men who helped by dragging out boxes and equipment while we searched for papers and ammunition. The ceiling above us was on fire and ammunition exploded in a cascade of sound. As we groped in the smoke, the ceiling fell down around us and on us, and we rushed for the door in a fog of smoke as blazing fragments clung to our backs and crackled in our hair. I was rolled on the ground until my smouldering clothes were smothered. Dr. Conlon, luckily, was near to us and he was able to bandage my hand and neck.

Everyone was in good humour now and there was a feeling of spring in our mood. We had needed encouragement for the men and for ourselves and here it was in the arms heap. Rifles were examined carefully to find if bolts had been damaged or sights injured before surrender; men counted ammunition, and a careful watch was kept, as ammunition and small arms had a way of suddenly disappearing. For weapon-lacking men, any expedient had been used for years to gain a few rounds even of shotgun ammunition, and now honour was elastic. The rifles were touched by many who placed their hands on them as if it was a ritual to finger a weapon which had lately been used against us. That it was indeed a ritual, we could see in the satisfaction even of non-possession as we watched their faces when they gave back the rifles to the custodians.

Letters and papers were quickly read through in search of information. A barracks, like a presbytery, was often the receptacle for anonymous information engendered by jealousy, in spite or in feud, or through loyalty to the British. In addition there would be direct information, although trace was unlikely to be found. One man who was busily reading a letter, shouted: 'Now, lads, listen to this, will you?' It was at the end of a letter to a sergeant and it was signed 'your little lump of love.'

The men sat down in delight and they savoured all the fun without any feeling for the romance of the words. 'The fat peeler and his little lump of love,' shouted one man to another, and they laughed again.

I had been reading a History of Ireland which I had taken as my treasure trove. It had been specially printed for the Royal Irish. As was fitting, it had a green cover. The writing was an interesting rearrangement of information and facets of history to assist in what amounted to the mental conditioning of janissaries. Long domination had worn down a large percentage of the race to subservience or aping snobbery. Security held others in its grip, who changed religion to hold their ancestor's lands, or those who ran the gamut of whatever privilege would be given to serve faithfully even on the lower rungs, as bailiffs or landlord's spies. Here again with the RIC was another version of service, trained in the use of rifles, bayonets, bombs and revolvers for any emergency, but opposed by a stiffening strength which had somehow fruited unobserved to their peering eyes. The Depot training of young country men had sent them out with the crown above the harp. In the medley of divided loyalties, split up by wedges of ascendancy, was a recent growth of loyalty which served the harp alone and which was presented here this morning.

The Volunteers who had been at work close by during the attack were drawn up on the street and thanked by the Brigadier for their help, before they were dismissed. Some of the outposts had already been sent home and the converging roads, save for their strong obstacles and a few scouts, were free for the movements of the British. We said goodbye to Tommy Donovan whose battalion had made the success of the operation. He was soon afterwards to be numbered among the fighting dead.

Séamus Robinson, Seán Treacy and I halted near a crossroads by which enemy troops might come from Fethard. We were given cans of milk and thick buttered farrels of cake by women who had remained up all night when they heard the rifle-fire in the distance. They were pleased as they brought us out mugs, and disappointed when they found that we could not wait for the tea which they were getting ready. We remained there in position for a while, thinking that the gunners might come out in our direction and that we could give them a surprise *aubade*. There were no khaki figures to be seen in the distance as we turned up the only road which had not been blocked the previous night. The morning air blew sweetly in our faces.

CHAPTER THREE

REARCROSS BARRACKS

JULY 1920

I had been working in East Limerick Brigade for close on a month in the summer of 1920 when, one July evening in Kilteely, I heard that there was to be an attack on a barracks in North Tipperary. I cycled on towards Doon which lies on the road that limits the southern edges of the hill country, and there, I felt, I would get more precise information about the project. I was able to meet Dan Allis, Brigade Vice-Commandant of East Limerick. He told me that Rearcross barracks was to be attacked that night, and already groups of men from the adjoining brigades were on their way to help the North Tipp men.

On the mountain road, which runs along the Bilboa river on the edge of Knockastauna, I met the Yank Carty, commandant of the Doon battalion, tramping up through the hills with about twelve Volunteers from Doon and Cappa White. A few of his men had heavy sacks containing weighty cart-box bombs which had been left over since an attack on Doon barracks in March. Others carried two-gallon tins of petrol as their contribution to the intended blaze. The Yank Carty had known of this proposed operation for over two weeks. Paddy Ryan Lacken, who had been company captain of Knockfune, close to the mountain core, was then, I think, vice-commandant of the Newport battalion. He it was who had told the Yank to bring men, rifles and petrol for the job, but he had also warned him not to talk about it. Ryan Lacken, it was thought, had not informed his own Brigade headquarters officers about this proposed attempt on the constabulary post, and so the Limerick officer was afraid that the deliberate oversight on his part might make for trouble. In almost all brigades at this time, plans for the attack on a post had first to be sent on to GHQ for approval. That procedure had been occasioned by half-hearted attempts on posts, by unnecessary loss of life, or by the casual misuse of ammunition when attackers preferred to remain at a distance rather than shake a garrison's morale by closer acquaintance. Even in the burning of empty barracks and courthouses, Volunteers had been lost either through carelessness or in the unthinking use of petrol. As I saw the regulation, it was an attempt to make officers first thoroughly think out their plans. It did not affect me personally, but it did, I think, bear on all IRA field officers.

In the heavy twilight the hills were double steep as we followed the muddy road along the wriggling valleys, and it was dark when I reached a small hut behind a Diarmuid and Grania bed. There I found Ryan Lacken who told me that they intended to burn out the Rearcross barracks from the roof. A spraying pump had been brought from Upperchurch and there seemed to be plenty of paraffin, but there was only a small quantity of explosives.

Normally, Ryan Lacken had a free flow of talk; he showed a certain reticence that night. He had not consulted his Brigade Commandant about the planning for this attack, and now he was nervous that the Brigade, if it was made aware of the project, might cancel it at the last moment. My questions, I could sense, were disconcerting to him, for he was in doubt as to whether I might use my authority to cancel the attack. These questions were to him, I expect, a categorical indictment of the undertaking, and he did not realise that even if the attack went ahead despite my authority I would be with him. I was merely anxious to find out what preparations had been made to ensure a good return for the venture and what were his alternative plans, but his main idea was to begin on the barracks, and he was more concerned about telling me who was there to help than with getting down to details of the plan of assault, outpost men, signallers and the time it would take to throw up effective road blocks.

Seán Treacy, Dan Breen, Ned Reilly and Jack the Master had come from South Tipp, with Jim Gorman and the Dwyers of Hollyford. Jim Stapleton and Paddy Kinnane had arrived from the Borrisoleigh battalion of Mid Tipperary. I had myself met East Limerick Volunteers from Cappagh and Doon proceeding to the place of mobilisation, and Knockfune and Kilcommon companies from two adjoining battalions of North Tipperary were out on the roads preparing obstacles. A veritable litany of names of men who had already left their mark on the enemy was recited by Ryan Lacken in proof of the measure of support that had been obtained for the Rearcross venture. Indeed there were enough good men present to take any post, for all of these outsiders had been in previous actions against barracks of the Royal Irish. For all practical purposes RIC barracks were strongly-held block-houses established by the enemy to assist in keeping the Irish in subjection.

I had already met Ryan Lacken when I was wandering through the North Tipperary mountains the previous year, engaged on the staid monotonous business of training companies of men and building up a dependable organisation. It was difficult then to judge a man save by his eagerness to learn, through the way his mind worked, or later on by his willingness to fight by himself if the military or the constabulary attempted to arrest him. As there had been no fighting as yet in their area, these two mountain battalions were more difficult to assess, particularly as they did not bother about routine or the building up of staff work.

Ryan Lacken was tall and well made despite a deceptively slim appearance, with a rapid eagerness of speech. His large eyes stood out of a well-shaped face, and his interest in any subject he discussed was apparent from his flow of eager questions which helped to skim off his curiosity layer by layer. His zest for information was at times insatiable, but his freshness of words showed that he had his own ideas to add in return. When he was persuasive he had charm which lighted up his face, but he held stubbornly to his own arguments despite an accumulative sapping from steadier reasoning. He had no more appreciation of organised discipline than had most of the men from the mountain parts. They wanted to be let alone, to be permitted to work things out in their own way, free of interference from headquarters. Their inattention to detail was no virtue when they came to plan an operation. This was, however, offset by their eagerness for action. Intangible, intractable, they transformed their early seed of distrust for peelers' activities into a steady indifference of contempt. They had all the essentials to wear down an organised force, save this essence of organisation at the base of effort, which when irksome was as easy to shed as a snake's skin. To them, such organisation seemed to weigh down their personal freedom rather than to enhance it. A brigade with headquarters well on the far side of the mountains was thought to be a necessary evil. To them, the plains increased distance, but the mountains were no obstacle in time or space, for they preserved a breath of freedom, and freedom had no measuring stick. A General Headquarters was some strange far-off force which pinched but little, and which they assumed would be better used for control in other areas, since to men who developed in their isolation the outside world was dim in effect and a kind of chimera. Movement itself seldom brought men beyond local fairs or market towns and the impact of outside chance was an ebb tide in their pattern of life. Even their battalion officers were doubtful quality unless they had the hill wildness in them.

This hill area was peculiar because it allowed Volunteers from four brigades to meet and permitted them to discuss ideas for a coming attack, or plans for making British rule improbable if not impossible, as they talked, perhaps, in the interval at a dance. Men from the high ground had a stronger fabric of resistance as their ancestors had been driven out from better land. There was a firm warp of native tradition and a weft of aloofness against hostile penetration. Contact on borders usually depended on the worth of a brigade staff's endeavours and its radiation to the circumference of the area, or on the qualities of the battalion staffs nearest the boundary line. Often enough there was little touch on brigade borders if the edges held men poor in quality. It was difficult enough to pass on ideas or to assess officers, as adjoining staffs were not inclined to meet. Sometimes an adjacent market town brought men from adjacent counties together, as might Mitchelstown or Fermoy, yet border companies were always familiar with each other. There was one place where officers and men could meet freely, talk to overplease themselves — and that was in gaol. Even while a gaol war was continually being fought, prisoners could also help to unify their political, governmental and IRA concepts, adjudge each other and realise their own strengths as part of a national effort. By the late autumn of 1920, however, untried prisoners could be sent to internment camps and further removed from outside influences.

It would have been more satisfactory if a mountain brigade had been formed from adjoining areas of the four brigades, but then the brigadier, unless he was a good hill man in spirit, would find himself in trouble. The South Tipperary battalion which bordered on Borrisoleigh had already wanted to join up with such a new brigade, but except for IRB circles which brought these hill battalions together there was no other central cohesion save in action.

They were individuals, the hill men, anarchical, to be understood through action, and they wanted to solve problems in their own way. Hill isolation had made them throw up a rampart of tenacity about their own methods. They would be more inclined to get an idea into their heads, think of the men who would carry it out, then go ahead, but planning was not their strong point. Up to this time they had been concerned with attacks in Mid Limerick at Murroe, and in East Limerick at Doon and Cappagh White, but none of them had been successful. Two of these attacks had relied on explosives, but the method was faulty and when the gelignite failed there was no alternative to be used at once. Mid Tipp had made onslaughts on Drumbane, Roskeen and Shevry. South Tipp had staged a feint attack on Clonoulty barracks, and with Mid Tipp men they had waited patiently at Rathcannon for military and RIC from Thurles who, they hoped, would attempt to relieve their distressed comrades. In the roadway they had dug a deep cutting, out of which they cleared stones over a bank. The gap had been carefully covered by supporting canvas deep in road dust, but no relief force came their way. In the meantime Clonoulty was sniped from long distance by a few men, one of whom, young Carew, was a natural shot. He had, when firing at a light within, put a bullet through the loophole. It wounded the sergeant, but when the garrison came out to surrender, the snipers remained unaware of their intention and the surprised police went back to their post. None of these attacks had been pushed as hard as that at Hollyford, from which the garrison left on the same day of the attack. In the Drumbane raid there was such assurance in the effective use of gelignite advocated by Jim Gorman that it was thought petrol as an alternative would not be necessary. The result of the explosion was only a cracked gable, but the shaky condition of the whole building forced the garrison to evacuate.

The pressure of hill country onslaughts induced a sense of tension among military and RIC, an increase in their awareness of unseen dangers. This uncertainty was not relieved by the burning of creameries and houses, or by the deliberate killing of IRA men in or near their houses by night. Following the killing of Brigadier MacCurtain in Cork, the first RIC murder gang to operate in Ireland in the darkness, masked in the moonlight tradition, came from Dovea and Thurles. When the constabulary searched for a Dwyer, a Ryan, Gleeson, Kinnane or a Stapleton, they shot a brother if the wanted man was not at home. Eugene Igoe, who later led his gang in Dublin, as an RIC sergeant was eager in such prowling.

For the remainder of the Tan war the mountain areas challenged British occupation through command of the roads, but although men lay out for convoys and lorry patrols there was no successful fight which resulted in the capture of vehicles and arms. Yet behind main roads the country became reasonably safe for the people who farmed the land, unsafe for their sons when they slept at home, and easy enough for small columns which wandered around searching for a chance to strike. They were secure enough, for being armed they had a chance to fight when surprised, but the people had no such chance. Meantime, Dublin, the capital, was comparatively protected by the British against their own indiscipline, because it was too available to press correspondents, too close to the outside world, and its property, shared by numerous imperialists, had to be safeguarded.

Attacks out in the country resembled a wake where if you were friendly with the deceased or with the family, you put in an appearance, for the news of death was quickly passed on by word of mouth. In a hill attack, if you were friendly with the officer in charge you would be certain to hear of the proposed undertaking, or you would receive an invitation which expected you to bring along your group with arms, helped out by explosives or incendiary materials. Moreover, when invited, it was taken for granted that there would be no talk about the job to be done, save among other men who had similarly been made aware of what was to happen, and that such far away institutions as brigades had nothing much to do with this neighbourly gathering on a mountain road.

The unsuitable type of pump, the absence of heavy explosives and the lack of Brigade sanction were three difficulties which I saw for this proposed attack on Rearcross barracks. The neighbouring battalions, with the aid of the men who had come in from outside areas, could hold the approaches to Rea, as Rearcross was called locally. There were British military posts at Tipperary, Thurles, Nenagh, Newport and Limerick. Limerick, about seventeen miles away, was a brigade headquarters, and Newport was a little over eight miles distant. Nenagh was over twenty miles through the mountains, and twenty-three miles from Rea if the road through Newport was used. The headquarters for the constabulary of the North Riding was in Nenagh, therefore police reinforcements would most probably come from that point. Kilcommon barracks was less than four miles distant. There was an RIC post at Shevry and a strong military garrison at Castlefogarty on the way to Thurles, which was twenty-one miles distant by road. East Limerick had barracks on the edge of the hill country at Doon and Cappagh White, the former being controlled from Pallas, one of the toughest problems in the country, ranking with Bruff in height and masonry strength. Pallas was an offensive heritage from the Land War. Cappagh had its constabulary centre at Tipperary, eight miles away, where there was a burden of Tans and always a battalion of infantry who should not find it difficult to cover the seventeen miles to our focus of discussion. The smaller enemy posts would continue to mind their own business, and as there was a hollow between Newport and Rea, which had blanketed even the sound of heavy quarry blasting, there was no liklihood that Newport would learn of the Rearcross attack through the medium of nocturnal explosions.

There were some map problems which I worked out as we looked down on the microcosm of our surrounding difficulties. The hills had imposed their own authority on the posts which were now held by their strength of rifles and not by any co-operate allegiance to law.

I found it difficult to winkle out the strength of the Rea garrison. Shortly after an ambush at Lackamore in April, two barracks, at Birdhill and Killoscully, had been abandoned and the dark coats had been added to Newport, Rea and Kilcommon. This redistribution had taken the constabulary away from weak points and had given a garrison such as Rea a depository of information from years of prying, which could be used by RIC in their raids, or enable them to serve as scouts and intelligence agents to the British military. Accounts varied between a garrison of eighteen and thirty, in the barracks at Rea, but in the end I took the strength to be about twenty men and two sergeants. The majority of the garrison were Tans, but there were a few Corkmen, together with local RIC who knew the people well.

One of the sergeants had served as a British officer in the world war. His particular work was the organised defence of the post which held one of the lines of blockhouses between Limerick and Thurles. He was responsible for the training of the garrison to fit into his preconceived plan against attack, and he was paid a pound a day which gave him a moneyed status. He had no power to interfere with the normal police routine which now generally varied between drinking bouts, gathering of information, and the frequent halts of transport, but as soon as hostile presence was suspect he immediately commanded the garrison.

The barracks was built under a gradually sloping hill from which it was difficult for a sniper to get in a shot. Indeed, little sniping had occurred here for there was small cover, save from a wall twenty yards away to the east, and to manage successful shooting would mean the use of other men to protect a withdrawal. On the other hand, the Kilcommon garrison less than four miles away had been frequently irritated by snipers at inconvenient hours.

The barracks had been prepared as well as it was possible to strengthen it. It stood back a little from the main road, but its well-loopholed porch jutted out to protect the flanks. Behind, the garden wall had been cut away down close to the butt and the top slanted towards ground level to increase the angle of fire from the upstairs windows. The hill at the rear could easily be swept by fire from the top and bottom storeys and although there were low banks on the hillside which could screen a man from eyesight if he lay low, they were too thin to stop a rifle bullet. The yard behind was covered with loops of barbed wire, leaving clear only a sinuous, narrow path that led back towards a small concrete outhouse and to an outdoor lavatory. The front windows were steel-plated, with projections of netting wire to prevent strangers' grenades from entering, whilst allowing sufficient opening for the defenders to use their rifles and hand grenades. Towards the east and in the direction of Kilcommon there was a haggard behind a low fence and backed by a schoolhouse wall. This haggard could control the front of the barracks, the gable, and part of the wired enclosure at the rear. In front of the building a wide bank had been levelled to the ground. That removal had uncovered to police fire a stretch of flat country that extended south for some hundreds of yards.

I had a doubt about the gable. It was difficult to know if the ground had been mined beneath it, as that position was an obvious place to mine although it was already well protected by loopholes. End walls and gardens of police barracks in many dangerous areas had been mined during cover of darkness and, as here there were no houses except one shop within some hundreds of yards of the gable, the Rearcross garrison could have worked at night without the local Volunteers becoming aware of their pick work. It was easy for police patrols to hold up the outskirts at night while digging went on. And there was a story that on successive nights, after midnight, the sound of picks had been clearly heard in the distance from the direction of the gable.

Another factor that had to be taken into account was the possibility that there were additional loopholes, hidden merely by a crust of plaster and ready to be broken open in the event of an attack. I also expected, judging from the thoroughness of outside defence, that the interior of the building had been partitioned off in water-tight compartments of protection.

A man named Flannery owned the entire barracks building at Rearcross; it was large, as there were ten windows on the top storey. He also owned the store to the left, in which he sold mowing machines, clothing, groceries and drink. Flannery had helped the thirsty constabulary by lending them men when they were busy on fortification work. They had drawn sand for sandbags, helped to remove the earth from fences, stones from walls, and they had also drawn turf to the barracks.

There had been a boycott imposed on the police. They were ostracized socially. No one was expected to salute them, talk to them, serve them a drink, or give them food or help in any way. This was, of course, a counsel of perfection, but in many towns and villages it was enforced, to their loss by the shopkeepers, and then by the people. Police would order a drink, be refused, draw their revolvers and threaten the shopkeeper, and if he persisted, the RIC and Tans would help themselves, with or without payment. The intensity of the boycott varied with isolation and the strength of mind of the shopkeeper. Flannery had been previously warned by the IRA of the consequences that would attend a continuation of his help to the RIC. Horses belonging to him and to a relation of his had been shot, and lack of a necessary animal kept him within the limits of Republican law.

Outposts had already been manned before I approached Rea and came to the 'Dane's house', another local way of describing the Dolmen. The boundaries of the 5th, or Newport, battalion ran slightly to the east of Rea, and Ryan Lacken's former company was just inside the eastern border limit of this area. He had instructed Killeen company, whose territory ran down to the northern hill slopes, to block the road near to Dolla, as that position would delay Nenagh military and RIC from using the mountain passages. In addition, he had told Newport company to cut trees beyond the park on the main road to prevent Limerick reinforcements from passing through. The military had occupied a dwelling-house on the Turnpike road outside of Newport and they would be the first unit to respond to a call for help. However, a hole had suddenly been made in this plan of attack, putting the entire project in jeopardy. Commandant Doherty of the neighbouring 6th battalion, having learned what was afoot, had gone into Nenagh to inform the Brigadier. This was the first intimation the Brigadier had received of an attack planned to take place within a few hours. The battalion concerned had not discussed plans with the Brigade staff, nor had Brigade officers been invited to attend. Because of that act of indicipline the Newport company was ordered not to block roads, and it is possible that other North Tipperary companies were given similar instructions. The Brigade decision meant that the most important roads which could be used by the Newport, Limerick and Nenagh garrisons were now left open to them.

In the next development a despatch rider brought a message to the South Tipperary outpost to the west of the barracks. There was no light there by which the despatch could be read, but at a house nearby, Quigley's, the order was looked at by candle light. The South Tipp Volunteers were ordered to withdraw immediately from the battalion area which they had entered to attack a barracks without permission. Treacy was worried. He had not been asked to enter their territory by any North Tipperary Brigade officer; on the contrary, he was now definitely ordered to leave. He was Vice-Brigadier of South Tipp and consequently it was a particularly serious offence for him to invade another area or to remain on when his presence was unwelcome. All senior officers would come under this ban, but I decided that, under the circumstances which prevailed, attack was more important than authority when plans were ready to be acted on. Accordingly, I assumed charge of the attack and also undertook responsibility for whatever losses in men or materials might be sustained by the Volunteers who helped us. I was solely responsible to General Headquarters who already knew this area through my detailed reports on each battalion, and on its Brigade staff. It would be with me the North Tipperary Brigade would have to deal concerning the participation of the South Tipp men and my assuming charge of the attack. Often enough it was difficult to induce brigade and battalion officers to undertake an operation, so now that men were both willing to fight and were actually on the ground of battle, a definite order from me to withdraw would be unjust to them and to the fabric of the offensive intention which we had helped to weave. Indeed, I was as anxious to attack as were any of the mountain men, so it was not difficult to solve this dilema. An additional reason, if any was needed for an attack, was that the RIC in this post, three months before, had helped military and police from Newport to burn Rearcross creamery, the first co-operative building in Ireland to be destroyed.

I talked the matter over with Ryan Lacken, the Mid Tipp men, and with Dan Breen in the small hut, but Treacy, perhaps owing to his invidious position, did not wish to see me, a representative of GHQ, as I would be considered another focus of authority. By this time some of the roads would have been cut or blocked, but others would have been left open and daylight would be on us before the omissions could be turned into obstructions. I then decided to postpone the attempt until the following night.

The road towards Kilcommon had already been blocked by heaped-up stones which could be removed before morning, but the blocks towards Doon and Cappagh were seven to eight miles away. I told the Yank Carty to snipe the barracks at Doon, and as he was a reliable officer the constabulary there would feel that an attempt had been made on their security. Rifle fire would enable them to inform the military and police in Tipperary town that their post had been gallantly defended, that at least one hundred attackers had been engaged and, as usual, traces of blood over many points would prove that some of their opponents had been seriously wounded.

It was late in the morning by the time the Doon men had returned home, however, and as sniping would draw concentrated fire they would now endanger people who had shortly to be on their way to first Mass.

A morning's reflection on the change of plan led into Sunday, which was a very gossipy day. People had leisure and leisure meant talk. Around chapel walls after first and second Mass the week's news would be discussed with a special interest in local attempts against the British, or any accounts of their raids and dragoonings. As a result of the destruction of local creameries the daily procession of carts which brought milk from the farms had to be discontinued. Men and women would now be all the more eager to talk with their neighbours on their way to and from Mass and later during the day. In the evening men often went into a pub for a few drinks and there again talk would begin.

Added to these dangers from the countryside was the number of men who had been present this last night from four different areas, and the ill-luck which might be expected from postponement, for that would lead to relaxation in security and a leakage of words. Many of the men would be relaxing over a pint with the gossipers in the pubs or at home. Despite the risk, we felt that the hill country was a special area and that the people could be trusted implicitly. On the following night, road blocks were to be more thoroughly managed; in the meantime rifles were to be sent on from Mid Tipp in Patsy Murphy's outside car, and explosives would be sought in Cappagh White.

Hollyford and Upperchurch Volunteers marched back to their company areas, though a few officers and men remained behind. Seán Treacy, Breen, Ned Reilly and I were brought beyond the Long Stone, up a narrow lane to Ryan's in Bottomy.

When we wandered around that Sunday morning we discovered that almost everybody knew what we had intended to do on the previous night, and that they suspected our continual presence in the area meant some further kind of operation. We were beneath the flanks of Mauherslieve and as we climbed the hill at Bealaclave we had a good idea of the land around us. The Silvermines hills could been seen on the edge of Slievecamalta, and below the barracks to the south-west were the clustered tops of the Slievefelim range. Valleys and hollows receded into a cool depth. This is a treeless land, then at its softest green, a dairying land where the grass produces a sweet butter. The slopes were cropped close to summits by dry cattle, and the holdings were comparatively large. There were sturdy sheep on the high hills and there were very few relicts of resident landlords. Four of the creameries in this district had already suffered in reprisals made against the people by forces of the Crown who had broken up the intricate machinery with sledges and had then made heated use of their petrol. Rearcross was the first of these buildings in Ireland to be burned, and in the case of Reiska, Knockfune and Kilcommon, British military had assisted the constabulary in destruction. This holocaust was a deliberate attempt to punish and intimidate a neighbourhood by eliminating one of its main money-making sources. The British Cabinet may have thought it would turn the people against the IRA or make them unwilling to give shelter or food. The lads who had carried on the fight were the sons and relatives of the neighbourhood, who by this time had assumed a new influence which, instead of being controlled by parental authority, now directed it. The district took its share of the burden. The people complained when it irked, but their loyalty was not breached.

We cleaned our weapons in the evening and inspected some of the heavy cart-box bombs. Each metal cart box had been filled with gelignite packed with scrap iron, and a hole had been drilled in the metal for the fuse. Bolts strengthened the box and clamped it to maintain resistance. When fully loaded it might weigh from twenty to twenty-five pounds. It was more convenient to throw its weight from a height, but it would also be a most useful missile on a road block, especially at night.

For the attack on Rea barracks we intended to enter Flannery's shop late at night, when the RIC in the adjoining building would probably be asleep, except for the men on guard duty. We would break out through Flannery's roof to gain access to the roof of the barracks from which slates would be stripped in order to permit petrol and paraffin to be poured into the building, and a jet of incendiary liquid would be played on the roof by the pump. From the yellow clay collected we had made our mud bombs which would help to blow out the slates and open the barracks roof to a rush of oil and petrol flames.

In the evening we talked about some of our problems. Up to

this we had not been able to work out the most satisfactory incendiary mixture to use, nor had we been able to find what was the most efficient pump to handle. Already we had captured a barracks in this county because we had been able to use a workable pump, but the South Tipp men had not brought that pump with them. These two worries, the type of pump and the proper incendiary mixture, seemed simple enough, perhaps, to solve, yet we had no one to guide us and our headquarters did not supply us with practical information. Outside of our IRA organisation, which by now was close-mouthed, there were few people we could trust to help without the British inadvertently being made aware of our intentions.

It seemed easy to put a house afire. Even a match, a lighted cigarett butt, or sparks from a grate could begin a lasting blaze; but when we poured in petrol and paraffin from the roof by the gallon we found the attacked house swallowed the dangerous liquids as easily as the *Craos Deamhain* once engulfed like amounts of curdle and buttermilk. We knew that in the night-time we would have to carry tins of fluid over the exposed rising ground to the north of the barracks, and we wryly thought of the advantages of misapplied matches in the safety of our homes.

By night-fall it was raining heavily and a westerly wind blew strongly. We assembled by the hut under Bealaclave behind the traditional bed where the lovers had slept. Outposts had already moved off to their positions, but I had to wait until I knew that Newport company was ready to block the road close to the town. There were heavy trees at the park about half a mile on the road to Rea, which could be used for that purpose. This side of Lackamore, Knockfune Volunteers were to begin work on a small grove of trees there, immediately they were informed that the Newport men were at work. Up at Toor, on the winding road which circles Slievecamalta, a barricade of stones was to be built at the bridge. There were four relays of signallers and observers: one at Glencroe, at Knockfune hill over Ryan Lacken's house, on the hill behind the barracks, and the final group over towards Lackamore. Men had sods of turf which had been steeped in paraffin, and the blazing sods should be able to send their messages across the darkness. Martin Ryan had set out earlier to make sure of the obstructions near Newport, and not until I knew that men were in position there did I move on with the assault group towards the barracks.

We had long lengths of rope, spaced for the men to grip, for the night was as black as a Kerry cow. We were laden with buckets, petrol tins, paraffin, heavy bombs, ladders, a forty-gallon barrel, the pump and our weapons. Volunteers had been warned to walk quietly and not to talk or murmur, even when they slipped — and fell. The long string of men went down the hill. The wind roared in our faces and lashed the rain until we had to turn sideways and backwards to breathe. Men stumbled and sprawled on the slippery grass or bumped against one another with a clatter of buckets and tins. The barrel swayed unsteadily like a crow's nest in a gale. I swore inwardly as the stumbling shapes bumped, halted and held each other up at disconnected intervals. We needed but an engine whistle to sound like a goods train shunting at night, but the wind was kind; it blew our suppressed laughter, curses and rattles away to the east. We were like the Brugel painting of the blind leading the blind, and the darkness seemed to increase as we blundered onwards past the barracks, until the steadying knowledge of our scouts directed us with ease from their memorial observation as if they were walking up a winding bohereen to their own homes. Inside, the constabulary slept like the enchanted warriors in medieval stories, heeding not the clank of armour, but awaiting a spell that would awaken them from the depths of their long sleep. Our spell was a sledge-hammer, but it could not be put to work just yet.

At last, all of us sopping wet, we reached the Newport side of Flannery's shop. Then Treacy, Breen and the South Tipp men pushed on to a grove about four hundred yards distant, where the few trees would give them a little shelter. They were to protect our most likely danger-point of enemy penetration, since if enemy reinforcements arrived they could control the rising ground at the back of the barracks with their rifles from a distance of six hundred yards, and they would then command our line of retreat. In addition, the South Tipp men could act as a reserve in emergencies. There was nothing we could do to prevent the RIC from leaving their barracks in the darkness if they were sufficiently determined. The old RIC would know the vicinity in terms of square yards, and we already had learned that night what difference our scouts' knowledge of a few square yards had meant to our shunting advance.

Paddy Kinnane and Jim Gorman induced Flannery to open his door to admit us on the pretext that we badly needed a few drinks, and by the time he had opened a door, persuaded by the persistent whisperings of my companions while I kept my ears apart for movement in the barracks, a good drink would have been a relief. When we got inside I told him we were taking over his place for the night, to use it as a base for operations against the barracks, that we would help him to remove his family to a place of safety, but if he himself wished, he could remain to see that none of his property was interfered with, without his knowledge.

'Why didn't you attack Kilcommon?' he asked. 'It would have been easier.' That was true, but our business was now with Rea. He was not to sell a drink to anyone, I told him, or I would hold him responsible for the breach of discipline. Some of the hill men had a good stomach for drinks, I knew, and the mountains had supplied good poteen to their own, but our job was to deal with the barracks.

Jim Gorman and I went up a short ladder, through a trapdoor, to the rafters and we crawled forward to the partition wall. Previously, the barrel had been brought upstairs by Paddy Kinnane and Stapleton, where it had begun to be filled with gurgling liquid, and the silence with which we had moved up to this moment seemed now to my ears to be disturbed by a mountain cascade. The RIC guard might, however, think that the liquid sound was due to sudden wind swirls of rain.

The men who were helping went about in their stockinged feet, but Gorman, I noticed, wore heavy socks over his boots. Buckets of paraffin and tins of petrol had followed us upstairs, and we spaced them out at intervals in case of fire. At the far end of the room were about fourteen cart-box grenades, mud bombs, improvised grenades and a few real hand grenades.

With a few quick wallops of his sledge Jim burst a way

through Flannery's roof which opened to the rain, and we got up on the barracks roof. Within a few seconds we were flaking away with sledges at the slates, and I flung a few grenades into the gaps we had made, to keep the police a room's length away from us. Immediately that we had started operations on top, our men posted outside opened up on the barracks with their rifles, to divert the attention of the police from the roof.

I held the long hose while Gorman pumped away. Spread by cotton waste and paraffin-dripping turf, the blaze fought the wind and rain, but the swirling wind was best able to impose its mastery. I tried to light the fuse of a mud bomb, and cursed when foiled by the lashing rain. There was nothing for it but to get back under cover of Flannery's roof to light a couple of cigarettes for use as torches, and to smear some gelignite to the end of the wet fuses so that they might light. Out on the roof again, and when I reached the chimney I was able to start the fuses from under the shelter of my coat by applying the burning end of a cigarette to the smear of gelignite. Slates began to fly as I flung bomb after bomb, stripping off quickly large areas of the roof within my lobbing range. The wind was in our favour. It blew flames across on either side of the roof ridge, but rain did its best to help the constabulary. Always, it had seemed, in our few hundred years of outside help, as if the elements aided the British Navy, but here the elements had divided their allegiance.

Suddenly the pump gave out with an enervating squak, but by this time the blaze had taken a good hold and there was steady rifle fire from the garrison below us. We could hear the bullets as they smacked off the chimney behind us, or buzzed their way over our heads. I laughed at Gorman's taut remark, 'When you hear a bullet, it's all right.' I could hear Paddy Kinnane and Ryan Lacken cursing well and hard below while we laughed on high, and Kinnane was dancing with eagerness; he was very light on his feet for his height and breadth, for he was a grand step dancer. Lacken's language was directed mainly against the RIC and not against the defaulting pump; he had a bitter contempt and hatred for the peelers and it eased his mind to overflow with language as vivid as the flames beside us. What had happened to the honoured pump which we used at Drangan, I have not remembered, but it would have made a big difference that morning at Rea, for with it we would have got the barracks roof blazing in short time. It had been close to one o'clock when we reached Flannery's and that, to my mind, was two hours too late for the beginning of an attack. We had to make the best of the night now, and a bad night it was for the easy spread of flame.

Gorman and I had rifles. We rattled bullets downwards at an angle through the slates from room to room. At times we held each other's legs to steady the rifle shots when we fired straight down to reach the first floor below us. As we sat on the roof edge I said to Jim: 'What happened to you that night at Cappagh?' He was very reluctant to talk about Cappagh White, which had taken place the same night as our attack on Drangan, and he was since sorry that he had not gone along with the Rossmore men. However, Gorman, who was anything but talkative save among his friends, sat on the slates beside me and I listened to his story of Cappagh. I knew something of it already, and I could throw in an odd remark to rekindle aspects of that night's work. Gorman had thrown heavy Headquarters' percussion grenades which were specially prepared for attacks on buildings. Some of them had rolled down from the slates, but others had made a shattering roar as they went through holes in the roof. Gorman became impatient of the result as the police had refused to surrender. He had carried up buckets of paraffin which were splashed on the flaming roof from his ladder, but the wind swerved and threw back the flames on top of him. His clothes went on fire and he had to fight his own burning garments. Two men from Knockfune went up the ladder, helped him down and put out his blaze when they reached the ground.

While we talked, the light gleamed into leaping thrusts of orange-red flame as the wind veered round. We saw small patches of hill behind the barracks and the mouths of dark chasms where the roof had been stripped between us and the end chimney. Then the flames were beaten towards us by the wind until our side of the roof was on fire too. A sudden spark or a piece of smouldering timber could reach our combustible reserves on the floor below where we had close on two hundred gallons of paraffin in Flannery's top storey, as well as explosives. Quickly sacks were steeped in water by Jim Stapleton, Kinnane and Ryan Lacken, and together with them we tried to extinguish the fire advancing on our side of the roof. Before we had it smothered, our hands, faces and clothes bore traces of the struggle.

Seán Treacy came up then to see how the barracks was suffering, but he found to his consternation that the barracks' fire had now attacked the shop and that it was the shop that was in most danger of immediate destruction. There was nothing he or his men could do to help us from their outpost positions, for they could not alter the situation on the roof. We had been dependent on the pump to keep the flames well forward and away from Flannery's, and the pump had now turned traitor.

I threw a heavy cart-box bomb into a flame-ringed hole in the barracks' roof. Heavy thuds, like the fall of a cannon ball down wooden stairs, came up from below, but that was all, and we waited vainly for the shattering sound of an explosion. We listened for a while, but no further sound came to our straining ears. 'A faulty detonator, I expect, or maybe the gelignite was frozen,' I said.

The pump, which had been screeching after continuous elbow thrusts, again kept quiet. More cart-box bombs were thrown with better results, exploding on the first floor with satisfactory reverberating noises that must have caused the garrison to wonder what was happening. Flames were no longer visible from the barracks roof, so that when Gorman hurled a tin of petrol through a gap and nothing happened, we thought that the fire below had subsided. On that account we went below Flannery's roof to examine the possibility of getting the paraffin pump to work again but, having written it off as a bad job, we had barely returned to our post when a shattering explosion shook the barracks, followed by a high geyser of smoke, edged like a Van Gogh cypress. Late contact with the remains of the fire had apparently made a delayed-action bomb of Gorman's tin of petrol. Flames started up once more.

Jim Gorman turned to me suddenly. 'I'm hit,' he said, holding his arm.

'Do you think it got the bone?' I asked.

'No, it's not bad.' He would not complain of the pain, I knew.

I helped him down through the man-hole we had made on Flannery's roof. Down below I examined the wound and found that the bullet had travelled along his arm from the wrist. I bandaged the entrance wound, and when he had taken a drink he wanted to return with me to the roof, but I could see that he was in pain and that his wounded arm was useless, yet he was reluctant to admit either pain or his state of relative uselessness.

'You can't use two hands above, Jim, but you can be a reserve down here.' I said, making it clear that I could not allow him back on the roof.

Again we tried the pump and it played a weak dribble of paraffin on the burning roof. Paraffin thrown out of buckets was much more effective, but the roof was long and to cover all of it we thought of hurling bottlefuls.

Sometime just about dawn a sergeant wearing a soft hat came out the front door of the barracks with a rifle and looked up at the roof, evidently trying to find the riflemen whose bullets, when they penetrated through slates and the top floor, had been a source of danger and of irritation to the garrison. Rifles cracked by the haggard and he stumbled back against the door. It was a brave and hopeless gesture, that of his. A brave man, he had served with the British Army in France, and had been promoted sergeant for his share in the defence of Kilmallock RIC barracks, but he bore no bad name among the local people, as did the majority of his swaggering comrades. We had a contempt for the RIC, who trailed our men for years, picked them out from other suspects when they were made prisoners, led marauding groups or murder gangs to plunder or burn, and practised their brutality on prisoners. The Tans aggravated the destruction, intensified the ill-treatment of prisoners, and dealt with the average country man as if he were actively hostile. It was only in action that we respected either of them. It was a pity that the British could not supply men we could respect in peace as well as in war.

We were in a good place to look for empty bottles and I sent Kinnane down ahead of me to organise these makeshift incendiaries. When I followed him downstairs I saw that rows of porter and naggin bottles had already been filled with a mixture of petrol and paraffin. Ryan Lacken and I threw some of them from behind Flannery's place, but instead of smashing against the slates a fair number of them rolled intact to the ground. The glass was too strong. We tried using loose paper stoppers instead of corks, but that did not work either. Then we hit upon the idea of filing the necks of the bottles so that they would smash on impact. Seán Treacy came up again from the grove when a good pile of bottles was ready for use and I had already tested a few of them. They smashed along the roof and flames had spread.

There was one drawback to an intensive roof fire. It made the roof too insecure to move along later when the heat had died down, and so it would become of no use to fire further portions of the building. That approach was therefore unworkable, and the lower storeys, owing to the heat, would prevent storming parties from proceeding by way of the ground floor in a progressive advance. By this time, however, there were large gaps along the length of the slates and we could now make use of these breaches. If we stood well out in the open we could lob bottles against the slates right up to the far gable and down towards the back windows. Seán and I threw bottles with a rapid swing, and the fire trail grew from our every smash. A wall separated us from the barracks. To our left flank, men had originally been posted who could have covered us with their rifles on the barracks windows, but they must have moved away since I had talked to them there. Anyhow, they would have scarcely had cover for themselves.

As I swung a bottle into the air I saw a dark object curving down towards me, a grenade I guessed, and as I flattened myself against the ground it burst beside me with a deafening report. I felt myself being lifted upwards, and a soft spot in my stomach melted at the same time. My equilibrium was badly shattered by the blast but I had retained sufficient of my scattered wits to get up and run with Treacy like the hammers of hell for Flannery's back door. We had just made it when another grenade exploded. I felt blood on my right hand; it had flowed down from my shoulder.

Flannery, whose house we had forcibly entered and whose

paraffin we had already used to the tune of about two hundred gallons, now got me a good glass of brandy as I sat down for a few minutes. The drink eased the stomach shock, but I remained in a shaky condition for some time.

Though further pelting of bottles continued, the morning moved on to a stalemate. Most of the police were probably in the concrete shelter behind the barbed wire, and some were in the end rooms farthest removed from the flames. They had moved along with them the body of the dead sergeant to prevent it from being destroyed by fire, as they were slowly driven back by the flames.

It must have been nine o'clock when a scout hurried in to report. 'They're coming, they're coming'! he exclaimed, and promptly made himself scarce.

'He won't stop now till he reaches Nenagh,' said Gorman drily.

I waited for Treacy's report. He was angry when he came up to us, for some men had gone up the hill without waiting for orders. Enemy soldiers were not in the vicinity but they might have been a distance away; a white flag had been seen on a distant hill where an outpost had been left, and that pre-arranged signal meant that there was danger now on the Toor road, yet there seemed to be no additional information as to the strength of the reinforcements. Later on, the flag had two interpretations: it had waved in the wind as it was carried on the shoulders of a man who was on his way home; against that, Ned Reilly at the grove had seen it wave for some time and it seemed to be a warning. All of the men on the Toor road, and the signallers, must have gone home around six o'clock, as we learned afterwards. A man carting milk to a creamery threw aside the piled-up stones of the road-block which should have been defended with force of arms, and a wagon that came along some time later might have been mistaken for a military lorry. It was, in fact, Jack Meehan's old hearse and was carrying a coffin. Military came along that road some hours after and they searched houses on the way.

We climbed the hill behind the barracks, under cover of low

banks, and the last look we gave the object of our nocturnal labours showed that smoke was still eddying through its shattered roof. Beyond the Diarmuid and Grania bed the South Tipperary men fell in with others whose way home lay in the same direction, and I went with them. It turned out a fine, fresh morning, bright with shafted sunshine on the wet grass and earth scents strong in the air. With protective scouts thrown out around us at a distance, we went across the hills in sections. People came to their doors and called across the fields to us, or ran towards the ends of bohereens to talk to us. They were anxious for news, as they had heard the noise of rifles and grenades; for them it sounded trebly loud on their hill slopes and must have seemed like a pitched battle. All that we could say was that the barracks was nearly burned out, and at that they were pleased. They wanted us to go to their homes for breakfast and they were eagerly persistent, but we knew we had to get the Volunteers back to their own townlands. Men on the run now wandered around their battalion areas but they, and the others who were yet able to remain at home, liked the security the feel of their own brigade land gave to their minds.

We did not know what disturbing projects British reinforcements from numerous compass points might suddenly unfold, but there was no feeling among the people we met with that we had failed in our attempt, and our own fighting values were elastic enough. Even though we had not captured the arms of the constabulary there was no tradition of result for effort to weigh us down, and instead we were brimming with the ease of gaiety. We heard stories of the weight of the British burden on the neighbourhood. An old man, close to Rea, said 'The police in the barracks were pure devils and they'd do anything that was mean and bad.' They had repeatedly pushed his sister into the fire one day, but one of them, however, had always pulled her out again. Convoys or lorry patrols which passed on the road to Thurles had a habit of opening rifle fire when they came under certain hills, or of spraying houses close to the road as they rode by.

The sun warmed us as we climbed up by the long slopes which gave us a view of hill and valley for miles around. There had been a big number of men present from Hollyford, and some from nearby companies who had gone home on Sunday morning had walked back on Sunday night, but they were men accustomed to stretching their legs. The fresh air, bright sun and the familiar contours of hill and valley helped to wash fatigue from our bones. Our lack of success did not weigh us down, for we had not lost men and we saw things through the eyes of youth. When we came to Hollyford, people came out to watch us as we marched through the village, stiffly at attention. We saw the broken barracks, and there the Hollyford men were dismissed. Treacy, Breen, Ned Reilly, Jack the Master and I went on our way to Glenough, about twelve miles away from our recent bonfire.

We never found out the RIC casualties of that morning, though the British admitted the death of a sergeant. Another sergeant was said to have been seriously injured when a cart-box bomb exploded, and a number of constables were badly burned. The number killed would vary either with repetition or from desire. We had not even the satisfaction of having destroyed a post, but the garrison was removed that morning for a long rest; some of its members did not return. Flannery's shop was taken over as a barracks, and a Scots regiment commandeered the school, remaining for weeks until suitable defences had been built for the new garrison, when its bottle-green occupants were once again ready to make their King's writ an empty tin can tied to a dog's tail.

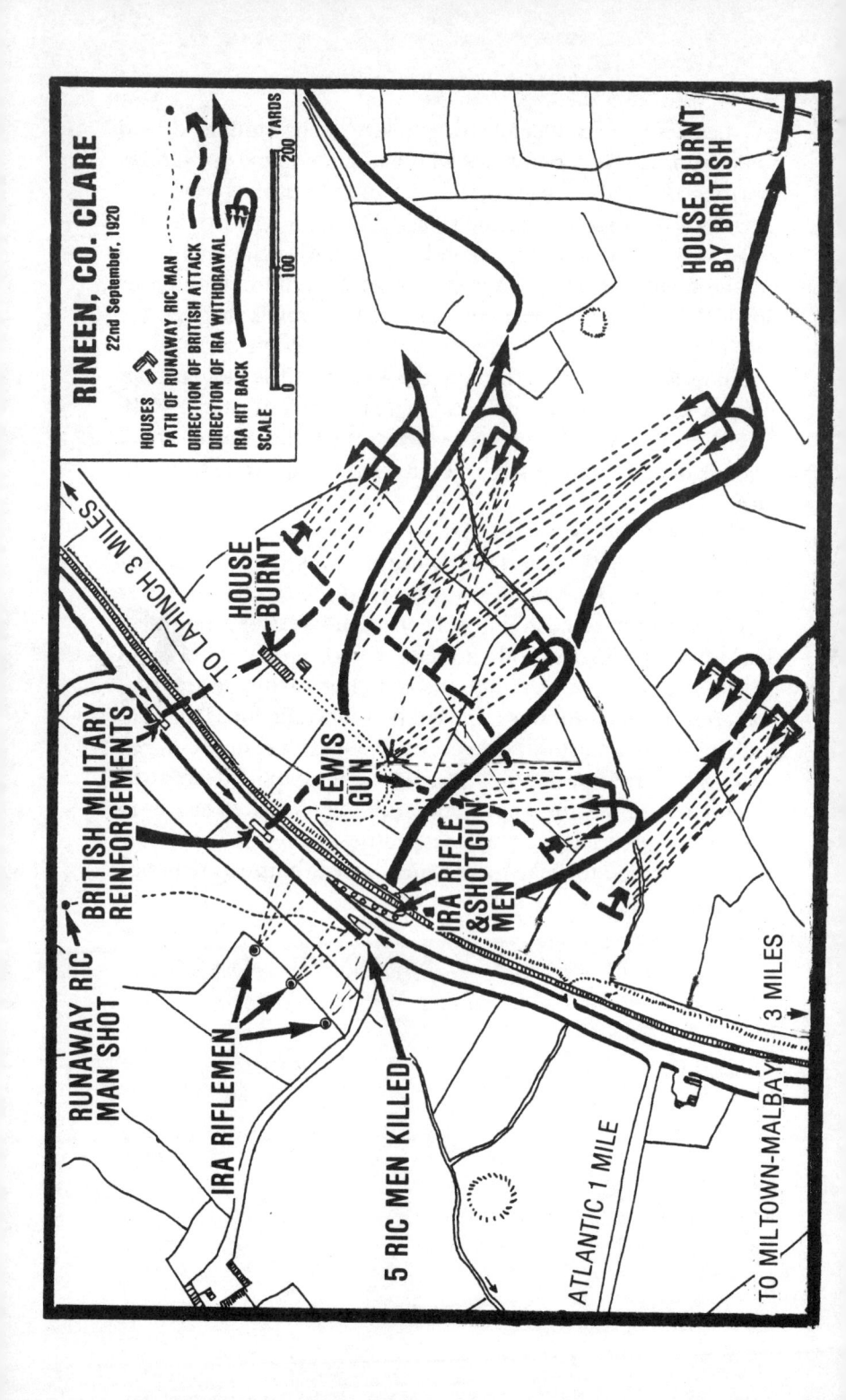

RINEEN, CO. CLARE
22nd September, 1920

CHAPTER FOUR

RINEEN AND REPRISALS

SEPTEMBER 1920

Volunteers in the Ennistymon battalion of Mid-Clare Brigade kept an eye on the RIC and British military in 1920. In each company there were men attached to intelligence whose particular duty it was to observe patrols on foot and in lorries, their movements of themselves and their supplies by rail. The gathering of gossip material is a congenial occupation in Ireland, but accuracy, being another matter, meant a more thorough investigation for the IRA. In a sense, every Volunteer was a gatherer of information about the enemy, but then the entire countryside, as could happen in a staunch area such as this, were also on the prowl for any stray tags of talk. A company area, as a result, could be a hive for the honey of rumour.

The battalion staff had been told of a small Crossley tender of RIC and Tans which left Ennistymon on the way to Miltown Malbay twice each week. Ignatius O'Neill, a fair-haired ex-Irish Guardsman who had a way with him, was in charge of the battalion, and as soon as he found from reports that there was a regularity in the movements of the Crossley he decided to attack it. Previously, ambush positions had been selected at random along the main lines of police and military traffic, with a view to the possibilities of ground. Now that there was a specific vehicle to attack, there was again an inspection of possible positions. Finally, it was decided to select an ambush place at Rineen, or Drummin as it is also called. Beyond Lahinch to the south the country in from the sea edge rises slowly into a series of broken hills. Farther on a sharp rise of low cliff backed the narrow-gauge West Clare railway to the east, but at Rineen the railway was lifted steeply above the road. There was a sudden curve to the left on the Lahinch side of the line, which would help men in ambush. A car would slow down on this bend and it would be abreast of the position before it could increase its speed. Fowlers and shotgun men could, indeed by themselves, hold the selected site, but if there was more than a lorry the hidden men would not be able to deal effectively with the second of the vehicles without the protection of riflemen.

As there had been no previous engagement in this Moy company area the commandant decided to get as many men as he could into the action. This would give a wider sense of participation and it might encourage Volunteers to be eager for another attack on the British. There were nine companies in the battalion, and as the area was thickly populated there was ample man-power to draw from. It was arranged that each company, except Lavereen, would furnish Volunteers. Séamus Hennessey was the company commander of Moy, and as the operation was to take place in his area he was responsible for guides to direct the incoming companies to their mobilisation centres. At two o'clock on the morning of September 22, 1920, three companies, Inagh, Ennistymon and Lahinch, were at Moy chapel. They had brought rations with them and they lay on trams of hay to rest while the Moy Volunteers acted as a protective screen in the darkness. At four o'clock the commandant moved the companies off towards the Carrig at Ballyvaskin where they met more men from three other companies.

It was a fine night with enough sea wind to cover the unusual noise of feet. The sea was beating heavily against the open coast in long rollers as the men moved inland to skirt houses and to circumvent the attention of any late ramblers on the road. Also they had to avoid showing their figures against the skyline before dawn. Across the bay at Liscannor was a coastguard station which was held by marines. From their watchposts the marines swept the sea with telescopes and they kept as well a wary eye behind them on the landward side. Well trained and disciplined, they took pride in the alertness and prestige of their force.

Men lay down close to the railway line while battalion and company officers were brought together to discuss the problems on the chosen ground. If more than one lorry came their way the provisional arrangements would have to be changed quickly, but as they would have timely warning from a sucession of signallers and scouts to the north and south their plan could be changed with some ease. It was felt, however, that there had been a continuous regularity in the movement of the police patrol and that only one lorry could be expected. Yet O'Neill and his officers were aware that both RIC and military had a disconcerting habit of suddenly changing both their formation and their travelling strength. Scouts had been sent on the main by-roads and signallers were out on the hills behind the railway in three directions. Moroney, who had expected to be given a rifle, was sent to take reluctant charge of the numerous scouts.

The armament, as was customary in Volunteer battalions, varied widely in pattern and in efficiency. In July six rifles had been captured from a military patrol in Ennistymon, and to these were added a few carbines which had been taken previously from the Royal Irish. The rifles were in good condition. When O'Neill inspected single and double-barrelled shotguns, however, his language was redder than the rust which pitted some of them. He found extractors to be faulty and he rejected a number of weapons. The precarious manner in which weapons had to be hidden often made them useless. For the past year houses had been thoroughly raided by RIC and British military for weapons and for incriminating papers. Successive raids on suspected houses would increase in thoroughness until a technique of quick destruction had unearthed most hiding places. Lack of attention by quartermasters and the men themselves influenced the proper use of arms, but shotguns were particularly difficult to keep in condition as they were for the most part now concealed away from houses. Shotgun ammunition was a great problem to solve, for if the cartridge was swollen through dampness the extractor would be useless in action.

At the selected position the railway was about forty feet above the road and it continued to overlook it for more than a quarter of a mile. Leading up from the main road at an angle was a narrow sunken lane which turned back on itself when it crossed the railroad, forming, with the track above, an alternative line either for attack or defence. The western side of the sunken lane was about eight feet higher than the road. Along it the riflemen were to be placed in position, and the shotgun men were to be higher up towards the railway crossing.

Two hand grenades, proud possessions of the battalion, were given to Peter Vaughan, an ex-American soldier who had used these explosive missiles in France during the world war.

Thick furze bushes were cut down and stuck in the ground where the lane left the road. The prickly green branches hid the men from the roadside view. Below the road the land dropped suddenly from eight to ten feet. That drop would be an advantage to the four men whose task it was to prevent anyone crossing the road towards them. They had a mixture of rifles and shotguns and they would have the cover of low walls and banks to lie behind. They were placed in position first, and were given instructions to withhold fire until they saw the constabulary leave the road to get cover on their side, otherwise cross-fire might hit men in the laneway. Further to their west was the sea, but these men below the road and the riflemen on high ground could fire over land in that direction for about five hundred yards. O'Neill picked riflemen and took charge of them. Higher up, Séamus Hennessey was responsible for the first small group of shotgun men.

Behind the railway line the land rose in hilly out-thrusts. The ground was bare, yet there was cover behind low banks, the edge of hills and in unexpected hollows. These rises and undulations would be of use to riflemen in the event of a pressed retirement, for when forced from their chosen positions men could retire only to the east. Further back, the country dropped into bogland which had rough heather flanked by deep drains. Away in the distance was the only considerable elevation in the western landscape, Mount Callan, over 1,200 feet.

There were numerous armed scouts on by-roads in the neighbourhood and more than sufficient unarmed scouts to thoroughly protect the waiting men at Rineen. There were also Volunteers then in the area who could not be of use, but their presence close to the scene of attack would sharpen their wits in experience and would help to start a legend in the making. Every man who was contributing in any way to the event would help to build up in the minds of the neighbourhood, and strengthen in the thoughts of the IRA, the symbol of an unarmed people emerging to fight for freedom against a formidable enemy which had successfully come through the greatest war in history.

In later years, in Europe, various underground movements would set their own patterns of resistance. Each country involved would have to contend against its own Quislings and a traitrous police, the counterpart of the Royal Irish, but no country in that war would have to face the long-nurtured hostility of what had once been a garrison, then an ascendancy and finally a settlement which held land and money securely and whose allegiance was mainly to the Empire.

The European Resistance would persist in spite of torture, the abuse of hostages and the iron-heeled ruthlessness of soldiers and intelligence services. In the Irish countryside all of these approaches to resistance and to despotism were budding in a token manner which had almost burst to flower before the end. Even so, imaginative fear in a small town ran to the full its gamut of apprehension and terror when forces of the Crown were deliberately loosed.

The Volunteers settled down for a long wait, hidden from passers-by. There were the incongruous interruptions of heavy cart wheels grinding the road surface, and the steady pounding of waves from the west. In the quiet morning the mooing of cows was answered by the barking of dogs and the shrill harshness of geese. Away across Liscannor Bay was the rising edge of ground which topped the steep cliffs of Moher. Over the ridge the long blue lengths of the Aran Islands were rimmed with sea haze. To the south-west lay Spanish Point and Mutton Island where ships of the Armada had been dashed against the shore when Spanish pride foundered. Further westwards a long promonotory pushed itself seaward at the mouth of the Shannon.

In the distance a syncopated noise became clearer as it was translated into the laboured puffing of a small engine. The West Clare train was on its way. The men settled well down against the opposite bank of the laneway where they were hidden from view, yet any passenger who leaned out of a window could surely see what lay beneath. There was even the possibility that troops might be aboard but that was most unlikely since at that time engine drivers and guards would refuse to carry armed police or armed military, and the line of carriages passed by with their swaying buffer clashes.

At last word came from the signallers. 'Three cars coming.'

There was a short interval while men listened for the sound of lorry engines and the officers attempted to make a rapid change of plan. O'Neill gave orders that fire was to be withheld until the second lorry was outside the lane. Riflemen could then fire at the first car and the shotguns could deal with the second.

As a car came around the curve and passed below, the Angelus bell rang, but no further engine sound reached the hidden groups. The mistake was explained shortly when a scout was hurridly summoned to the laneway. The message, 'Police car coming', from the farthest signallers had been changed in the interpretation by a winded scout.

Now the position would have to be held until the police returned and that meant another weary stretch of waiting under cover. John Clune, an Inagh cyclist, was immediatly sent into Miltown to find out where the patrol had gone and to try to get information about its return. Soon young Clune was back to report to O'Neill that the Crossley was outside the RIC barracks and would be returning shortly.

From rising ground which overlooked Miltown the approach of the car was signalled before its engine noise could be heard. As it passed below the sunken road there was a loud scattered volley from shotguns and rifles. The driver was killed, the Crossley halted with its dead, but one policeman was seen to leap out, jump down the far side of the road and make wildy for the sea. A considerable amount of rifle ammunition must have gone past him before he dropped five hundred yards away. Michael O'Dwyer, a noted fowler, and John Joe Neylon, among others, were said to have brought the lone blue-green jacket to earth.

All other occupants of the Crossley had been killed by the opening volley. Five rifles and one revolver were gathered up.

Some of the rifle stocks had been torn by shotgun and rifle fire. There were black bandoliers and black canvas slings of ammunition on the dead bodies. In addition there was a large reserve of rifle ammunition which came close to three thousand rounds, an unusual supply for such a small escort. The tender was sieved by the concentrated fire which had struck it, and the five police sprawled out in a bloody mass.

Suddenly another car was signalled from the same direction. The IRA slipped quickly into position, but when it came close it was found to be a car of civilians. The people in it were warned to keep their mouths shut about what they had seen, and they were then permitted to resume their journey.

The scouts had returned out of curiosity when they heard no further gun noise. The ambush at Rineen was successful and the Volunteers were inclined to take it easy. A few sat on the road bank for a chat and a smoke, but Dan Kennelly, who had served in both the British Army and the RIC, urged the talkers to get back quickly towards the hills which were now their only line of retreat. He knew that a number of men had come from the north of Ennistymon and north-east from Inagh over nine miles away. Military reinforcements could be expected from Ennistymon, from their county headquarters in Ennis and maybe from Kilrush. Roads had not been blocked in any direction, nor had telegraphic wires been interrupted, for fear police and military might be put on the alert and the motor patrol increased in strength. Behind them, to the north and north-east, was a patchwork of small roads leading from valley to valley through the hills. These roads were badly surfaced but skilled military drivers in their heavy lorries would make quick use of them to lay a ring of troops in a pressing encirclement.

As the IRA went up the rising ground Séamus Hennessey waited behind for a comrade of his, Steve Gallagher, who had gone down to collect the rifle belonging to the constabulary man who had rushed towards the sea. Séamus shouted to him to hurry up towards the road, as he heard the noise of what seemed to be a lorry approaching from the Lahinch direction. Some of the men had halted below the first hill, but he shouted to them to push upwards as he indicated the direction of the noise.

A couple of minutes later a military lorry came around the bend below the railway. As he saw the shattered car the driver halted abruptly. Khaki figures jumped out and rushed up to the railway from which they could see men in front of them running uphill. The sudden crash of rifles and the patter of a machine-gun spread the alarm. Now all the Volunteers were aware that they were being closely followed and that for many their way to safety would lead across unfamiliar ground. A second lorryload of troops halted close to the bend and a further thin khaki line went up the hill. The British fired at random, too eager for the chase to lie down at their ease and sight their weapons carefully.

There was a succession of small hills to the east, and when the soldiers reached one hill which they thought would give them an advantage over the men who should now be below them they saw only a few targets, and in front of them was another hill. Their legs were not trained to such a ground. For their own protection they had by then become accustomed to the ease and comparative safety of their lorries. Now when at last they saw their enemies they also met with as formidable an enemy, the hills. They were not as physically fit as the country men whose chance of survival now lay in their legs and in the commonsense of their officers.

A machine-gun and its crew burdened with heavy boxes of ammunition slowed up on the inclines, but often when the gun had a field of fire the gunner continued to run forward, followed by his other weighted bearers. Targets appeared and disappeared behind hand-cocks of hay which gave no protection but upset the gunner whose breath was not attuned to his vanishing sight-fields. Nevertheless, the gun drummed its bullets along the tracks of the retreating IRA, cutting ground ahead of them and close in to their flanks.

A number of riflemen, including Pat Lehane and John Joe Neylon, had gone towards Lahinch through the hills. But Seán Burke, with the few riflemen who had been west of the road, had kept close to the sea-edge. O'Neill, Kennelly and O'Dwyer the fowler had their rifles, but the shotgun men, with their out-of-range weapons, carried extra and useless weight in the race. The numerous unarmed scouts who up to this had taken no part in the action were suddenly a joint part of the reaction, and their former passive relationship to the ambush had now become intimate activity in a relentless pursuit, announced more closely by the shrill wind-blast of bullets.

A small group of soldiers led the advance of the extended line of khaki which by this time had been sadly dinged by lack of breath and by obstacles. By their pace the group seemed to be trained runners. In front, as was afterwards discovered, was their best cross-country runner who had set the pace. They made for a scattered driblet of unarmed men, shouting their customary expletives. Such frequent use of noun and adjective stole what they most needed, breath, but then they were sure of their prey.

The three IRA riflemen, O'Neill, Kennelly and O'Dwyer, lay down slowly until their breathing was natural and then began to use their weapons. Kennelly wounded the leading runner and his khaki followers sprawled so quickly into the heather that some of them were probably hit. Behind them, the leading wings of the long line settled down on the ground, so that the IRA rearguard had sprinted over the bog and had got down again to fire as soon as the soldiers advanced once more. The three riflemen were now widly separated, although within hailing distance, for it was felt that dispersal might deceive their pursuers who must have thought they were numerous, and the occasional use of rapid fire would also sustain that illusion.

Séamus Hennessey and some of his shotgun men were making for a gap in a bank when Vaughan shouted at them, 'Don't go out that gap, for they're like to set the gun on it. Roll over the bank when I shout.' Sure enough, the gunner had his sights trained on the gap, and when the men simultaneously leaped up and tumbled over the brow, the gun, in a long roll of fire, cut the edges off the gap and the top of the bank on either side of it. O'Neill and his two riflemen lay down to fire whenever a clump of soldiers induced them to take aim. They concentrated on the machine-gun which was the focal point of danger, and must have hit one of the gunners for there was a long delay in its noisy threat, longer than would be accounted for by a normal stoppage. The gun resumed firing in a succession of long bursts, but then there must have been another casualty, for there was no further reply. The captured British ammunition was invaluable in the retreat. It was returned generously to its late owners and the steady use of it held up the military until the shotgun men and the unarmed scouts were well on their way to their homes.

Ignatius O'Neill was wounded in the thigh. Michael Curtin also received a bullet, but both were able to walk for a while. By this time the squelchy bog surface and the irregularly-placed deep drains had helped to impede additional infantry detachments that were followed up by cavalry, and not one of the fast retreating men had been captured. Men who had been making trams of hay on the edge of the bog helped to carry the wounded to houses a few miles further on. Doctors were sent for, and they came out at once from Miltown, Lahinch and Ennis in spite of the handling they would get, if intercepted, to explain their presence or to force them to give information about casualties. The wounded were later carried back across the hills on stretchers to Moy company where they rested until they were able to walk again.

Near these hills, in the spring of 1919, I had carried out manoeuvres with five IRA companies against an extended position held by four lighter units. During the advance I watched a tall, fair-haired officer, O'Neill, who had attended my classes on tactics. He had served in the Irish Guards during the world war, and he bore himself with an ease which had not been blotted out of him by his rigorous training. He had a haversack filled with small balls of kneaded clays. When he noticed men who were disregarding my instructions about the use of ground he beladoured them accurately with his missiles from behind until he had converted their hump-backed approach into a wriggling and snake-like flatness. He had a way with him, I could see, and he was as wild as a March hare.

A few hours before the time I had fixed to dismiss the battalion on that Sunday evening, scouts brought the news that British troops from Lahinch were coming in our direction over the hills. The tactical scheme was now quickly changed. Some of the battalion officers took charge of the retreat and I remained behind with Ignatius O'Neill, Maurteen Devitt and a group of Volunteers, as a very conspicuous rearguard. Maurteen was impetuous, I knew, and I was afraid he might detach some of the rearguard and order a charge with the long sticks which were carried for arms drill and for bayonet fighting but which were now useful to us in probing the chocolate non-resistance of the ground. The British tried to outflank the rearguard, but our legs were more nimble than theirs, hardier on the hills and surer on the soft brown of squelching turf. We expanded and contracted, luring the expectant enemy abruptly into the softest bog we could find, while our main body, out of sight, split up into sections which scouted the way back to their company areas. We sat down to laugh at the hopeless position of the eager British.

There was an amount of rashness in Ignatius, but he had a fine quality of ease combined with a surging gaiety which made him popular with his men. He had the alert instinct for combat of the natural soldier, and he had handled his men well that day. He was a contrast to his senior officer, Maurteen, whose speech was as rapid as his energy, which was like a rainstorm when it was given head and as difficult to control. He was hound-eager for action and careless of his own safety.

British reprisal parties had been at work since early in the afternoon of the Rineen ambush. As the IRA crossed a rise they had seen smoke and flames from Honan's, the house nearest to the ambush position, and from O'Gorman's, a little more remote. An old man, Keane, had been carting hay to a rick with his horse and cart. He was found to be a good cock-shot for soldiers who had followed up the two lorries, and they killed him.

In the nightime an RIC raiding party went to old Dan Lehane's house at Cragg near Lahinch. He was a very independent type of man. They questioned him about his IRA sons and they threatened him with revolvers when he refused to answer. They explained in tortuous detail what they would do to his boys when they found them, but the old man answered them abruptly and finally told them to go to hell. They brought him out to the strand with his wife and, as he stood close to her, they fired a surplus of lead into him, but he did not die before some weeks. Early next morning, when they were on their way to Miltown, the Ennistymon police burned his house.

In the darkness reinforcements of Royal Irish Constabulary crowded into Ennistymon where their enmity was sharpened by an official report that the bodies of the RIC at Rineen had been mutilated by the IRA. Drink added intensity to their bitterness which was constantly being kindled by their officers, by themselves and by the presence of the bodies. When the town was quiet, blue-green uniforms began their attack on the neighbourhood.

In Ennistymon, the town hall was first set on fire about nine o'clock. Shortly after ten o'clock, about twenty police under a sergeant came to Tom Connole's house. He was the local secretary of the Irish Transport and General Workers' Union, as well as being an IRA man. The sergeant told Connole he wanted him, but would not give his wife time to get his coat for him. They threatened to shoot her if she did not leave her house at once, and they refused to allow her to return for a shawl to wrap around her child of four whom she led by the hand as she carried her four-months baby in one arm. At gun point they forced her to a neighbour's house close to her own. From there she saw her house in flames and she heard shots. Early on the following morning a piece of a blood-stained skull was picked up near Connole's house and the charred remains of his body were found inside the house.

The RIC then killed a boy of twelve, P. J. Linnane, who was carrying water to help put out a fire that was consuming a neighbour's shop. The Tans and RIC, warmed by their night's work through fire and drink, made a bag of five houses and the town hall before they came to Lahinch.

They broke into Tom Flanagan's shop where there was ample drink for their incendiary thirst, but when they had drunk themselves into humour they gave warning to a few houses, one by one, as they came to them. That warning of from four to seven minutes was a help to children and to the aged. Flanagan's was the first house to be sprinkled with petrol, and when four houses were on fire the constabulary stopped for another thirst quenching. They gave no notice to the sixth house once they had put Mick Vaughan's aflame. Inside was an old woman, a young woman and a young child. The women had watched the kindling squads at work but they had thought that their house was safe. Here was used an incendiary bomb which fired the house at once. Luckily the young child was brought down the stairway by her aunt who collapsed on the way down, but all got out in safety. Even then they were fired on as they came out the front door in their night clothes. Susan Flanagan had an invalid sister who was bed-ridden. On her knees she begged the RIC not to burn her house as she would not be able to carry out her sister. 'We don't give a damn if you have five invalid sisters, we're going to burn', was the hopeful answer as they spilt petrol on the furniture. She had to go upstairs, drag down her sister and then carry her out on her back as far as the end of the yard, where she left her.

An East Clare man, Sammon, who had come for a seaside holiday, was killed as he was helping to bring a woman out of a burning house.

Pake Lehane, a son of the old man whom the police had left for dead on the strand the previous evening, had been at Rineen that day. He was asleep upstairs over a shop when police put the house on fire and he was burned to death. The fire toll for Lahinch was also five houses completely destroyed and a town hall, but many other fires had been started which were put out by neighbours.

Throughout the successive torch and petrol attacks the RIC eased off their rifles at movement or through sudden inclination. Their unsteady aim, weakened by drink, saved many people who were rushing away in panic to neighbours' houses, but the neighbours had again to leave their own homes and clear out to the relative safety of the hills before the RIC left the town. The clear moonlight was a menace to the fugitives as it silhouetted movement, made the flames more dramatic and rendered the streets safer for the Tans and RIC who could be fairly recognised at a distance by their comrades, generous in their distribution of ammunition. Women and children crept into gardens or lay in outhouses, but there was no sense of security as they could hear shouting and taunting from police threats against individual men whom they could not find, and the night terror of straggling rifle shots.

Great numbers of people made for the seashore where they lay on wet grass or on the damp sand. They lay low until dawn came for fear they would be seen, and rumours about the shooting of Dan Lehane and Sammon went on their round. Mothers sheltered their young babies in their arms, but elderly people shivered in the moist sea air, for few had time to clothe themselves properly. Fear, however, drove out cold. Young boys in their shirts tried to hold on to horses which had been rescued from burning stables and were again frightened by distant shouts and by rifle shots. Yet there was mercy shown to a few. A tall, fair-haired Tan stood at the door of a house which his comrades of the constabulary intended to burn. The woman of the house appealed to him in flickering light thrown from a burning building.

'Don't burn me out,' she said, 'There's only women and small children inside.' The police went away then.

At a lodging house which they had set on fire, police helped visitors to remove their luggage, although the man of the house, who had been drawing water to the blaze, had to hide from them. 'It's not women and children we want,' the RIC said. 'It's men we want tonight. We're out for blood.'

Miltown RIC were early out on the streets, waging war against the town. When the inhabitants saw that the dark-coats were busy drinking without cost in damaged pubs they left the town. The police used hand grenades against shop windows and their rifle butts on doors, but they were too interested in drink to burn more than a few shops. Later on, Ennistymon police in their lorries toured the town in an unsteady circus parade, with discordant song allied to roaring threats and invitations to fight as they proclaimed their intention by unsteady volleys. They had come over to assist their comrades, the local preservers of law and order, and additional people left quickly for the hills. Petrol which they brought with them was freely used. The houses which were set in flames were all quickly destroyed. British military, who were stationed in the town, worked under their officers to check the rapidly spreading flames and, due to their help, the fire was confined; yet, before daylight, eight houses were gutted and there was little glass in the town save what could be found in splinters on the foot-paths.

That night, a young Fianna boy, MacMahon, found a police rifle leaning against the wall of a pub and took it away with him.

The policy of reprisals organised by the Crown forces had a certain discipline in its supposed indicipline. Men, drivers, lorries, arms, explosives and petrol had to leave barracks and, however drunk the expedition became, they had to return. The punitive force, if it arrived from a distance, had to be guided on the way and directed towards the selected houses. The Royal Irish had prepared lists of houses to be burned in an emergency, and when destruction became more methodical Tans in each barracks had a copy of the names. Burnings or explosions were seldom carried out in daylight before martial law was proclaimed. The favorite time was the darkness which provided a certain security against recognition. Seldom was a foray made in hot blood. There was an interval of time, often a day's space, but more usually it took place on the night ending a day attack against British forces. The first wrecking of shops in a town took place in September 1919 when British garrison troops descended on Fermoy and picquets were not sent out to round up the troops until two hours later. The RIC garrison protected property by their absence. Constabulary, military, Auxiliaries, each organisation acted when members of their individual force had to be revenged, but except at the beginning of 1920 military and police seldom acted together. At Balbriggan Black and Tans carried out the sack of the village, and in Mallow RIC and Tans helped to save a few of the houses which British regulars had fired. In Tuam military foot patrols on duty left the streets when they saw constabulary and Tans from Galway busy with petrol and rifle, but during the second destruction in Templemore the RIC barracks became a place of refuge. The intention of this seemingly haphazard destruction was to crush a town or countryside so that its fighting men would be fearful or incapable of further effective resistance. As time passed, houses of members of administrative bodies from county, urban and rural districts, which had given allegiance to Dáil Éireann, were due for the petrol tin. The organised source of wealth in resistant country was a creamery, and when a creamery was destroyed it was thought the countryside would turn against the Republican Army. Strangely enough, even to members of the Republican Army, people did not blame them for the ensuing destruction or for the terror induced, neither did they withdraw their sympathy or support. This strength of the people was difficult to understand, for Ireland had not produced soldiers for well over two hundred years, and during that period, until the early land wars, the British, seemingly, had effectively crushed the spirit of organised resistance in a pacific people. The famine was an example of a nation unable to make an attempt to save its withered people by a few resolute attacks on those who took food or exported it.

Volunteers, indeed, were not soldiers but they had a stern sense of discipline, and each county was learning for itself how to make use of its ground and its arms. In a sense the vagaries of indiscriminate destruction defeated themselves. In Bandon the stores of a life-long Unionist were destroyed, possibly because he employed Republicans. Newport creamery was destroyed the evening a girl's hair was cut for paying attention to soldiers. In towns and villages many ex-soldiers had been killed at random by British forces, and these killings strengthened the support which men who had once served the British were now giving to the Volunteers and the Dáil Government.

It later became clear why British reinforcements came so quickly to Rineen. Troops were on their way to the west to search for Captain Lendrum, a resident magistrate, who had set out from near Kilrush to attend a petty sessions court in Ennistymon that morning. No trace of the Captain could be found and it was probably presumed that he had been taken prisoner by the IRA, or that he had been executed. That night along the coast, flames from burning ricks of hay and straw trailed the wandering of the Tans, RIC and military. It looked as if the British were celebrating an out-of-season Bealtaine of their own. The country from Ennistymon to the west resembled an Iroquis raid on an American frontier settlement in the middle of the seventeenth century— except that the British had not been encouraged to return with scalps. Their night's saturnalia might have been somewhat stimulated by the official communique from their headquarters: 'Dum-dum bullets were used by the attackers, and there is evidence that certain police officers lying wounded on the road were subsequently murdered by the attackers.'

Captain Lendrum had been held up that morning at a closed level-crossing in West Clare by two Volunteers who were waiting for their officer to arrive. They intended to take his two-seater car from him but, when they challenged him to halt, the ex-officer drew an automatic and was then mortally wounded. His dead body, in the hope of avoiding reprisals by the discovery, was buried that night at sea, close in-shore.

British regulars, in the night, lighted stacks of turf on bogs, hay and harvest crops between Miltown and Kilkee. They burned houses along the roadside at Creagh, Doonbeg, Bealaha, into Kilkee, but Doonbeg village was saved by its people when the soldiers had passed on their fiery way.

On the morning of September 26th, people in Kilkee found notices fixed to their doors, warning them that if Captain Lendrum was not returned by noon on Wednesday the 29th, Kilkee, Kilrush, Carrigaholt, Doonbeg and Kilmill would be burned. The flaming pathway of the RIC from Ennistymon to the coast at Lahinch, down to Miltown Malbay, and continued by troops down by the sea edge for close on twenty miles, had frightened the inhabitants, who left their towns and villages. Volunteers blocked roads and lay at night in position to defend forewarned villages, but there was no assault. On October 1st, a roughly shaped coffin was found on the railway line near to Craggaknock station. On the coffin, which contained Lendrum's body, was written, 'To Kilkee'.

Evidently the British placed the blame for Captain Lendrum's death on certain IRA officers. Early on the morning of December 13th, William Shanahan, Brigade captain of police, and Michael MacNamara, company commander of Doonbeg, were captured in an isolated house in Doonbeg where they had been sleeping for some nights past. At a quiet spot in Dallagh on the way from Kilkee, on December 19th, the military halted the lorry in which were their two prisoners. MacNamara was told to get down and to walk home. He had not gone many steps before a volley killed him. Shanahan was brought on to Ennis. A short time later a non-commissioned officer put a bullet through his head while he was a prisoner of the regulars.

When Hamar Greenwood, the official Government apologist, was questioned by a Home Ruler, T. P. O'Connor, in the House of Commons, concerning the burning of portions of Miltown Malbay, Lahinch and Ennistymon by the RIC, and the killing of inhabitants by Crown forces, he condoned both destruction and shooting. Nobody then reminded the House of what had happened at Miltown Malbay on April 14th of that year.

There was a large release of prisoners who had been on hunger strike in Mountjoy. In a number of towns there were celebrations in honour of this new freedom, for the hunger strike had compelled the British to free their prisoners. Blazing tar-barrels and heaped pyres of turf lighted up the crowds who listened to speeches, sang songs with conviction, and then danced to melodeon music around the fires.

In Miltown there was a garrison of fifty men of the 2nd battalion, Highland Light Infantry, who held the town hall. The RIC sergeant asked the British officer who commanded the detachment for a patrol at 9.30 pm to support the police, and this military patrol had passed a tar-barrel around which songs were being sung. As soon as it reached the police barracks, Sergeant Hampson joined it with nine police, and the joint party moved up past houses which had been lighted in honour of the breaking of suspense induced by the hunger strike. When Hampson came within a few feet of the bonfire the constabulary and soldiers knelt or lay down in firing positions.

'Clear away to hell,' Hampson shouted, but before anyone could move he fired into the crowd with his revolver. Then he turned to order his mixed force to fire. The crowd of men and girls rushed in panic, but the sharp rifle cracks continued. Ex-

RINEEN AND REPRISALS

soldiers who dashed in to carry away a badly wounded man were fired on and one of them was wounded as they brought him away, only to find that he was dead. Military, joined by police, manned the sandbags outside the town hall and volleys came up from this position. Three Irish Volunteers, John O'Loughlin, Thomas O'Leary and Patrick Hennessey, were killed, and there were ten people wounded, some of them seriously. Crosses were erected in the street where the men fell. On each cross was an inscription: 'May God have mercy on the soul of — who fell on this spot and died in the cause of Ireland.'

Volunteers from the three Clare brigades marched in the long funeral procession which brought the tricolour-wrapped coffins to the graveyard. There was a military inquiry from which the public were kept away. Soldiers swore that they had been fired on by the crowd and the RIC supported their testimony. Canon Hannon, the parish priest, as a result of Government replies to questions in the House of Commons which substantiated the military and police reports, gave an interview to the Press. There had been no provocation whatever, he said. There had been no flags or processions, and the demonstration was organised by people of all shades of opinion who were glad the hunger strike had released untried prisoners. Ex-soldiers and ex-sailors from adjoining parishes in West Clare and North Clare, to show their sympathy with the dead, marched into the town and recited the Rosary at each of the crosses.

An inquest took place while police with carbines held the courthouse. Outside was an armoured car, its machine-gun swinging on to the front of the courthouse, and strong detachments of troops with threatening bayonets held the space in front through which the people passed to enter. The evidence showed that Sergeant Hampson had been drinking hard for some days, that he had fired the first shots eight yards from the tar-barrel, killing a man, and that then the mixed patrol behind him had fired. One RIC man, Constable McDonnell, who was on the patrol but who had not fired, swore that there was no violence from the crowd. Seven weeks previously, Sergeant Hampson had issued an order, as directed by Lt-Colonel Murray in charge of the British military in County Clare, that shopkeepers were not to sell drink, food or other supplies to the military. As a result of this strange order, soldiers had commandeered goods from the shopkeepers.

After numerous witnesses had been heard, a number of them ex-soldiers, the inquest jury decided that 'that John O'Loughlin, Patrick Hennessey and Thomas O'Leary died as a result of shock and haemorrhage caused by bullet wounds on the night of April 14th, inflicted by Sergeant Hampson, Constables O'Connor and Keenan, Lance-Corporal McLeod, Privates Kilgon, McEwan, McLoughlin, Bunting and Adams. We find from the evidence that each of the above-named members of the patrol was guilty of wilful murder, without any provocation, and we also condemn the other members of the patrol for their action in trying to shield those who committed the murders.'

This verdict, on May 7th, was the fifth within three weeks which charged members of the police and military with murder, and the third pronouncement against named members of the British forces. Subsequently, jurors refused to attend inquests on military or police, and so alarming were the verdicts on IRA and civilian dead that in September 1920 inquests were abolished in many counties. Military held courts of inquiry on the dead, in their barracks, but the people refused to attend.

Later in the year, when the Chief Secretary for Ireland in the House of Commons was replying to a resolution sponsored by Labour MPs, he said in reference to the Rineen ambush and the subsequent actions of the police:

Four of the men were killed instantly as a result of bullets, and the car was bespattered with blood and the mutilated remains of the four. The fifth, though badly wounded, managed to crawl away from the car four hundred yards. He was pursued. Shotguns were used within a foot of him to blow his body to pieces. The car was on the road with these men mutilated beyond recognition when within ten minutes another car containing soldiers and police came along. They lost their heads. They went to the villages of Ennistymon and Lahinch. I am sure the House, whatever their opinion may be as to this resolution, will at any rate give me their sympathy in trying to bring peace out of chaos in Ireland. It is true that reprisals followed the murder of these gallant men. Sixteen houses and shops were destroyed, houses that were considered to be occupied or owned by notorious Sinn Feiners.

Here again, I am convinced that the people of these two villages knew of this ambush. The place of ambush covers a long stretch on both sides of the road, and from the evidence of the bandoliers, hay beds, haversacks, coats, blankets, meat-tins and so on, it was clear that the bivouac was within sight of many houses. I am putting to you the provocation that comes to brave men. I hope I have shown that the ambush must have been apparent to many people in the vicinity. The Irish Republican Army is particularly strong in that area. We have lists of the numbers. We have the muster-roll in that area. We know exactly, so far as is humanly possible to know, the persons who connived at and helped in that ambush.

Arthur Henderson had proposed the Labour resolution. He had voiced the opinions of certain British MPs who were hostile to, and alarmed by the planned campaign of reprisals in Ireland. It read:

That this House regrets the present state of lawlessness in Ireland and the lack of discipline in the armed forces of the Crown, resulting in the death or injury of innocent citizens and the destruction of property; and it is of the opinion that an independent investigation should at once be instituted into the causes, nature and extent of reprisals on the part of those whose duty is the maintenance of law and order.

The resolution was defeated by 346 votes to 79. The Labour Party then decided they would carry out their own investigation into what was happening in Ireland. Their Commission visited towns and villages which had been sacked, and the houses of people whose relatives had been shot dead, and they took evidence on oath as they travelled around.

The RIC reported on what had occurred during and after the Rineen ambush and most of Greenwood's material came from that source. On the morning of September 22nd, the District Inspector at Ennistymon had received an anonymous letter:

Dear Sir — I am giving you a warning to make your men look out for themselves for the Sinn Fein is going to make a raid on them some day. Let your men look out and the two officers that are going by themselves in the black motor. They will give them a downfall as sure as you are reading this. We cannot help our young innocent sons. The leading man of them all is John O'Loughlan who is going to all the races. He has plenty of powder and firearms.

The letter, which may have been the work of the RIC themselves, may also have been genuine. This habit of writing anonymous letters in the hope of getting neighbours into trouble prevailed in most Irish parishes until recent times. Parish priests and sergeants of the Garda received a supply of such letters. They were written because of jealousy, rancour and spleen, and usually the information was false or distorted. The reason for the habit was deep in the cross-currents of town and country life, and it epitomised the ineptitude and frustrations which mole their way continually through parish fabric. The RIC received such letters, but the raiding of mails by the IRA often reduced the local sergeant's share of information and helped in some instances to trace the writers.

The RIC report on Rineen shows their standpoint:

At 11 o'clock in the morning, an NCO in Ennistymon was told that a police car was to be ambushed that day. He went straight to the military barracks and reported. A party of troops from the garrison was dispatched along the Miltown Malbay road, with instructions to examine likely positions for ambushes. Shortly after passing Lahinch shots were heard ahead. The party pushed on and came into touch with the rebels as the latter were scattering inland.

The troops came under fire from both flanks, and the driver of the motor car was wounded. A Lewis gun was brought into action and a few minutes later a second small party of troops came up in support, whereupon the rebels scattered and fled. The rebels took skilful advantage of cover behind banks, whins and hedges.

The troops now came back to the road, and at a point where the road is about 25 yards from the railway line, they found the bodies of the victims and the wrecked car. There were signs of a regular bivouac which had clearly been occupied from before dawn. Hay was strewn about and there were a few haversacks and coats as well as meat tins. Empty rifle and shotgun cartridges, and also sharp-nosed bullets whereof the points had been carefully filed, converting them into dum-dum bullets, were found. The original wounds caused by the dum-dum bullets were bad enough, but the bodies showed that after the men had fallen the criminals fired at their victims at short range with shotguns. The evidence of this bestiality was undisputable. Search was made for the body of the missing constable, but it was not found until next morning. The wounded man had managed to crawl nearly 400 yards, but as the tracks showed, he had been hunted down and butchered in cold blood.

During the fight the rebels fired from two houses, and it is certain that not only were the occupants fully aware of the ambush, but also deliberately refrained from giving any notice, as they certainly could have done. However, they did not get off scotfree for their houses were set on fire and burned to the ground. There were other people who could have given warning and did not do so, and who are therefore accessories to the murder. Two trains passed within six to ten feet of the ambush, every detail of which must have been visible from the line. The guard and driver of the train must have known of the ambush, and it is impossible that some of the station officials at Miltown Malbay should not have been informed. It is worth noting that a priest wearing what appears to be military medals was reported to have formed one of the ambush party.

Local companies had a suspicion that information was given about the proposed ambush, but the question stayed unsettled. Either the search for the missing resident magistrate, or a leakage of information, brought out the military. The RIC would be more inclined to report that a leakage of information was the cause, as it would indicate a degree of uncertainty and doubt among Volunteers. This indeed was an old trick of the Royal Irish. Leakage of information was one of the most serious factors which could be used against the IRA, with their poor armament and their haphazard training. Their discipline, however, had slowly spread to their townlands. People who delighted in talk learned not only to keep all the miscellaneous information which they had concerning the Republican Army and government activity to themselves, but became skilful in gleaning news about the British Army of Occupation and its adherents. The bitterness of the RIC increased as they found that their former ample prying and sounding now brought little but dross to help them increase their garrison status. At most, the men of the Volunteer companies had only an imaginative idea of what fighting meant. However, even if the British had been fore-warned about Rineen they made little use of their information against the men whom they followed up across the hills. They had superior armament, they were fresh and they had had food that morning. Their lorries had saved their legs until they began pursuit, yet a few men with rifles and the intimate knowledge of ground which the local scouts possessed had taken the advantage from the British. It would seem that Crown forces were able to inflict real casualties and destruction only when they were opposed by the unarmed population of three small towns.

On the morning following the burning of Miltown, a few people came back cautiously. Then at intervals others returned, some to their wrecked homes. To their surprise they found that relatives and families of RIC men in the town were busy gathering together clothes, bedding and furniture. Tans and RIC helped them to remove belongings, and a wall of silence was suddenly built between the townspeople, police relations and their bleary-eyed helpers. The RIC families were afraid that the IRA would take reprisals on them and on their property, and the once semi-friendly town no longer seemed to be safe. They left Miltown that day, never to return.

A few days after the ambush the IRA carefully searched the ground over which some of them had raced ahead of the soldiers, able to reconstruct an amplified action for the ears of those of their comrades who had not been chased. They found a few discarded coats, metal ammunition clips full of cartridges, isolated cartridges and a few khaki slings heavy with their treasure. Crossing a short rise they came upon parts of a machine-gun which had been left behind.

CHAPTER FIVE

THE BRITISH ENFORCE MARTIAL LAW

DECEMBER 1920 – JANUARY 1921

On December 10, 1920, a proclamation was issued by Lord French placing the counties of Cork, Tipperary, Limerick and Kerry under martial law. Many English people who were opposed to what were called 'unofficial reprisals' were in favour of martial law because they hoped it would give additional authority to the military, would help them to prevent unauthorised reprisals, and would keep their own undisciplined forces in Army, Auxiliaries and RIC subject to military control. RIC, Auxiliaries, marines and coastguards were now controlled by the competent authority in the selected counties.

The next night, December 11th, a large part of Cork city centre, including Patrick Street, the City Hall and the Carnegie Library, was looted and burned by an Auxiliary company — 'K' company, aided by some military and by Royal Irish Constabulary. The 'K' company of Auxiliaries were then removed from Cork to Dunmanway. They now carried a piece of burnt cork on their glengarry bonnets as a symbol of their daring in destroying two and a half million pounds worth of property and possessions during curfew, while the British military were in complete control of the city. On December 15th, an Auxiliary officer shot dead Timothy Crowley and Canon Magner, the parish priest of Dunmanway.

From the time of the first proclamation dealing with the imposition of martial law — the counties of Clare, Waterford, Wexford and Kilkenny were further included on 4th January 1921 — many edicts were printed by the British military. By degrees military power seemed to be able to thrust its tentacles into most facets of Irish life. In the counties, in what was now called the Martial Law Area, a series of printed bills showed that people could be executed, if sentenced by a military court, for possessing arms, ammunition or explosives; for wearing clothing likely to deceive, such as Irish Volunteer uniforms, or British military or police uniforms; for harbouring or abetting rebels.

Brigadier-General H. B. Cummings, who was then in charge of the Kerry Brigade, issued a proclamation which said that owing to treacherous attacks from day to day by armed civilians on military and police convoys proceeding by road, IRA officers or leaders in military custody would be sent as hostages in all transport vehicles belonging to the forces of the Crown proceeding on the roads in the areas under martial law. Untried prisoners were carried in the lorries — members of Dáil Éireann or county council and rural council representatives, whose councils had given allegiance to An Dáil. Hostages were warned that should the lorry or convoy be fired at, they would at once be killed by their escort. As a result of this procedure men who had gone over from Ireland, as well as London-Irishmen, watched members of the British House of Commons. The intention was to sweep suddenly, take about ten prisoners and hold them as security for the lives of members of the Dáil who ran risks when used as hostages. The personal records of some of the British MPs were surprising. Their promiscuous sex lives made them move frequently from house to flat, from flat to hotel, and it increased the difficulties of the watchers. Cummings, who had begun the hostage procedure, was killed with other officers and men at Clonbanin, Co. Cork, on March 5, 1921, when his touring car, escorted by a heavy armoured car and three lorries, was ambushed by the North Cork men.

The English Labour Party Commission visited Ireland to collect information as to conditions through the country. On their return they published their report:

There is a state of war in Ireland and what are called 'outrages' and 'reprisals' are but incidents in a bitter campaign. On the one hand, there are the armed forces of the Crown; on the other, the Irish Republican Army. While we wish to avoid making any general accusations against a body of men with so distinguished a record as the RIC, we feel compelled to express the opinion, based on personal observations, that a by no means negligible proportion of the Force, as

THE BRITISH ENFORCE MARTIAL LAW 93

at present constituted, are men of intemperate habits and utterly unsuited to their duties . . .

The Auxiliary Division of the RIC is recruited almost exclusively from ex-officers . . . in other districts which we visited they inspired terror as the authors of reprisals whose brutality and destructive effects were only equalled by the skill and forethought with which they had been planned.

Several cases investigated by the Commission revealed the fact that these detachments had worked independently of, and brooked no interference from the other forces of the Crown. In view of their recent conduct, after the issue of orders forbidding all reprisals, they do not seem to recognise even the authority of Dublin Castle, and the question suggests itself — under whom do they serve? . . . .

The IRA is formidable because it is intangible . . . In its present form it lives, fights and disperses. It is everywhere all the time and nowhere at any given moment. Without the support and sympathy of the vast majority of the population, it could not exist. This support is probably more generous and effective today than it has been at any previous period.

So great has been the provocation by the forces of the Crown that 80 per cent of Irish men and women now regard the shooting of policemen and throwing of bombs at lorries with the same philantrophic resignation that Mr. Lloyd George displays towards arson, pillage and the shooting of civilians at night in the presence of their wives and children.

The Auxiliaries took their instructions from General Tudor who had served with distinction in France in the first world war. He had been personally selected for this police work by Mr. Winston Churchill. The Royal Irish, together with the Tans, were also subject to General Tudor.

The New Year opened with this military alternative to a truce in Ireland. Sir Henry Wilson was then at the War Office as Chief of the Imperial General Staff. He could always be found to be a believer in 'shooting by roster' and in what was called 'naked force', but naked force seems to have been well covered up in Ireland as it was too often used furtively. Wilson had been the adviser on the crushing of the Irish and, as is the way with certain old soldiers, he had the usual solution for a misunderstood difficulty, the spirit of freedom — force and increased force. Force, of course, involved time. Yet when the British use of force increased in Ireland one answer was an increased opposition. Archbishop Clune of Perth, who had previously met Lloyd George in Rome and had brought him to the Pope's Mass in the Vatican, had been meeting members of the Dáil Cabinet in Dublin. Conor Clune, his relative, had been one of three murdered in Dublin Castle on November 21, 1920. A truce had been practically arranged when Lloyd George, whom the Archbishop had understood to be anxious for peace, changed his mind.

Three things may have suggested an Irish weakening: a letter from Sweetman, a member of Dáil Éireann; a resolution from Galway County Council, and a telegram from Father O'Flanagan, Acting President of Sinn Féin. It might be that the British thought that Sweetman revealed a sign of weakness as he did not consult his Cabinet when he wrote. The Galway motion was passed by six members out of thirty-two, when the quorum should have been nine members. Father O'Flanagan's telegram was sent by himself without the authority of his colleagues. The military and Dublin Castle officials were anxious to find any wedge to drive into the soft underbelly of Irish unity.

Proclamations continued to be issued. They were pasted up on walls or on the inside of shop windows or house windows of Republicans who were usually members of public boards and councils. Although it would appear that the British military had unlimited power to be used against a province, words in print may have deceived them in relation to their strength of men and material, for in effect they had to rely on words to bolster their armed strength. The spirit of freedom is immeasurable and its strength can suddenly increase in unexpected ways.

The gentlemen of the British 6th Division at Cork were busy with their pens towards the end of 1920. Indeed they might have again published some of their former edicts, such as this more readable one used by Cromwell in 1650:

We come to break the power of a company of lawless rebels who, having cast off the authority of England, live as enemies to human society, whose principles are to destroy and to subjugate all men not complying with them. We come — by the assistance of God — to hold forth and maintain the lustre and glory of English liberty in a nation where we have an undoubted right to be, whereas the population of Ireland if they listen not to such seducers as you, may equally participate in all benefits to use liberty and fortune equally with English, if they keep out of arms.

Official reprisals within the Martial Law Area were carried out by the military in daylight. All the males in a small village or town would first be rounded up and searched. Soldiers with fixed bayonets guarded all approaches to the beleaguered place while furniture was broken up with pickaxes and crowbars and the houses demolished by explosives. A sheet of typescript was handed to the owner of the house before its destruction. It stated that he was bound to have known of the ambush and that he had neglected to give any information either to the police or military authorities. The RIC, who advised the military about local rebels, were as well aware as were the senior officers who ordered a reprisal, that outside of the staff or IRA commander of a column or a battalion few others would know what operation was being planned.

One method of holding up troops at night while an attack was being carried out had been the felling of trees, scattering of stone walls on to the roadside, or the caving in of culverts. Now British troops were more systematically held up by the digging of trenches in the roadways, by pot-holing the surface at intervals, or by tearing down the bridges without the waste of explosives. As time went on, each battalion in an active area made its roads impracticable to heavy lorries and tenders. Road-pitting or even odd stones scattered at intervals allowed drivers to go slowly, but the depressed road surface shook bodies and nerves of troops and police and damaged their vehicles. The answer was a round-up of the neighbourhood and forced labour on the roadways. Yet the repair material would tend to sink and cause the same depression. Fairs and markets were stopped by proclamation for weeks when roads were interfered with around the market towns. Creameries were forced to close down for months. People were tried by military courts for not informing military or police that the roads adjacent to their houses had been tampered with.

Destruction of houses in British reprisals continued rapidly in Cork, Kerry and parts of Tipperary as ambushes and shootings increased. Cork then began to burn hostile loyalist houses in the vicinity of the city and the other brigades soon kept pace. The British posted up proclamations stating that for every loyalist house burned they would destroy three houses of active rebels. The destruction of loyalist houses continued until the owners of yet untouched country seats were able to exert enough influence on the British Government to make them understand that a castle was an unfair pawn for a cottage or a public house. By this time reprisals, through good publicity from Dáil Éireann and from friendly and disturbed journalists, had made foreign peoples aware of British methods in Ireland.

There was another matter which concerned the Irish Republican Army and that was the talk of bishops in their cathedrals and their letters sent to be read by subordinate clergy, also the attitudes of parish priests and curates.

On December 13, 1920, Dr. Cohalan, Bishop of Cork, said that there was no doubt about it that these ambushes were murders and every life taken in an ambush was murder; if any section or member of an organisation refused to hear the Church's teaching about murder there was no remedy except the extreme penalty — excommunication from the Church.

Dr. Finnegan, Bishop of Kilmore, said on December 17, 1920: 'You are told you are engaged in a just war of defence and that you may kill, in any way you can, a member of the constabulary as a member of a hostile force. Any war, even a defensive war, to be just and lawful must be backed by a well-grounded hope of success. ... What hope of success have you against the mighty forces of the British Empire? None ... none whatever ... and if it be unlawful as it is, every life taken in pursuance of it is murder.'

On January 9, 1921, Rev. J. Murphy, administrator of South Parish Church, Cork, said: 'Such deeds [ambushes] are the work of men of distorted and perverted moral sense, and place the perpetrators outside the Church's pale.'

A letter from Dr. Gilmartin, Archbishop of Tuam, read at Mass in Headford, on January 24, 1921, dealt with an ambush at Kilroe in Co. Galway where members of 'D' company, the Auxiliary company in Galway, had been ambushed: 'The misguided criminals who fired a few shots from behind a wall and then decamped to a safe distance are guilty of a triple crime. They have broken the truce of God, they have incurred the guilt of murder ... they have come from outside to do a foul and craven deed and then, having fired their few cowardly shots, they beat a hasty retreat, leaving the unprotected and innocent people at the mercy of uniformed forces.'

Six of the Auxiliaries had been wounded. Their company, which had already killed in their beds Volunteers and representatives of local councils had, for the first time, met with men who were not in their shirts.

Rev. Dr. Hoare, Bishop of Armagh, on February 6, 1921: 'Our rulers have been unjust to us, false to their promises, have aggravated us by their coercive laws and now seem to have pointed out the way to lasting hate by these cruel and arbitrary reprisals, their audacious denial of them, and their prevarications as in the case of Granard. On the other hand, our young enthusiasts, instead of falling back on God, who can bring to nought the machinations of tyrants and give victory to the oppressed, have soared too high and have allowed themselves to be driven into devices and practices such as ambushes and the wanton destruction of property.... All this is contrary to the law of God and worthy only of the barricades.... How can a poor country such as ours ... hope to win.'

On March 20, 1921, at Cavan, asking the prayers of the people for young men killed in Leitrim the previous week, the Bishop of Kilmore said again: 'It was generally believed the young men were shot while running away. It was under these circumstances that I allowed the victims Christian burial, for had there been an ambush they would have been deprived of this consolation of their Church, as I have warned them ambushing is murder.' Dr. Finnegan was referring to five officers of the Leitrim Brigade —

a portion of a column under Seán Connolly from the Longford Brigade — who had been killed by the British on March 11th at Selton hill after information of their presence had been given to the District Inspector of the RIC in Mohill by a doctor who had served in the British Army. Men of the Bedfordshire Regiment were seen by a badly wounded IRA officer, who survived, to use rifle butts on the skulls of two wounded men, the Leitrim Vice-Brigadier, Séamus Wrynne, and Captain Baxter, until they killed them.

Pronouncements by the bishops did not, so far as I know, affect active members of the IRA in the Martial Law Area nor our adherents who housed and fed us and the columns. In weak areas it may have had an effect and must have added to the worries of senior officers.

On April 5, 1921, Eamon de Valera gave an interview to a correspondent of the *Illustrated News*:

One of our first government acts was to take over control of the voluntary armed forces of the nation. From the Irish Volunteers we fashioned the IRA to be the military arm of the Government ... under officers who hold their commissions under warrant from their representatives. The Government is therefore responsible for the actions of this Army ... The IRA is the national army of defence.

TD's had in 1919, as had all members of the Army, taken the Oath of Allegiance: 'I will support and defend the Irish Republic and the Government of the Irish Republic, which is Dáil Éireann, against all enemies foreign and domestic.' Successive county councils and boards of guardians and other boards had pledged allegiance to the Dáil.

In the Martial Law Area a brigadier had to solve each new problem in terms of his area with regard to strength and weakness. General Headquarters became remote, except through the exchange of intelligence reports and details about British troops, RIC and their adherents. GHQ could not provide arms in 1921, nor explosives in any quantity. When IRA Divisions were established in 1921 there were at first two in the Martial Law Area, the First and the Second Southern, under the command of Lynch and O'Malley. The Third Southern and First Western, formed later, had respectively one brigade and three brigades in that territory. Divisions established better contacts between brigades and some would now more often allow columns from one brigade to reinforce those of another. Already this co-operation had taken place on the Cork-Kerry and Cork-Limerick borders. In addition, good officers could be sent to organise battalions that were slack in training and activity.

The British 6th Division now made more use of aeroplanes, carrier pigeons and wireless for the safe transmission of messages and reports, as other channels had sometimes failed them. British intelligence was poor and Irish strength was misleading. Without the RIC the British were impotent and, even with them, in the Martial Law Area they were incompetent. The RIC had failed as an intelligence force in any area in which the people had given allegiance and their sons' and daughters' strength to serve An Dáil. The police did not know the names of the officers appointed after March 1920 in staunch brigades. They knew nothing of the movements of IRA columns nor of any battalion or brigade headquarters, with very few exceptions.

The British were driven to the expedient of using their officers as intelligence agents in certain counties. Brave men, often disguised in everything except accent, were dropped from lorries at night, but they were picked up within a few days, tried and executed. This was a sad story of forlorn courage when their seniors were ill-advised and hard-driven enough by lack of information to allow such men to wander into the countryside. They also made use of 'deserters' from the ranks, hoping that they would compile information from amongst the country people with whom they stayed, but again they filled further graves.

By degrees the martial law machine ran itself down. It could terrorise, slightly bend the opposing will, but it had no hope of achieving a result. Month after month the area demanded further troops and munitions from the Empire.

CHAPTER SIX

AMBUSH AT SCRAMOGUE

MARCH 1921

The Strokestown-Longford road was a tarred road in 1921. Almost every day British military lorries used it as it was a main communication route. But there were drawbacks to a much-used road from the viewpoint of IRA ambushes. Two lorries might be met with when one Crossley tender was expected, or an armoured Lancia with three lorries and perhaps an armoured car in the rear might have to be faced. Also, men in position might have to meet an enemy force coming in the opposite direction. The advantage of surprise was, therefore, sometimes on the side of the British, and all good planning by the IRA had to be elastic to deal with unexpected emergencies.

Volunteers from the slopes of Slieve Bawn in South Roscommon and from Strokestown battalion in North Roscommon had known Seán Connolly. He was the Brigade Vice-Commandant of Longford but he had been sent by GHQ to organise South Roscommon and to put it on some kind of a fighting basis. He made the area active by attacking patrols and by an attempt to use explosives on one barracks there. He had come down towards Ballagh underneath Slieve Bawn to discuss a possible attack at Lanesborough and while he was in the area he suggested the holding of an ambush position on the road crossing the bogland to the Shannon. He had inspected many possible sites along that road but the Scramogue position seemed to form the surest ambush place. During the Christmas he had been talking to a few of the South Roscommon men and had reminded them again of the use the British were making of the bog road. He had promised that he would come down to help them whenever they had decided to man the position, but then he left the county for Leitrim in February and now he would not be able to keep his promise. In March a portion of his Column was surrounded in Leitrim by the British. Five of the men with him were killed, he was mortally wounded, and as the bodies left Mohill that evening their soldier escort shouted 'Fresh Meat' as they displayed their wares. Connolly's Column had been betrayed by an Orangeman who brought his information to a doctor in Mohill. The Orange farmer had been executed but the doctor had escaped to England.

Kilgeffin and Curraghroe companies remembered Connolly's eagerness to increase activity in their county so as to help other hard-pressed areas by making the British withdraw some of the troops that now beset brigades which had better organised their offensive. His death, twelve days previously, made them eager to carry out the ambush in which he had hoped to take part.

The road had been watched by Volunteers for some days and as a result of this observation it was found that military lorries passed along its surface daily, but usually came and went more regularly in the morning time. Seán Leavy, who was in charge of the third battalion of the North Roscommon Brigade, had a house near a bend on the side of this road. When the position was first visited Leavy was there with Duffy and Seán Connolly; later some of Leavy's friends thought that his house would certainly be blown up if anything happened close to it. 'I don't care a damn,' the owner of the house said, 'if my farm and all belonging to it are destroyed, so long as you carry out the job.'

When the proposed operation was examined seriously the officers found that there was one great disadvantage. They had very few rifles and the long-range arms would be needed in this particular action to keep the enemy at a distance as men retired from their selected positions. Rifles were borrowed from Longford and from North Roscommon. Soon eleven service rifles, a Winchester and a sporting rifle were brought together, and this meagre collection when inspected was the largest quantity of arms the officers had seen at one place in their county preparatory to action. There was a good number of shotguns, for this was a country of lakes where good shots had practice, and as well there were a few experienced ex-soldiers available who had joined the British Army when John Redmond made his political gesture in 1914.

The brunt of the operation was carried by Kilgeffin company which was one of the most active companies in the county. The British made the company members aware of its standing in their eyes by their determined attempts to track them down. Raiding parties harried the parish and the adjoining parishes.

Pat Madden was in charge of the local South Roscommon battalion and he also commanded the Column formed from it, which was brought together only for an operation. It was he who had induced some of the ex-soldiers, whom he had known as a boy and who had served for the most part in the Irish Guards, to join the Volunteers. In the neighbourhood the men who had joined the British Army were the sons of farmers, and as country men they had been less influenced by war than men who had joined up from garrison towns such as Longford or Boyle. They had the background and tradition of land in their bones. When the war ceased they went back again to the land, which steadied their wildness and freed them from the authoritarian grip that had withdrawn them from personal responsibility. Madden might have been with them in France as he had tried to enlist on the evening of a fair in Lanesborough, but he was dissuaded by a friendly RIC man who prevailed on him to go back to his farm.

The night before the action, men had mobilised in their areas and the Flying Column, mainly made up of Kilgeffin men, had come together. The Cumann na mBan girls waited up to cook for them and they made sure also that all the men had a day's rations before they set off.

The men were on the ambush site at about three o'clock on a cold raw morning. There was a good deal of work to be done to strengthen the position which it was intended to hold, and as soon as each man was aware of the place he would occupy when the attack began, the work of improvement started with picks and shovels. Men from NorthRoscommon had been in the habit of asking Pat Madden and a group of Volunteers from his battalion to assist them whenever they carried out an operation in the two adjoining battalions of Strokestown and Elphin. Now, in return, companies from Strokestown area had been mobilised to block roads in the neighbourhood to prevent

British transport from quickly reaching the vicinity of the proposed ambush. Some of the North Roscommon officers were already waiting at the road bend.

Care had to be taken with regard to the line of retreat. The men were on rising ground looking down on to the Strokestown road and on to the level fields on either side of the road, but when the operation was over they would have to retire up the hilly exposed ground which led away towards Slieve Bawn. If anything went wrong with their plan the bare hilly ground would be under fire from the country below it. It was decided to remove the people who lived in the house near the roadside, and families in houses further back along the small road behind the main positions were placed in one house for safety. Sentries saw that none of them left that shelter. Men dug a trench behind the hedge which commanded the bend of the road so that they would have protection from rifle fire. The hedge itself was cut down to reduce exposure during action. Gaps were cut in hedges running at right angles to the road for ease in communication. There was a reserve of ten men kept a short distance away on the rising ground. The man who had been instructed to take charge of this reserve was very reluctant to command it. It would keep him out of the fight, he argued, but in the end he agreed to command men only some of whom had their fowling weapon, the shotgun. Shotguns had been carefully hidden for over a year and a half and their condition varied generally from bad to worse. The usual place for a shotgun was over the comforting heat of a turf hearth, but for a long time they had lain in earth banks, loose hay, or in underground dumps where they had become pocked and pitted with rust.

The roadside house was soon loopholed for three riflemen, and the barn at the rear of this house had an exit hole cut in the wall so that men would not be trapped inside. The men had sops of hay to rest on, and all kept quiet in their damp positions.

The main body was along by the hedge where the trench had been dug. They were about six feet above road level at the bend. Some of them could see the main road to Strokestown and look down it for five hundred yards, as could the Column men in the loopholed house. Further out, companies in a ring about the position had been ordered to block the roads leading to enemy posts.

Amongst the trees was Strokestown House, about a mile across country to the north-west. It had a garrison of the 9th Lancers. The Lancers could move swiftly across country on their horses when they heard rifle fire and they could outflank the IRA as they withdrew. Consequently, this post was the chief immediate danger.

Pat Madden, the Column Commander, inspected the men again as the slow morning ticked on, and he felt sure that his instructions were well understood. 'Cushy' Hughes, an ex-soldier, who was seated contentedly on his little bundle of hay, had been badly wounded in the spine in the world war. He had rejected the long Lee-Enfield which was offered to him. 'Be damned if I know about that yoke,' he said. Either Frank Simons or Luke Duffy handed him a short Lee-Enfield of the pattern he had used in Flanders and in France, and 'Cushy' was happy as he fondled the type of rifle that had served him well in the past. Most men had gone to confession the night before, but 'Cushy' had been late for parade. He had time to light a candle in the chapel for his intentions, and to have a long drink, and having satisfied soul and body he marched off to his position.

The Column Commander had time to reflect on the ring of posts, other than Strokestown House, from which British reinforcements could be quickly sent. Longford was twelve miles away, Roscommon an equal distance, Castlereagh and Boyle were further off. All these towns had an RIC garrison and at least a company of infantry. Athlone, a brigade headquarters, had a big force of all arms.

It was a clear frosty morning and as the men listened for the tuning-up of lorries in Strokestown they could hear the quiet noise of cows, calves and hens, and bird-song in the hedges nearby. The eyes and ears of the waiting fowlers behind the hedges were as alert for bird life as they were for the distant hum of a motor, and with reluctance they saw grouse and wild duck change their course when disturbed by movement amongst the men below them. At last they heard the sound of lorries. They had expected two of them and it was agreed that the first lorry

SCRAMOGUE
CO. ROSCOMMON

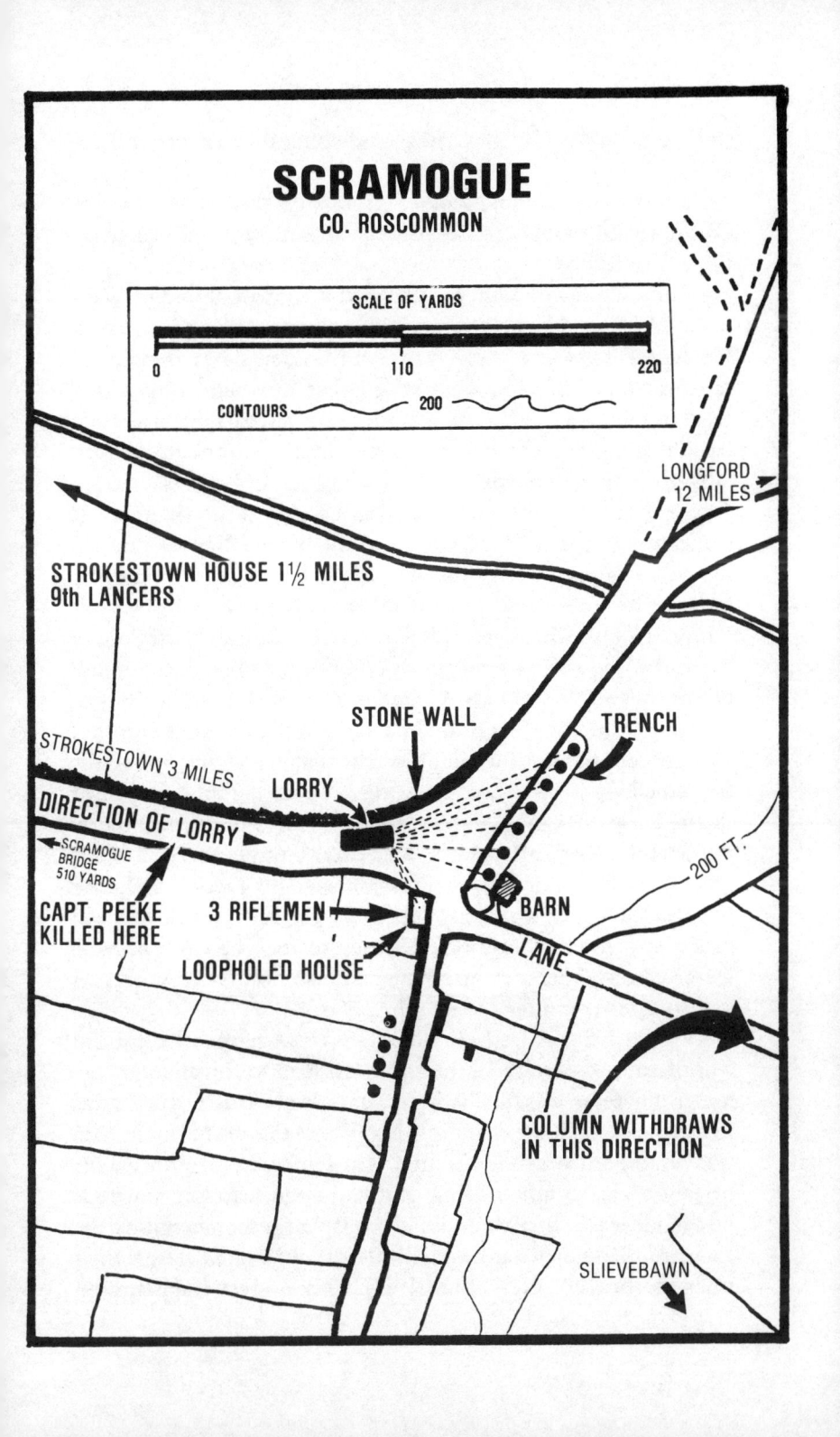

should be allowed up as far as the shotgun men beyond the bend.

Some of the men had gone in groups up the by-road for tea. One of them was playing the piano in a house while he waited for the kettle to boil.

A lorry came into sight but ahead of it, close to the bend, was a pony and trap. The driver was a man who was being boycotted. He was on his way to Longford. Pat Madden shouted at him to move faster. The men were afraid that lorry and trap would reach the bend together, but by intensive and earnest curses and by the strength of the driver's whip-arm the pony made the turn well ahead of the British.

The lorry was fired on from the house by the riflemen. It staggered like a hit bird on the wing. Khaki figures jumped inside a wall on the far side of the road but others of them lay outside on the road. One man, a corporal, sat beside his Hotchkiss gun which was bolted to an upright bar on the floor of the lorry. He was able to get in one burst of fire at the house before he was wounded. A lieutenant pulled a soldier out of security from behind a drain inside the wall and got in himself. The lancers behind the wall thought that the attack was solely from the loopholed house. They were exposed in the direction of the hedge as they faced parallel to the house, but the men there, Pat Madden and Luke Duffy, who had no target so far, now left their position and crossed the side-road to reach the hedge beyond the bend, which gave them a view down inside the wall of the straight road leading to Strokestown. The riflemen who were scattered behind the hedge had also fired at these targets and in a few minutes the action was over.

Captain Sir Alfred Peeke, DSO, a nephew of Lord Middleton, was wounded but he continued to run along by the hedge where he was finally hit four hundred yards away. He was to have gone on leave that morning. When the lieutenant in turn was wounded someone shouted 'Up Duffy.' Luke Duffy, the battalion vice-commandant, who had been a fowler since his boyhood, was a fine shot. That shout was remembered by the Lancers. Lorries would afterwards carry chalked up on their sides the prayer, 'GOD HELP DUFFY' — yet Luke himself was not suspected. The British had confused him with another man of his name, Seán Duffy, who was adjutant of the Longford Flying Column. It was he who in December of 1920 had carried a mine in his arms and placed it on the window-sill of a house in Ballinalee, which the Black and Tans and RIC held with four sergeants and twenty-seven men. The explosion blew a hole in the gable-end but the attackers had not been able to make proper use of the opening to set the post on fire. Seán Duffy's house and Seán Connolly's were burned a few days later.

When the firing ceased two civilians walked out to Madden with their hands up. They were being brought to Longford as prisoners, they said, but no one paid any attention to them for the time being. It was assumed that they had been picked up during a raid by the British and that they were being brought to Longford for interrogation.

The machine-gunner, who had been badly wounded, was carried over to the side of the road where he sat down stoically despite his grievous pain, and a man lighted a cigarette for him. Another soldier was found under the lorry. 'What's wrong with you?' one of the lads asked. 'My effin leg is broken,' he replied.

Towards the end of the action another lorry came along the Strokestown road towards the Scramogue river bridge. The men on the rise fired at it but the lorry reversed and turned down a side-road which led back to town. There were RIC and Tans in the lorry. The Lancers blamed them afterwards for not having tried to relieve their first lorry. The lieutenant's body was found near a hedge and close by were other wounded soldiers.

The Column now eagerly examined the Hotchkiss gun which was bolted by its upright bar to the floor of the lorry in such a way that it could be easily swivelled on a target. The upright had been frequently hit in the recent firing. There were metal strips of ammunition to supply the gun, in a case. None of the men present knew how to work the gun but admiring eyes gave it a toll of tribute. The capture of what was now a white elephant would give them prestige, and as other machine-guns had been captured previously Pat Madden felt that they would soon receive instructions in its use. There were a number of Lee-Enfields and Webleys to add to the Column's meagre equipment. It had indeed been dangerous for it to operate in such an open county as Roscommon with a preponderance of shotguns.

The most curious object of interest to the IRA was a heavy stock whip which carried a long lash. That whip was a cause of talk and speculation. Was it to be used on prisoners or what was its purpose, the men asked, as they fingured the strong lash.

The lorry was sprinkled with petrol from tin cans which it carried, and it was set on fire by the roadside. Pat Madden ordered the men to move off at once. The British wounded could see the direction which their victors were about to take, but there was no time to circumvent their observation. At any moment now an extended line of Lancers might come charging across the low long ground beneath them. The lorry which had gone back with police would already have brought information about the ambush to Strokestown House, but apart from this possible use of cavalrymen the Column Commander was easier in his mind about the inthrust of other reinforcements. By this time the roads in a wide circle would have been thoroughly blockaded so that obstructions would keep back incoming military and police. That time interval would give the Volunteers an additional chance of reaching those secure places which they had already decided to make for. They would now have until perhaps early evening to put a good distance between them and the road bend.

Men from some local companies and from the Kilgeffin company were sent home but others remained on to scout, while Fianna boys who had turned up to help were searching the rising ground, moving in front of the climbing men. The North Roscommon men went to their own areas, but the Column, with the men from Curraghroe, climbed up the slope towards Slieve Bawn. The mountain bulked in the low water-basin for it was the highest point between the Partry mountains beyond Lough Mask, fifty miles to the west, and Slieve na Callaigh away to the east. In the extreme west this rise of ground would be an insignificant hill but here in Roscommon it looked down on the plains beneath and, as is usual in mountain areas, the men on its slopes, who were known as 'the mountain men', had a spirit of their own.

The two rescued prisoners were questioned as they moved with the Volunteers, and to the surprise of their neighbours they were found to be Black and Tans. At once they were more carefully guarded. One of them was a Scot but the other was Irish. The Scot told Madden that he could work a Hotchkiss and he seemed anxious to explain the mechanism if he were given the gun. That knowledge was essential for its proper use by a crew from the Column, but there was now no time to spend in learning its intricate mechanism, and even if there had been time there was no one to check the accuracy of what was regarded as an untrustworthy source of information. The gun was indeed a burden. Instead of being a safeguard to protect the men and hold back pursuers it was now an inert trophy which would have to be closely protected.

Pat Madden talked to Luke Duffy and Frank Simons of this menace from the captured Tans. They could identify a number of men if their captors in turn became prisoners, and that would mean a death sentence, as by this date anyone who had taken part in an operation in which soldiers or police had been killed could be executed if it was proved that he had been present. There had been an order from GHQ to shoot Black and Tans at sight, but it was seldom observed once they had become prisoners.

It was decided that the Tans would be shot as soon as the men had reached a place which would make them secure from the inevitable round-up of the neighbourhood. The decision was not easy to take as it was hard to shoot prisoners; few men liked to be part of an execution squad even when it was concerned with a condemned spy.

The Column parted from the Curraghroe men who were given the Scottish Tan to look after, and retired to the long plateau on top of the rise. There the men sat down to rest and as some lay stretched out they could see across the plains, but no undulating line of dust mounting yet signalled the approach of lorries. Enemy reinforcements were on their way from Athlone, however, and were moving up from Roscommon town. Some of the roads to the south had not been blocked that morning.

The Tan told Column men that Captain Peeke had been in the lorry, but Peeke had not been accounted for. Some of them had seen a soldier run along the hedge towards Strokestown, and it was later they discovered that Peeke had indeed been killed about four hundred yards from their position. Maybe it was he who had stuck his revolver into the hedge when he was wounded, for twelve years later the weapon was found by county council men working on the road. Late on the morning of the ambush Peeke's body, standing erect in a lorry, was brought back through the streets of Strokestown. The dead officer and his blood-spattered face and uniform were to arouse the indignation of the loyal townspeople at the death of the local commander of the Lancers.

A week previously Captain Peeke and his men had set fire to whins on the mountains. They had fired into isolated bits of cover and the Captain had threatened to come back later. 'I won't leave a bush standing and I'll get all these effin Shinners,' he said. Earlier in the year he had been in charge of Lancers who, strengthened by other troops, had come from neighbouring towns and from barracks as far away as Renmore and Mullingar to participate in an operation directed against the area. They had crossed the rise of ground in extended formation and had fired at the mountain which they regarded as a base for operations, as a refuge for the men on its slopes, and as enemy territory.

The wide plateau on top now hid the Column from hostile sight, but the ascent had sparse cover save along hedgerows which ended before the summit was reached. As the men picked out familiar landmarks in the near distance they argued about the exact location of houses they knew, while the glint of water edged their focal knowledge. To the north, beyond Strokestown and Boyle, large lakes feed the winding Shannon, nearer to the west smaller patterns of water reach the river, while eastwards the curve of water rounds the province, and to the south the wider angles of Lough Reagh narrow as the flow reaches Athlone.

AMBUSH AT SCRAMOGUE

Meanwhile, in Roscommon town, District-Inspector Cole had made a bloodthirsty speech to reinforcements. A whippet tank followed by eight lorries of troops was the first force to move up twards the mountain. On their way they made a prisoner of 'Cushy' Hughes. He had changed his clothes and gone in to draw his service pension. The soldiers brought him around in one of their lorries and he saw that two North Roscommon men, Pat Mullooly and Brian Nangle, who had been with him earlier that morning, had been captured by the Tans. They were both driven to the Lancers' headquarters in Strokestown where the soldiers tried to get at them with fixed bayonets, but the Tans protected their prisoners. On the way to Roscommon barracks, however, they were beaten with a cat o'nine tails by a Lancer until the Tans protested, for the two men had faced up to their captors and the Tans had some respect for them. Their subsequent career was of death threats from RIC and Tans in Roscommon and bloody floggings from the soldiers on their road to Athlone. When they were later brought to the Curragh hospital where the badly wounded machine-gunner lay, the Yorkshire man turned his head away from them. He was not going to assist in their identification.

Mullooly and Nangle waited behind when Madden hurried away after the ambush, and had lingered when word was sent back to them to push on. The British fired on them as they rushed out of a shop and they were surrounded and taken prisoner before they had made any distance. The Column men were barely half a mile away when they heard the noise of rifles which warned them of the enemy's presence, but they could not guess that it was at two of their ambush supporters that the firing was directed. The British decided that there must be additional men in the area who had taken part in the attack, and from halted lorries soldiers were spread out along the Lanesborough and Roscommon roads from Curraghroe.

The day after Pat Mullooly's capture his brother Michael went home although he knew it was dangerous for him to do so, but his teeth were troubling him and the pain upset his judgment. Tans and RIC from Roscommon town under the command of the County Inspector raided the house. They found Michael inside and he joked away with them for he felt he had no hope of escape from their plans for vengeance that he sensed. As the County Inspector was leaving the house there was a sudden rattle of firearms from inside. The officer did not halt for he knew what the shots meant. Some of the Tans and RIC had killed Michael.

The Column men carried the Hotchkiss which they intended to leave in a prepared dump. Their prisoner was inclined to talk at first.

'I had great luck to escape in that attack', he said, as they coursed along the sheltering hedge.

'If you had,' was the reply, 'you'd better say your prayers this evening.'

After that he tried to drop behind on one excuse or another, but the men were careful. At a cross-roads one of them saw a piece of paper on the ground and, suspecting that it had been dropped by the prisoner, he handed it to his commander. On it was the Tan's name and an indication of the direction in which he was going. His name was Evans. A prisoner usually had an amount of freedom as his hands were seldom if ever tied. The chief danger about holding prisoners was that if they remained among the men for a few days they would gather a good deal of information. The general tendency was to be decent to captives. This meant a cigarette, the sharing of a cup of tea, and talk. When this human equation had been reached the prisoner could often find a sense of ease and if he was astute he could, and often did, direct talk into grooves which gave him personal names, places and miscellaneous information.

'Look out, they're coming,' Evans shouted suddenly to Cooney who was the Column man nearest to him. As Cooney turned to look in the direction of the supposed enemy, the Tan jumped on him and tried to snap at his revolver, but Micky Collins, who was behind him, held him up as he struggled for the weapon.

In the valley between Aghamuck and Fairymount the men found British around them but they got through slowly to the heather stretch of Clonberry bog where they shot and buried their Tan.

After the Column had parted from them, the Curraghroe men pushed on towards their townland below the eastern slope of the mountains, but before they reached Killyackan the British had spread out close by. The men had intended to make for Derryhannen, a townland in an isolated bog about a quarter of a mile from the Shannon banks. Here they had previously cut away dut-outs in the turf banks. They had floored them with boards, arranged for proper drainage and had covered them with turf and scraws so that an observer nearby would not notice any alteration. In this open stretch of bogland and long grass along the river edge the dug-outs would be the only safety for themselves and their weapons if they were squeezed in by an enveloping movement, or if they had to lie up quietly for a few days. British activity now cut them off from their prepared safety. The ground on which they lay flattened out was low-lying, and movement was cut off by deep drains and bog holes, but the broken nature of the ground was well known to men who had fowled and frequently rambled over it. The variation of clumpy heather, long rough grass and ferny growth gave extended cover for movement if they had to retire or advance. The British had the rise of ground on either road which was raised above the bog, to observe them. They made use of the slopes of Slieve Bawn as observation posts for officers with prismatic glasses who had a wide view of the country between them and the Shannon, and as well the Longford edges of the river on the far side.

On that Spy Wednesday the Cumann na mBan girls played the spy to save the men of their mountainside. They went to the local shops as if to buy food, and to the neighbours as if to visit, but all the while they gathered their harvest of gossip about the movements of the British. Whatever stray talk was dropped in pubs or shops and in the presence of listeners on the roadside by the men in khaki or by the bottle-green prowlers for information, had been carefully gleaned by them. As soon as the British moved to pay attention to another stretch of country, one of the girls was before them with her story of their doings and conversations.

The Curraghroe men then crawled away until they were held up by what looked like another rounding-up by khaki figures.

The second captured Tan lay down with them. He had been a prisoner himself, he told them, and he had been on his way to a court in Longford when the lorry was ambushed. But he did not tell them that one of the charges against him was that of breaking the windows of the chapel in Elphin. In a way he sensed what would happen to him when the enveloping movement of his khaki friends was finished, but the men who guarded him were reserved in their talk and in their attitude towards him, although there was no hostility. Already he had attempted to expose himself when he was crossing drains and banks and he had to be told to crawl under cover. He had made a few attempts to drop behind, thinking he might conceal himself from his guards, but all his movements had been quietly watched.

The men waited until the light went out of the sky. The welcome darkness folded around them as they resumed their way across the uneven surface broken by drains and by the sudden rise of turf banks. Here many of them had handled a shotgun against the quick jerky rise of snipe or had lain out for wild duck, and that compass memory now served their movements. Some of them went off towards the dug-outs, but a few under Martin Fallon moved with the prisoner towards the river. They had intended to get one of the boats which were kept secure for crossing the Shannon at certain points, then bring the prisoner to the Longford side where they would shoot him. The finding of the body would direct investigations away from Roscommon and make the British concentrate their attention on the far side of the river — but their reprisals might then fall heavily on an area unconnected with the shooting.

The Tan had been pleading for his life every now and then, but whilst some of the men went to look for the boat which they expected to find close to a pier, Fallon told the prisoner that they intended soon to shoot him. If he needed them to pray with him they would help him to prepare for his end.

The Scots Tan suddenly made up his mind. He swung a punch to Fallon's jaw and as his captor dropped in a surprised heap the Tan ran hard towards the gleam of water.

When the boatmen returned they searched about in the narrow reach of the Shannon until a dark shape was seen against some bushes. Orders shouted in that direction met with no response, but when fire was opened against the bushes the Tan cried out. He was found on the edge of the flood under sally branches to which he had clung, but he was wounded. He was shot on the river bank, taken out into the current and thrown overboard. His ghost, it is said, haunts the bank and though there is no reason for a bias of friendship, the story has it that he is now hostile only to those people who were friendly to his side during the fight.

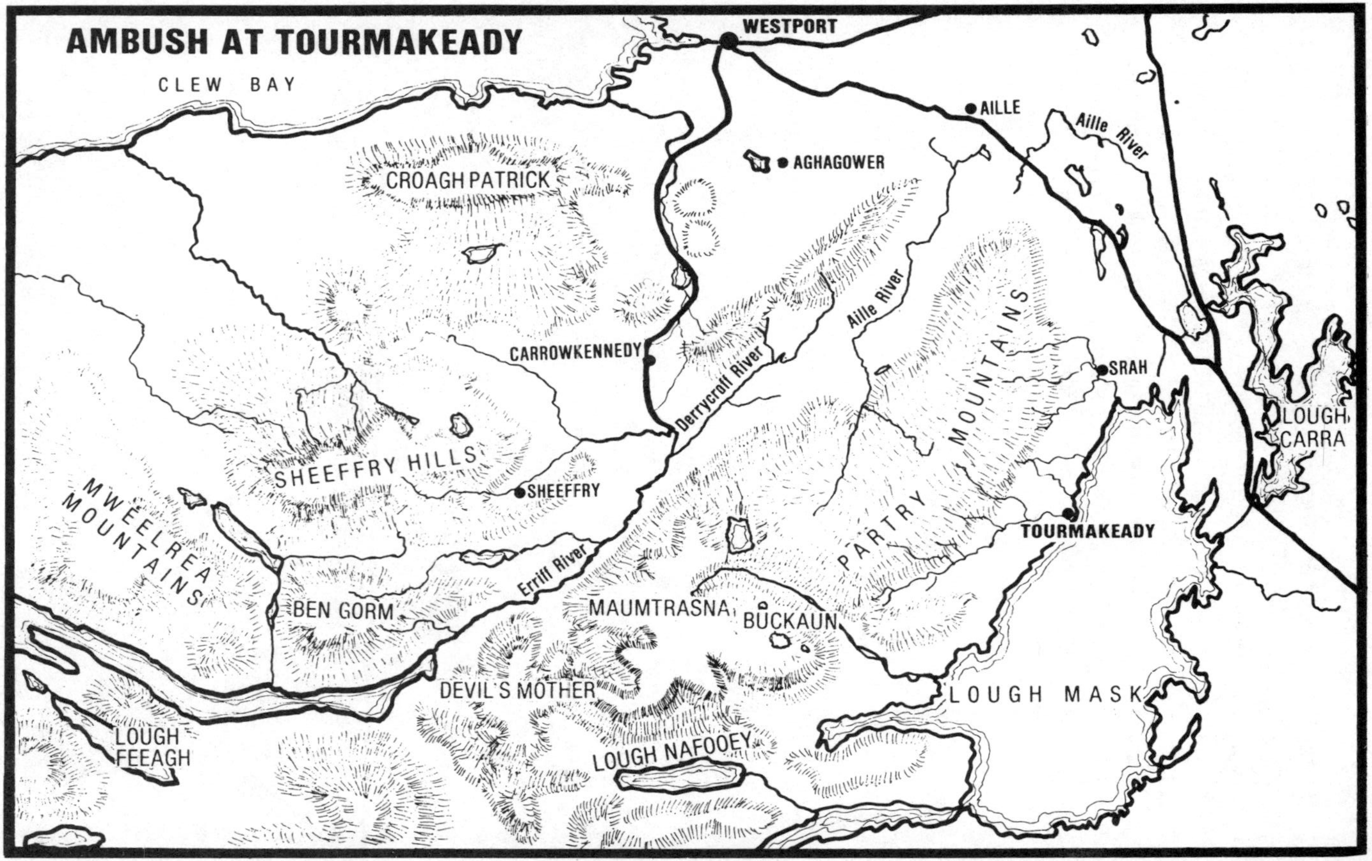
AMBUSH AT TOURMAKEADY
CLEW BAY
WESTPORT
AILLE
Aille River
AGHAGOWER
CROAGH PATRICK
CARROWKENNEDY
Derrycroff River
Aille River
SRAH
LOUGH CARRA
PARTRY MOUNTAINS
TOURMAKEADY
SHEEFFRY HILLS
SHEEFFRY
MWEELREA MOUNTAINS
Errill River
BEN GORM
MAUMTRASNA
BUCKAUN
DEVIL'S MOTHER
LOUGH MASK
LOUGH FEEAGH
LOUGH NAFOOEY

CHAPTER SEVEN

AMBUSH AT TOURMAKEADY

MAY 1921

Derrypark RIC barracks was a strongly-built house under the cliff-edged brows of Buckaun Mountain. The post looked down on Lough Mask and across to the wooded eastern shore of the lake towards Ballinrobe, the local police headquarters, which was about eight miles away as the crow flies — though by road it would be closer on twenty miles. The barracks was built during the land wars when certain constabulary posts were strengthened as forts rather than as stations, wherever landlords by their actions had sown dragons' teeth. Their sturdy walls yet served to reawaken memory. Lord Plunkett, Bishop of Tuam, following his eviction of tenants for not sending their children to his prosleytising schools, had needed protection on his land. Indeed he had required three other temporary barracks nearby as he had evicted people from the two Tourmakeadies — Gortfree and Gorteenmore. The constabulary had to pay rent as these three houses were his property, but the people had to pay additional tax for the maintenance of the police.

Now there was a garrison of twelve RIC in Derrypark but of late it was isolated, as two barracks, Partry on the way to Ballinrobe, and Ballyglass in the Castlebar direction, had withdrawn their garrisons for safety. Although their fighting and aggressive strength had been stiffened with Black and Tans, the uncertainty that existed among the constabulary in small posts in remote districts helped to wear down their nerves. In many places they were an outpost beleagured more by the withdrawal of the surrounding people and the menace of encircling hills than by the threat of IRA efficiency.

It had been the custom for some months past to send out a small convoy of RIC with pay and provisions to Derrypark on a fixed day each month. The IRA watched the convoy, which varied in strength from a motor car and a Crossley tender to two lorries, and when their reports had been forwarded through the battalion the Brigade decided to deal with this force.

Tom Maguire, the Brigadier of South Mayo, commanded a Column of twenty-five men who had been on the watch for random movements of British military or constabulary by road. They had been out many early mornings in frosty weather when long waiting was hard both on nerve and body, but nothing had recently come their way. The rainy climate of the West added another burden to late winter and the early spring. The men had been sleeping out in the woods on straw, covered by blankets given to them by local friendly people. This method of protection meant that if one portion of the Column was attacked it could be relieved by another group, but this also put an additional strain on the outposts to prevent the surprise of the concentrated unit. Nonetheless, if attacked in the open, the Column men felt they could fight without endangering the people of the nearest houses.

The Column, with minds centred on the convoy, had been for two days in the friendly neighbourhood of Srah under the eastern flank of the Partry mountains. In the morning of May 3, 1921, the Column and men from local companies met near the scattered village of Tourmakeady, eight miles north-east of Derrypark. There were close on sixty men when all their force had assembled. They were expecting two lorries and a touring car, spread out at intervals of about three hundred yards. As the intervening ground was wooded in places and the road wound quickly out of view, each section in the attack would have to be self-contained.

The Commander divided his Column into three units of sixteen men each, and as he wished to divide the available force fairly with the officers who would take command of two units, he allowed them in turn to select their pick of the men. One group under Michael O'Brien, the Brigade Adjutant, was then placed at the fair green to the north of the village. Tom Maguire's command post was at the centre of Tourmakeady, while Paddy May commanded the men two hundred yards further along the road, near the entrance to Drumbane House.

May was to be the first to open the attack and by that time it was hoped that each vehicle would be a target for a section. Linking files of Volunteers were scattered to maintain touch between the parties, and flanks were protected by the units themselves.

Armament, slenderly effective for the attack, consisted of six rifles only, so that shotguns of varying degrees of usefulness had to pad out the striking power. The wooded ground, however, suited smaller-range weapons; success would depend upon their initial use.

The people in the scattered homes which formed the two Tourmakeady villages were brought away from the danger zone and placed in an end house under guard. This ensured that the villagers would be sheltered from possible danger which the attack might occasion them, but it also meant that their movements and their talk would be restricted through this security. Among the temporary prisoners was an RIC pensioner and his wife. The woman attempted to escape at about the time she expected the convoy would arrive, but before she was able to warn them of the hidden groups of men she had been recaptured.

The post office was occupied by the Volunteers and as they waited for the enemy they examined the recently-posted letters. Often it had been found that real, or supposed information, from people friendly to the enemy, about the activities of the IRA or of members of the Sinn Féin clubs, could be found in the post bags. Deliberate intention, jealousy, petty spite, or the country closeness which rubs raw spots until they fester into a rash of rancour, were at the base of this type of petty spying. In this instance the letters would be forwarded either to the District Inspector of Police in Ballinrobe or to some of the constabulary who had formerly served in Tourmakeady and who had since been withdrawn to the safety of the strong post in the next town. When the letters had been read through they were sealed up again, but across the envelopes was a new notice 'Censored by IRA.'

Amongst the Tourmakeady post office mail was a letter from England from the wife of a Black and Tan. Her husband, who was serving in the massy isolation of Derrypark, had not been sending home what she regarded as her due of his good pay. Tans were usually heavy drinkers and the local porter helped to soothe outpost uncertainty and remoteness. The wife's furious letter of protest wound up with the intriguing question: 'How do you expect me to go out to my friends' houses when I have no blasted shoes?'

In Ballinrobe, scouts watched both the RIC and the military barracks. When the police in a car and a Crossley tender had drawn up at Birmingham's to buy provisions for the Derrypark garrison, in keeping with the recently-established routine, Pádraic Feeney set out by bicycle to bring his information but he did not reach the Brigadier in time. Another scout was able to get through and take a despatch to the IRA in the village just ahead of the enemy convoy. It was then decided that the first vehicle, lorry or car, was to be allowed to pass through as far as Drumbane gateway over five hundred yards on, where Paddy May and his men lay waiting. The car was first and the driver was killed immediately by a rifleman who occupied a position behind a wall nearly opposite the entrance to Drumbane House. The vehicle crashed through the gateway, but the other police got out on the road and from there they engaged May's men.

At the sound of the firing the Crossley halted between the first and second IRA positions and was fired on by the unit led by Michael O'Brien to whose assistance the Column Commander sent half of his own men. Then, with the remainder of his section, the Commander advanced down the road to join in the fight against the first police car, and after a short exchange of shots this group of RIC were out of action, all of them being dead. Arms and ammunition were stripped quickly from the outstretched bodies, but as a noise of rifle fire was coming from the village the Commander was anxious to move in that direction so that he could find out exactly what was happening.

The remaining police from the Crossley were under the charge of a head constable who directed them while they carried their wounded and held off their attackers until they reached a hotel a little in from the roadside, beside a crossroads. They were then secure enough in a well-built house and they knew that if they were able to maintain their position the RIC in Derrypark, who had probably heard the firing, would be able to get a message through to Ballinrobe for reinforcements. There was a small plantation nearby from which the two rifles in O'Brien's command were being used. As soon as the RIC located the sound they used rifle grenades against their hidden attackers, and the bursting metal splinters made the shelter of the young trees a lesser security. O'Brien felt he could not achieve anything from his position and withdrew his men.

Tom Maguire had no immediate plan for attacking the hotel, and to organise even an impromptu attempt on the building would take some time. There had been no preparations made to cut roads, fell trees or destroy culverts so as to delay reinforcements, as it had been thought that the police would be forced to surrender soon after the action had begun. It was essential to move the Column away into the mountains and to disband the local Volunteers.

Soon after the IRA had left the village the RIC were able to venture out. They made use of the telegraph in the post office, but a wireless transmitter in the barracks at Derrypark had already sent information to Ballinrobe about the attack on the convoy.

Tourmakeady lies under the Partry mountains, but to the west and south-west are steeper heights: Buckaun, the great mass of Maumtrasna, and the Devil's Mother. The only cover is given by gullies which tear the denuded flanks of the mountainside, or that provided by river beds, cliff edges and dips in the ground. South-west from the village a road borders Lough Mask and continues along by Lough Nafooey over a pass to the Maum valley fourteen miles away. To the west of the village a rugged road crosses the mountains and drops down the far side towards Westport. The road from Castlebar to Ballinrobe borders the north-eastern mountain edges, and another road on the western mountain slopes connects the Castlebar road with the mountain road running across the heights from Tourmakeady.

Maguire intended to cross the road from Castlebar to Ballinrobe as he knew there was insufficient cover in the hills.

When he reached a point two miles above Srah he rested his men. Most of the local lads had already been dismissed and had made for the hills, but Maguire kept a few of them to act as guides. While the men were resting he used his field-glasses to search for enemy reinforcements and as he looked towards Partry across Lough Mask he saw swirls of dust. Very few roads were then macadamised and in dry weather a lorry's path lay through several inches of dust, but a depth of mud whenever rain fell. As he counted those dust clouds Maguire knew that they signified enemy reinforcements which were already making for Tourmakeady. He counted twenty-four dust storms. That meant, he surmised, that Galway, a brigade headquarters, and possibly Claremorris, had sent on troops.

The lorries passed on towards the village while the Column men took cover, but evidently the soldiers knew where to seek their quarry. Lorries halted at intervals along the lake shore, soldiers and bottle-green police jumped out and were soon slowly making their way up in extended order towards the hills. Some of the lorries passed on to Tourmakeady and the Column Commander guessed that they would cross by the mountain road to Westport, and when they reached the far slopes they would steadily help to encircle his Column.

The Column now moved northwards. With it were some Srah men who knew the lines of the hills as they knew the creases in the palms of their hands, but the Column itself consisted mostly of men from the Ballinrobe battalion and they were not so limber as the Srah men.

The direction of the Column was changed again, further to the north, for that point would bring it across the hills which were about 1,200 feet high, topped by a plateau, but as soon as the men commenced to climb, the British followed them up. The men scattered out along the hillside and used their few rifles, but the British picked out the direction in which they were moving by the sound of their rifle shots and tended to close in on them. The Column hurried up the hills towards the road from Westport to Ballinrobe but, as the men climbed, their scouts found that military and constabulary who had come on from Westport and Castlebar were now stretched across the eastern slopes, barring their way to safety. These fresh reinforcements were still at a distance but they used their machine-guns at long range, prior to moving close.

The Column men looked about them for a position which might give them cover and which they could hold when the ring tightened around them. By this time they were high above Tournawoad village. The Commander with his officers picked a fold in the ground formed by a table of stone with a steep drop to the south and behind it a rise of ground. In Irish the place is known as 'Rock of the Sally Trees', but there are no sally trees there any longer.

It was now one o'clock and the men extended lines and settled down for a long fight. Below them they could see the shores of Lough Carra with the light green sheen on its waters, the oak trees around Moore Hall and the tiny islands of Lough Mask standing away from serrated lake edges. The peninsula between the two waters stood out clearly with its steep western end, and below it were the many islands in the Corrib until it narrowed on the way to Galway. Men could pick out their homes far below or guess at their location with the aid of well-known landmarks. Around them on the mountains were the British forces together with that old historical tradition of Irish mercenaries who now in their bottle-green uniforms helped to guide the troops and later would identify the prisoners and the dead.

Lewis guns began to find the range as they cut up the heather and scraws of earth; then when the gun bursts were observed British officers gave the range to their riflemen. It was a fine May day but to the waiting men it meant that sunset, which in the West is an hour later, would not creep down until close on half past ten. If the Column could hold out until then, the men would have a good chance to get through in the sheltering darkness, but the hours in between would be long. The rock sloped behind them and gave them cover, but in front Lewis guns cut away the torn earth and fire crept in gradually until it reached the extended Column position. It would seem that the British hoped to solve the problem of making the Column surrender by an intensification of rifle and machine-gun fire directed now from scattered groups of soldiers on the mountainside, who had closed in. Terrified by the sounds of battle and by the unusual movement, cattle and horses rushed through the heather and hares darted out of cover. The real danger, however, would come from 1,500 to 2,000 yards away. Bullets from these ranges would drop down at forty-five degrees and could then search out the defended position from on high.

Tom Maguire was wounded by a burst from a Lewis gun and from the pain in his upper arm he knew that the bone was smashed. He lay on his uninjured side while Michael O'Brien crawled to his assistance. O'Brien knelt beside him, eased the jacket off the injured limb and ripped up the shirt sleeve to expose the wound. Then he tried to staunch the blood by pressing on arteries and by binding the arm tightly with a bandage from his first-aid kit.

As O'Brien crouched beside Maguire his back was towards the enemy rifle fire. Suddenly Maguire, who was now lying flat on his back, became aware of a tall, bareheaded man in his shirt sleeves a short distance away. He was carrying a rifle. By his build Maguire took him to be Costello, an ex-soldier from Tournawoad. Costello had served through the world war in the Irish Guards and had been wounded. He later became a good Volunteer and had fought in a recent ambush at Portroyal where a number of rifles were captured from the military, but he had not been at Tourmakeady that morning.

'Costello is coming up now,' the Commander thought, 'because he knows we are in trouble.' A good shot and a man who had seen arduous service, he would be of immense help to the Column. The Commander saw his mistake when it was too late. Behind the tall figure he now noticed eight khaki soldiers with rifles, who had suddenly rushed forward from behind a low ridle of ground.

'Look out, lads, look out!' he shouted excitedly.

'Hands up, boys!' called out the tall man as he brought up his rifle towards his shoulder.

O'Brien, when he heard his Commander's cry of alarm, was pressing tightly on a bandage, concerned about the spurts of blood which had raddled his hands and seeped on to the ground. He grabbed his rifle and turned quickly towards the new menace. Maguire watched in helpless anxiety.

Both men had their rifles in a firing position and, for what seemed a long time to the wounded officer, they faced each other as if time had suddenly stood still. Some of the hurrying soldiers had stopped and were fumbling with their weapons. Then there was a sharp rifle crack and O'Brien slumped heavily across Maguire's legs. To the right of the Commander a shotgun man replied. His buckshot struck the stranger and knocked the rifle from his grip. Shotgun men on the left used their weapons as the soldiers ran back with their leader towards cover and safety. Some of them dropped into the heather, wounded as they retreated. O'Brien lay where he had fallen. Men crawled up to him and lifted his weight off their Commander's legs, but when they turned him upwards he was dead. The tall man who killed him was subsequently found to be a Lieutenant Ibberson of the Border Regiment then stationed in Ballinrobe. A good long-distance runner, his training had helped him to make the breath-catching ascent ahead of his comrades. Ibberson's legs and his stomach were severely lacerated by the tearing buckshot. He was operated on, and recovered, and was promoted to a captaincy for his bravery on that day.

Two experienced Column leaders were out of this fight. The Commander was an additional burden as he was bleeding profusely, and if his men could hold out until dusk he would have to be carried off the mountain. Ammunition was becoming scarce. Fire had to be directed only at movement and against Lewis gun positions. Shotgun men waited for the inevitable charge, but the riflemen were learning to squeeze their triggers, as they had been ordered, only when they felt sure that they could hit a khaki figure. Previously the British had advanced under concentrated fire but they had run back again when a few good shots in the Column flattened out some of their number.

The Column Commander was wounded several times as the day for him slowly filtered out its light. Although his men bandaged him as best they knew, he had lost a good deal of blood, and the wounds and anxiety were wearing him between dual millstones for, unlike the British, each IRA unit had to continue its resistance by itself. That was a burden which often weighed heavily on a senior officer or column commander. If he worked out an action he was responsible for its success, and if it was drawn out in time he might have to meet British reinforcements which would attempt to support an endangered barracks or a convoy threatened on the road. Unexpected sequels to a deliberate attack had to be provided for in his planning. If the fight was prolonged he could not hope to receive help, either in men or munitions. As well, he would feel responsible for losses in action and for whatever reprisals the enemy might take against the lives of people in the area, or against their property. As the British tested out their ring squeeze he would find that some of the shotguns, probably worn thin by rust and lack of care, had burst their barrels when the buckshot of refilled cartridges tried to rattle down their sides.

Gradually the British came as close as they could find cover; at intervals heavy fire was directed at the Column position, both from near at hand and from far away. The British could afford to wait. They had ample ammunition and could rely on fresh men to reinforce them. The Column men had intended to get food and water at Srah that morning, but while they were on their way to that village their Commander had first sighted the enemy lorries, and his men had withdrawn up the hill again, without provisions. In the evening they were very thirsty from their hurried climb and from the excitement of action. They had neither food nor water and their wounded Commander suffered badly from thirst.

Reports had gone regularly into Ballinrobe, which was now a minor expeditionary headquarters, about the day's work on the mountainside. IRA prisoners in the military barracks had heard the soldiers there discuss the situation. The last report was that the rebels on the mountain were completely surrounded and it was now just a question of time before they surrendered.

The men waited on the hills anxiously until the long twilight slowly settled down over the rise and on the bright surface of Lough Mask. Then, in a blaze of colour, slowly adjusting itself as if painting a series of tone relationships to be seen only in the West, the sun dropped over the edge of height. In the darkness the men could see Very lights from scattered British positions shoot up into the night sky to outline the countryside as a red-blue blaze in the strange unreality of their dramatic light. They heard whistles shrilling, then lorries started up on the roads and it would seem from the noise that their engines made in the quiet evening and their spaced headlights as they moved along, that the enveloping forces on this side of the mountain were returning to the shelter of their barracks. The dead and wounded British were carried down the mountainside, and as there was an anxiety to conceal casualties the wounded were sent on to Claremorris in carriages with the blinds drawn down. The British left picquets behind them on the lower slopes to guard the ground until daylight, but the fear of hill darkness and a night swoop by the hill men kept the skeleton force so strictly on the defensive that there was no difficulty for the Column men moving through them in the dark.

Maguire had already advised some of his men to make their way beyond the western cliff surround of Buckaun. They could then skirt the narrower out-thrust above Sketia, and on the heights of Maumtrasna, over seven miles away, they could follow down towards Lough Nafooey and along by the Finny river to Finny. The men did not know the sharp cliff edges of this journey and there were now no guides left to help them, but their sense of direction and the clarity of danger brought them safely across country that would daunt most men in daylight, to the lowlands near Finny.

At midnight the Column Commander was slowly carried downhill. The jolting movement of descent and the insecurity of footing in the darkness made progress difficult, but the bearers were anxious to spare him unnecessary pain. The first house they came to was Lally's and there they decided against taking him any further. Some of his men had now to get back to their own countryside, although reluctant to leave him behind. They went towards the eastern edge of Lough Mask, round by the water close to Ballinrobe, and they made their way some miles below that town to the security of the Neale. Bourke, a Column man who had been slightly wounded in the thigh, crossed the mountains with a few companions to the western slopes and by the morning's light he had reached the friendly houses of Clady, about nine miles from Westport. There he was helped on his way with a horse which would take him further away from the wide encircling movement to be expected that day.

On the evening of the fight a message detailing the plight of the South Mayo Column was brought to Michael Kilroy, Brigadier of West Mayo. He was then in the valley between Bengorm and Buckoogh near to the salmon leap at the foot of Lough Feeagh on the northern side of Clew Bay. The Newport Column men were with him, waiting for more definite information about British movement on the Mallaranny road before they got ready to prepare an ambush position at the winding curve beside Burrishoole bridge. Kilroy told them that the South Mayo Column was hemmed in on the eastern slopes of the Partry mountains and that he intended to go at once to its aid, but as men would have to go outside the Brigade area he must first ask for volunteers. All the men present, he found, were willing to go with him. Most of them carried rifles. They waited until the light began to fail, then they left the shelter of the mountains in the soft freshness of the May night. They moved eastwards by Newport and by unfrequented ways until they crossed the main road between Castlebar and Newport. Broken hills led them onwards until they reached the district around Aghagower which was also a core of safety and discretion. Their way wound on through bare heights towards the further mountains, in which the South Mayo Column was hemmed. Dawn came early, around four o'clock, and as the light slanted softly into the valleys of the Partry mountains the Column had to end its long march. At a house where they halted for information, Kilroy was told that the encircled South Mayo men had got through the enemy lines in darkness.

That same day the Westport Column had been lying out in ambush on the Ballinrobe road some miles beyond Westport, hidden in a tangle of scrub. In the early evening, tired from the disappointment of not finding any sign of British movement on the roadway, the men had moved out of their position when their Commander received a despatch. It brought news of Maguire's men on the distant heights. The Westport men went quickly towards the hills, hoping that they would be able to engage some of the British outposts to draw their attention away from the distressed Column. They had come as far as Derrycroff river, which runs below the Partry mountains, when they found that they, too, were not in time to assist in the break-out.

Young Pádraic Feeney who had tried to bring out word from Ballinrobe saw the military escort pass him on the way. He was too late to bring the required information but he thought he might be permitted to join the men who were ready to fight. When the Column had withdrawn from the village he was captured by some of the RIC who had been defending themselves, but who had then left the hotel and were now in an ambush position. He was taken as a prisoner to the hotel. Sometime later a few of the old RIC took him out of the hotel by a backdoor. Shots were heard, and his dead body was found after the police had left Tourmakeady.

At dawn on the morning following the fight the local men came to Lally's with the intention of carrying Maguire away from danger, but they were unable to help him. He was so weak that he could not put weight on his feet. During the night Dr. Murphy had come out from Tourmakeady to attend him, but he had been unable to bring either bandages or antiseptics for fear of meeting British patrols or piquets on the way. The doctor would have been spared none of the brutal methods practised by intelligence gentlemen to extract information had he been found with equipment suitable for a wounded man. In Lally's he made a rough splint for the injured shoulder and he cut up a hastily emptied flour bag which served for bandage material.

With the morning light, troops emerged from the comfort of their barracks. Extra reinforcements had made the proposed day's work easier and the full resources of military equipment, from field-kitchens to aeroplanes, were released for this mimic of a minor war. Houses were systematically searched and the occupants laboriously questioned in a ponderous manner, but evasion and astute anticipation of the ambiguous nature of questions were bred too deeply in the bone, so that the people hermetically sealed off whatever information they knew in a pretence of innocent unawareness.

As the soldiers moved upwards they came close to Lally's house. The women, who had observed the military movements from their first dust swirl, carried out the wounded Column Commander towards the bed of a dried-up mountain stream where he lay under the shelter of overhanging whins. His blood-stained bed-clothes were placed under him in the stony roughness of the stream-bed and there he stayed until twilight put an end to military mountaineering. That night he was carried down the mountain to another house where he had to remain because of the increasing seriousness of his wounds. IRA men who remained in the area came in with the news that the British were approaching the house where he lay in bed. Again the women helped, this time by carrying him on slings made of their shawls. As they hurried upwards, stumbling under their burden, Maguire heard the clear engine-sound of an aeroplane which was directing troop movements. He told his bearers to set him down at once and to seat themselves on the ground. They first covered him with their shawls so that the aeroplane noised overhead of a group of women who were having a good chat.

The women carried him uphill until they reached a sheltered spot on a hillock where they laid him down. During the day they watched in turn and brought him news as successive parties of troops came in his direction. A few times he heard English voices as sections moved up and down the hill, but when the shrill noise of whistles came to him in the late evening he knew that another day's search had been ended. Later, as he was being hammocked down hill in his net of shawls, he heard the sounds of lorry engines as the troops prepared to return to their bases. Dogs barked their annoyance at these unusual interruptions of their stewardship.

News about the Column and the local IRA, stories about searches and interrogations, came in regularly to the Commander. Women, girls and children got through the British outposts and returned with information and with a well-seasoned curry of neighbourhood talk. The people had been frightened as they watched the British attack the hillsides. They had listened to their rifle and machine-gun fire for part of a long day. Now they could see how formidable the British were in numbers and in armament. They could hear orders in the distance as khaki groups scattered like mountain sheep over the hills. Yet they knew the British up to this had failed, and in addition they were well aware that the wandering lines of troops had tightened their net only on their own disappointment. The ponderous British effort no longer had any meaning for them. Their hearts now cheered as they talked to each other in Irish with an ironic sense of the ridiculous aspect of the mountain climbers.

For four days the British combed the mountains for the numerous IRA dead whom they boasted they had killed, but particularly for the wounded who should have been hemmed in by their outpost lines. Constabulary men with their steadily accumulated knowledge of the hills guided each khaki column. The young men and the middling young were missing from their villages whether they were members of the IRA or not. In the mountain area the heights were but stepping stones to their strong leg muscles which were accustomed to spend the day tracking down their cattle and the climbing propensities of their wandering sheep. These men knew that raiding parties would interrogate them, and if they were of an active age they would be suspects to the military, Auxiliaries and Tans who would not accept their ignorance of the previous fight. They would be presumed guilty as aiders and abettors. That implication of connivance would mean variations on themes of manhandling, from rifle-butts through heavy boots to fists or even to shots as threat or intention.

Two young men were found the morning following the retreat, near Glenmask, exhausted and asleep beside their shotguns. The military awakened them by the use of heavy boots. They had been searching the heights for foxes, the men said, which killed the young lambs whenever they found them isolated during the lambing season. The explanation cut little ice with the soldiers who beat them unmercifully with rifle butts, again and again, and laid into them with their heavy boots, while the two wove their stories around the ravenous foxes. On their way to Ballina they were again given the close-quarter attention of their captors, so that on arrival they were a bloodied mass. An

RIC man who had served in Tourmakeady confirmed that the men of the district did lie out to get the fox. The British had decided that possession of arms in the vicinity was sufficient to implicate these men in the deaths of the police and British military, but the explanation of the RIC man saved their lives.

A troop train which ran a pilot engine in front of it to test the railway line for loose rails or a land mine was sent on to Recess in Connemara. Troops searched the mountains on either side of the Maum valley and across by the pass which led to the enclosed shelter of Lough Nafooey. The prowling eye of the aeroplanes helped the ground forces in this difficult country, but their quarry, the Column which had confronted the mixed force on the mountain, seemed to have vanished like mountain mist. On the troops' way back, the Twelve Pins were investigated on foot.

The only result of this careful combing of a mountain district was a tired-foot impression of rugged scenery, the capture of two unmounted hunters, and the finding of the body of Michael O'Brien, which was to have been removed by the local Volunteers the night he had been killed. It seems that his body could not be found when it was searched for in the darkness.

Pádraic Feeney's body was placed in front of the main altar of the church in Ballinrobe. The RIC dead rested before the side altars of the same church. When the British protested against the place of honour being given to a rebel, the Canon refused to make any alteration in the distribution of the dead. Daily papers, however, announced the following: 'The Archbishop of Tuam and Canon Dalton, PP, called at Ballinrobe barracks and expressed their deep sympathy with the police, describing the victims as men of excellent character.'

Following the ambush at Tourmakeady the Royal Irish in the isolated posts of Derrypark and Kinnury were withdrawn at once for their own safety and to strengthen the constabulary posts in Ballinrobe and Castlebar. Thus, as a result of the ambush another large stretch of mountain area was freed from continuous constabulary espionage and from immediate constabulary contact with civilian sources of information. On the other hand, IRA columns had an added portion of difficult country to use as a retreat in emergency. Constabulary usefulness was now limited to the identification of prisoners, the tutoring of Tans in local knowledge, and the guidance of raiding parties who rarely sallied forth except in considerable strength.

The enemy had to use additional men for patrols and for convoys, and this increase, when multiplied by the demand for more troops in other centres of unease throughout the country, fixed the strain on imperial defence at too tense a breaking point.

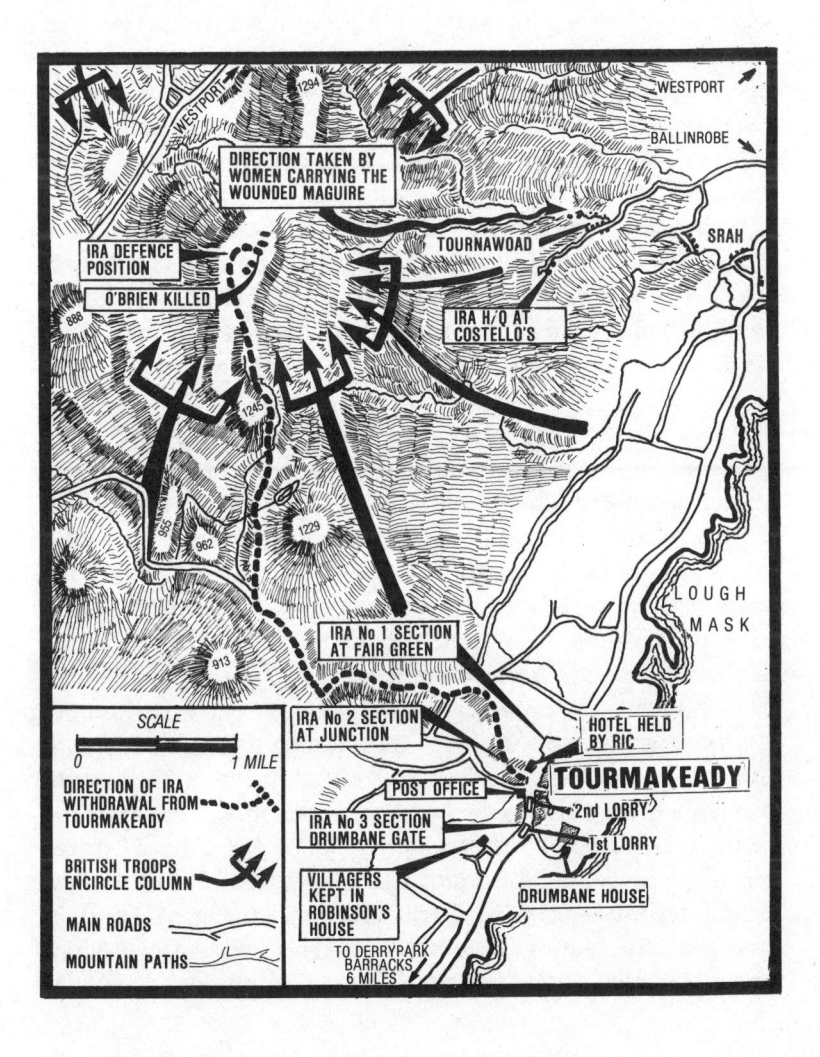

CHAPTER EIGHT

MODREENY

MAY–JUNE 1921

The North Tipperary Column acted as guard while officers were being trained by Captain MacCormack from GHQ. A large house and its outhouses, not far from the Shannon, were made use of. Officers from battalions to the west had already received some training in another part of the Brigade; now officers from nearby battalions were attending classes while guarded by the Column and by detachments from local companies — though the Column men would have preferred their wandering life of waiting for a chance to hit at the British. Word was sent out by a friendly RIC man from Cloughjordan that the police were aware of armed men somewhere close to the Shannon and that Birr military would soon be detailed to carry out a raid.

More attention was then given to protection by day and night. Offshore from the Shannon there was a motor boat in good engine condition, which had been commandeered from a Major Williams in Portumna. It was commodious, it had a powerful engine, and it could be handled by men who knew Lough Derg with its many shallows and jutting rocks. The intention, in case of an enemy raid, was to hold the position until a large number of the officers had been brought away by boat. The RIC man came out to the training camp one evening to tell the Column Commander that the British would sweep a certain section of the countryside early on the following day and that they would probably come close to the headquarters house. The searching of countryside was a slow enough process, especially when the enemy were looking for armed men. They would have to cross fields, drains, hedges and woodlands, and they would move in strength. The Column Commander and his senior officers knew that all day they would be kept informed of approaching parties by a thin spread of scouts. It was decided to allow the British to come close enough to engage their advance parties while the boat removed surplus men. Reports about the moving troops came in regularly to local company officers. An extended line of troops was moving steadily across country, but when they came close to the positions held by rifle and shotgun men, the British turned about and moved obligingly in the opposite direction.

On two occasions the Column had united close to Cloughjordan in the late evening. A heavy patrol of about twelve or fourteen RIC was said to advance in extended double files up and down the town every evening; when they reached the outskirts they would halt, break their formation and go back in close order. The town was lighted by electricity, so that both IRA and police would be in a strong light covering a few hundred yards beyond the limit of the streets. Local Volunteers with shotguns reinforced the Column on the verge of the town, but no patrol came that night. On the following evening the RIC moved out again. This seemed to indicate that there was some leakage of information in the district and the Brigade finally traced it to the Moneygall area in the Toomevara battalion. The proof was not decisive, but it made senior officers more guarded as other movements of the Column seemed to have been known to the British.

An ambush was prepared on the Middle Walk on the old Bianconi road from Birr to Nenagh, in Bill O'Dwyer's company area, and the Column, under Jack Collison, was strongly reinforced that morning by local companies. Police, normally strengthened by military, were due for the opening of the assizes in Nenagh, the occasion being both an opportunity for a ceremonial display of force by the visiting police and a protection for the court and its adherents. Jurors had often to be brought to court under escort because they might be held up by the IRA, and although legal advisers and officials were also so protected, the business of courts, due to non-attendance of litigants, was now very slight.

Three lorries were expected that morning and three positions had been prepared. Shotgun men were close to the road, their refilled cartridges weighted with bicycle ball bearings, and each section with a few hand grenades. Trenches had been dug in the roadway for the first lorry, and the road surface had been carefully covered with propped canvas, its own surface dusted to resemble the neighbouring area of road. As the morning went slowly on for the waiting men, passers-by were held up by outposts and escorted to a local house where they were kept under guard. A clergyman who had been made a prisoner was evidently informed that a Volunteer officer from another battalion, whom he knew, was in charge of a group of men below near to the road. The officer went to see him. The clergyman told him that he had intended to go on a sick call and promised on his word of honour to return. The officer was reluctant to allow him to go; he released him, but he did not return.

The assizes party did not come by the Middle Walk. Volunteers thought that somehow the holding-up of numerous people might have created anxiety in their homes and that information might have been passed on by a loyalist. On the following morning, the officer concerned was told by a garage man in a neighbouring town that the clergyman had spoken to the police as they were preparing to leave their barracks in the lorries. Subsequently, British officers from Nenagh and Birr inspected the positions on the Middle Walk. They were impressed with the preparations for the reception of their friends. 'There would have been nothing left of them save their buttons,' said one of them.

In May the Column under the command of Jack Collison was close to Terryglass on the Lough when it was joined by the Brigade OC, Seán Gaynor, who was the proud possessor of an automatic shotgun. It was a rare weapon then, though often carried by members of Auxiliary companies. Five of the Column had gone home on leave, so there were then fifteen men to command, armed with fourteen rifles and the repeating shotgun. In deference to the presence of the Brigadier in the Column, Collison handed over command to him.

Gaynor had a talk with Felix Cronin who commanded the local battalion. When Cronin was questioned about the possibilities of making use of the Column, he said, 'Well, you missed a great chance a few days ago,' and told the Brigadier what had happened. Tans and RIC had been drinking heavily in the quiet seclusion of pubs in Borrisokane when a report came in that telegraph wires had been cut outside the town and they were ordered out on the road at once to investigate. Fourteen of them went off along the main road, *on duty and patrolling 0* as did the Bansha peeler in the time of the Land War. Having patrolled part of the line, the heat of the May sun and the strength of the drink inside of them had exhausted their zest for such martial activity; they had thrown their rifles alongside a ditch and slept on the bankside in the soothing arms of Bacchus. Fourteen rifles, ammunition and revolvers for the picking up. What a treasure lost, just as if they had dreamt about it.

By this time the British had become wary and had learned to avoid routine movements in the countryside, whether on foot, in lorries or by train. This absence of regularity now made it difficult for a column commander to plan attacks. In any battalion area he would have the complete assistance of the local intelligence officer, but unless chance talk from police or military could be gathered up about their intentions as regards movements, or direct information be obtained from telegraphic offices, a definite objective would not be revealed. There was, however, if the local intelligence system had been thoroughly organised, the possibility that chance information would be given by a friendly policeman, or that a military or police message in the now quickly-changing code would, when unravelled, betray enemy secrecy either about movements or the approach of important officers.

The IRA tried again. The Brigadier thought if the telegraph wires were cut once more this would result in an armed patrol being sent out to investigate what the enemy would call 'an outrage' in that quiet area. The wires were severed by some of the Borrisokane company while the Column remained hidden near hedges from early morning until late afternoon. This time a scout was watching Borrisokane barracks, ready to bring word to the waiting men should a patrol move out of the town. He was surprised to see an RIC man walk leisurely from the barracks and approach him. 'Go on out,' said the policeman, 'and tell the boys in Ballinderry that we know well where they are, and get them to move off at once before they're rounded up.' The astonished scout had no more than turned to get his bicycle when the policeman added: 'We're going to the court in Cloughjordan next Friday and I hope now that nothing will happen to us.'

At about five in the evening, when the Commander was ready to move the Column, the cyclist came hurriedly up the road with his message that the RIC knew that men were lying out in wait, that military in Birr had been informed, and that it was expected that troops would come on shortly to surround a portion of the district. After Gaynor and Collison had listened to the news, they moved the Column away across country to Arderoney which was looked on as safe.

Gaynor had also been given a despatch from the local IRA intelligence officer informing him that a lecture was to be held in the courthouse at Borrisokane on Friday, June 4th, and that between twelve and fourteen RIC men would go there from Cloughjordan. The Borrisokane courthouse, as the Brigadier was aware, had been burned down by the Volunteers as part of the destruction policy by which the administration of British law would be made difficult to function, and then only through the help and protection of the armed forces of the Crown. An Dáil, through the resolution of the Republican Army, was determined to show that British rule now rested on force. Local police, reinforced by outside troops, usually guarded a courthouse to protect such jurors, litigants and officials as might attend the court. Often the police and the local magistrate had the courthouse to themselves, while in the open bog or in an isolated house the Republican court held session, giving swift judgement as a rule. These Dáil courts had to be carefully guarded by scouts and Volunteers with shotguns, as the British, who had not at first interfered, were now doing their utmost to raid for the courts and to arrest litigants, solicitors, court officials and Republican police.

It was intended to ambush the RIC patrol on the following Friday when it went on its way to the courthouse for the assizes, but the decision was not mentioned to the Column men. That procedure was unusual. Ordinarily a column would know the previous evening or on the morning of an operation what part they were to take in the proposed action. The men would then be more alert. Weapons would be thoroughly cleaned and ammunition examined; each Volunteer would take an extra interest in protection until he arrived at the chosen spot. Recent strange mishaps, however, had made Gaynor and Collison cautious. There were so many soft bog surfaces on the surrounds of this Irish life that firm ground could so often give way to a sinking depth. This was the heritage of a conquered country, the unprepared, the unexpected in the middle of seeming security. The British now had their sense of insecurity when they left their strongholds, yet their long domination had prepared its own kind of mental ambush for the men who fought them.

On Thursday night, eight shotgun men from Cloughjordan company had been added to the Column. They were intended to be used for close-quarters work and especially at the onset of a surprise attack, and their addition brought the total strength to twenty-three. The country through which they moved shortly after dawn had slight hills and fields densely fenced. The land was rich, as could be seen by the short, slender shoots of barley and wheat. Its worth was attested also by that sure indication, the high incidence of names of Cromwellian troopers. One of the Protector's regiments had been disbanded in the district. Now some owners of the homes were known as Orangemen, who kept the ceremonies of that Order, including the Orange Walk. They also became members of the Ulster Volunteer Force, though they had not been as active as their friends in the neighbouring Roscrea battalion area, who had an intelligence service of their own and who lay out to surprise wanted Volunteers until their zeal had been suitably discouraged. At all events, the presence of a tentatively hostile element amongst the population made officers and men more careful of their movements and kept them more seriously alert in their protective precautions as they went on their way. As strangers in the neighbourhood, the Column Command felt they might be reported by these Orangemen to the nearest post, or else the

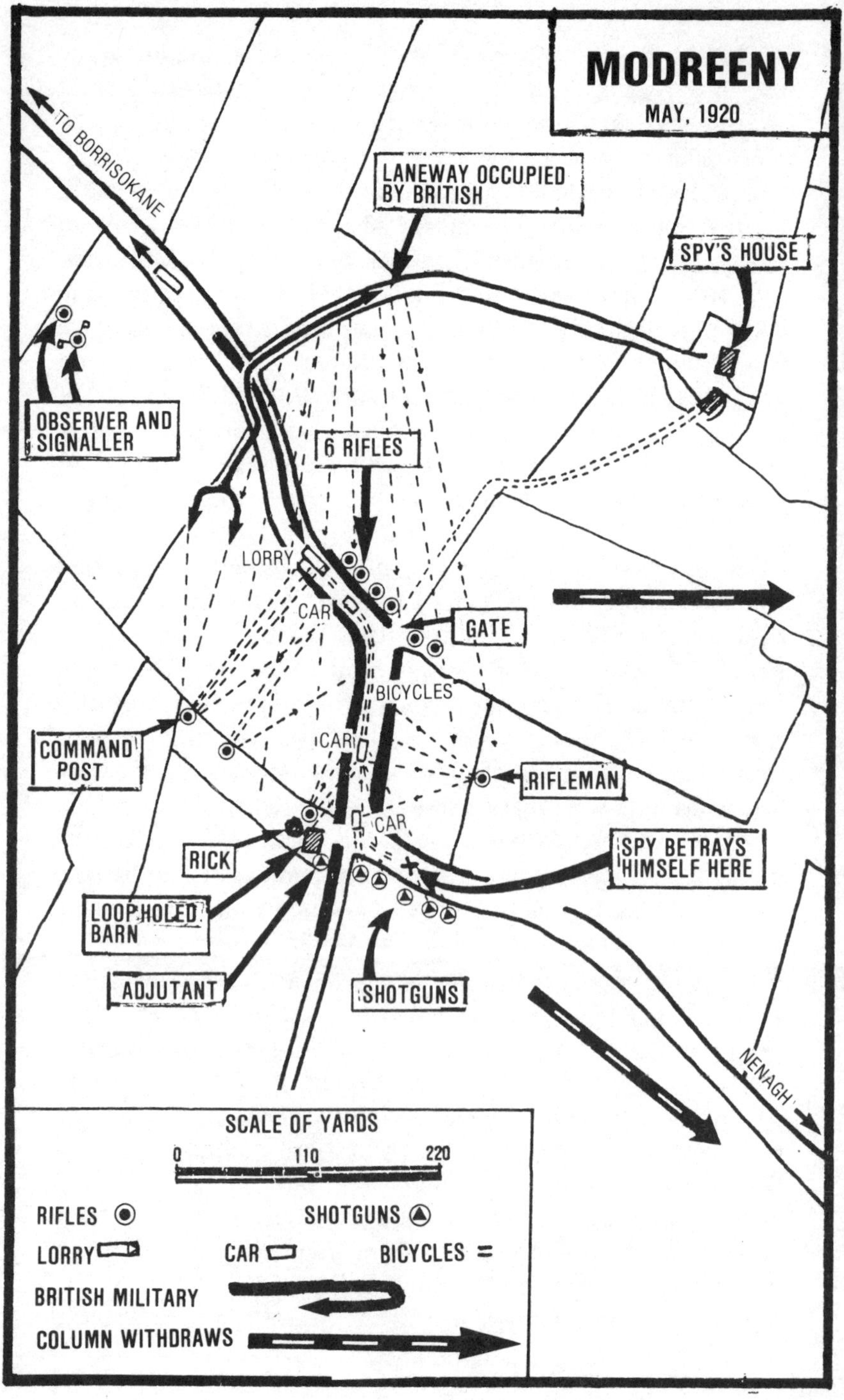
MODREENY
MAY, 1920
LANEWAY OCCUPIED BY BRITISH
SPY'S HOUSE
TO BORRISOKANE
OBSERVER AND SIGNALLER
6 RIFLES
LORRY
CAR
GATE
BICYCLES
CAR
COMMAND POST
RIFLEMAN
CAR
RICK
SPY BETRAYS HIMSELF HERE
LOOPHOLED BARN
ADJUTANT
SHOTGUNS
NENAGH
SCALE OF YARDS
0
110
220
RIFLES
SHOTGUNS
LORRY
CAR
BICYCLES =
BRITISH MILITARY
COLUMN WITHDRAWS

Column might be dogged until their halting place was definitely located. It was all in contrast with the freedom and ease they enjoyed when travelling in the mountains from Slievecamalta to Knockfune, where the people helped to protect them and the close-mouthed schoolchildren were eager scouts and quick reporters of information.

Dew was heavy on the grass on the fresh June morning as the men crossed through the fields. Suddenly, at a double bend, Gaynor and Collison halted to inspect a position at Modreeny on the Borrisokane-Cloughjordan road. They were in advance of their men as they talked about the RIC cyclist patrol which was due for the court assizes and might pass some time before noon that morning. They ordered the Column to halt and to get within a bank. The two officers went from field to field. They looked out over hedgerows and across banks whose thickness they gauged with a rifle; they lay down behind stone walls and sighted their weapons; they crossed the fields on either side of the road and then from a distance looked back on the roadway where finally they carefully examined the ground from firing height beneath the cover of hedges. The Column men, who had been watching every movement, now burst into a quandary of talk. What were they up to, and what was expected along the roadway? Maybe at last they would have a chance to fight, and they began immediately to look at the surrounding landscape with more calculating eyes. When the two officers returned they looked grave as if resolving a difficulty, but they knew from the expectant faces what they were supposed to be anxious about. The Brigadier told the men about the day's problem and outlined the plan of attack and the distribution of sections. Then the delighted men were sent off to examine their new positions.

The police patrol would be on bicycles, strung out in twos at roughly twenty to thirty yards apart and extending over two hundred yards of roadway. There was a double bend in the road from Borrisokane to Cloughjordan at Modreeny, which was three miles distant from either place, with a straight stretch of road of two hundred and fifty yards long, between the bends. This distance would permit the head of the patrol to be at the Cloughjordan bend at the same time as the end pair passed the men who would be lying in wait at the Borrisokane bend.

The men lay down early, resting out of sight of passers-by, while the Column officers went through the fields to decide the position of their force. Rifle and shotgun men were theoretically placed and replaced in tentative arrangements until all the arms had been satisfactorily accounted for. When the officers were satisfied that the most effective use could be made of the weapons their strength possessed, action positions were occupied and each selected unit was placed in its firing position. Each group knew what part it was expected to contribute in relation to the Volunteers in other positions and also what part in the action each group itself was responsible for. Ranges were estimated, then distance was stepped out across the fields and along the roads until each rifleman had a succession of targets. There in the soft freshness of the early morning the concealed men lay close to earth.

It was agreed that the last police pair would be allowed inside the position before a shot was fired. From a barn about twenty yards in from the road Gaynor and Collison were about a hundred yards from the second road bend and near a rick of straw. This gave them a view of either bend and a glimpse of the road towards Borrisokane which ran uphill from the first turn where there were five riflemen under the command of section leader Seán Glennon, who could fire either up the Borrisokane road or down the straight stretch to the second bend. Some distance to the north, in from the hedge, was an observer who could watch the Borrisokane road in front of him for over five hundred yards and could tell a signaller with flags, of any movement; the signaller, who had been trained by Collison, would send back the information to the Column Command.

Paddy O'Brien of the Silvermines was on the road edge below the straw rick, in command of Paddy Kennedy, Paddy Daly, Paddy Nolan and his brother Jimmy who had a repeating shotgun, an efficient weapon for close-quarters work. Beyond, and at right angles on the corner across the narrow laneway which continued the road view, were the two Bouchiers whose shotguns could spray the road reach in front of them. They had the cover of a stout bank on top of which was a small hedge, and were to prevent the RIC from crossing it. The ground behind them was level for nearly four hundred yards as far as the hedges which enclosed a large field. Along the road bank a hundred yards further down was Joe Mangan, a very steady Column man, and two of the Cloughjordan shotgun men who protected the extreme flank. Diagonally across from them was a good shot, Dinny Whelan, who lay with his rifle behind a low bank some hundred yards in from the road, to prevent the police from getting over the road hedges on his side. Along O'Brien's side of the fence, further down the laneway, were a few more shotgun men. O'Brien was to allow the RIC to pass as far as the bend, or beyond it towards Cloughjordan, before his men opened fire. A whitethorn bank led up from the low wall beside the road gate where O'Brien and his section lay. It went up past the rick of straw for about two hundred yards. Behind this bank a rifleman had a good view across the long open field to the Borrisokane road about three hundred yards away, as his position was five or six feet higher than the distant road hedge. In addition, he could command the hedge bordering the straight stretch between the bends, also the ground beneath it which dropped about four or five feet below the road level.

Everything now seemed satisfactory as Gaynor and Collison again went over the position and viewed what the groups could see from their rifle and shotgun heights. The Column, they felt, should be easily able to deal with the police, and the result would mean the capture of thirteen or fourteen carbines or Lee-Enfields and a fair supply of ammunition, if all went well. Here again were those fourteen rifles, though under the aegis this time not of Bacchus but of Mercury. The sections settled down for a long wait. In the early morning hours there would be a few passers-by, and the only chance of a meeting would come from people who were out to milk cows in the open or from men who came to inspect and count their bullocks.

While the morning passed on and the Column waited, a young lad came wandering across the fields. His lazy morning meander had brought him close to where the section was concealed near the barn and he became aware that there were men behind the hawthorn hedge. Questioned by Paddy O'Brien and another of the men, he said he was out looking for the donkey and that his father was in the house, across the fields from them.

'Go in and send out your father,' he was told; 'we want to talk to him.' The father, an elderly man, came out across the fields to meet Gaynor, Collison and O'Brien, whose intention it was to tell him and his son to keep indoors. But as he walked towards the hayrick, with a bridle in his hands, Gaynor was told by Cloughjordan shotgun men that he was an ex-soldier who was not friendly to them.

'It's time for you to come,' he greeted the IRA men before they had time to talk, 'and you're heartily welcome. Maybe you're watchin' for the lads who might be raidin' the mails, and some of them are busy enough at times, around here.' His first cheerful greeting made it plain that he had mistaken these armed, trench-coated men wearing Sam Brownes, with their caps at rakish angles back to front, for Auxiliaries.

There had been a company of Auxiliaries close to Templemore for the past eight months, and another at the Lakeside Hotel, near Killaloe, on the edge of the Brigade. Auxiliaries had often raided around by Roscrea and Moneygall as far as the Shannon and into Offaly. Each carried a rifle with bandolier and two revolvers in somewhat fancy quick-draw holsters. Two lorries of them had been defeated in a County Longford ambush and when they surrendered arms, all were found, when searched, to have had a .38 revolver in hip pocket, of which no surrender had been made. They would wear khaki or bottle-green RIC uniform, with khaki shirt and either a khaki or a blue-green Glengarry, or there might be a sprinkling of naval or airforce tunics as well, as the Auxiliaries had been drawn from all three services. Or they might wear mufti. Sometimes they dressed for a mood to show their formal authority, but also they were aware of a sense of masquerade stressing their disregard of conventional army authority. They were a formidable fighting force which had once been well decorated and mentioned in despatches for valour. But as was usual with imported British troops, they knew nothing about Ireland, their first colony, except what lack of information suggested or their prejudice dictated.

O'Brien, who was over six foot in height, was spare and hardy and he held himself well. Jack Collison was of equal height, broader in the shoulders, with a well-trimmed moustache, and this may have helped to confirm their visitor's first impressions. Taking their cue from this unexpected development, the three questioned him about dangerous 'Shinners' who lived not far from his house and mentioned by name those on whom they pretended to be particularly anxious to lay their hands. Jack Collison referred to O'Brien as Brown and changed his accent as the loquacious intruder told them about Bill O'Dwyer and when he was most likely to be found at home. As he spoke, Bill was out watching the Borrisokane road for police cyclists and signaller Maher's information of 'U' for bicycles, 'R' for motor cars and 'L' for lorries.

Auxiliaries, Tans, RIC and military, when they questioned people, were usually met by a wall of silence, or by a bog of ignorance, concerning the names and movements of the IRA. Accordingly then, in the easy histrionic manner which the situation induced, the officers showed their pleasure and delight at this unexpected windfall of words, although beneath their questions was a fabric of humorous irony which had a feeling of contempt.

'And what do you know about Seán Kenny,' asked O'Brien. The man replied that he was the local company captain and lived on the main road to Birr, knowing a great deal about his comings and goings.

'Well, where did he stay the night before last,' they asked, and he was able to tell them where Kenny, who was then a field away, had spent that night. Having probed his knowledge of local IRA affairs in general, they discovered that he could give an accurate account of the active men in the parish, where they could be found, and how dangerous they were from the British viewpoint.

'But as you know so much, why don't you give your information to the local RIC?' they asked him. 'They'd make use of it and they'd know how to deal with those bloody Shinners in their own way.'

'Indeed I do,' was the reply. 'Sure don't I meet the Cloughjordan sergeant, and a decent man he is to me, every Saturday inside in Nora Ryan's, within the snug, and it's then I pass on to him what I know. Then he asks me questions and no one is a bit the wiser for it.'

Taking his lead from the questions put to him by the Column officers, the ex-soldier unfolded his record of spying and its reward until he had thoroughly compromised himself and left no doubt about his guilt in the minds of his listeners. His information was found to be both correct and abundant. When the officers were satisfied that they had heard enough, they told him that he was not dealing with the British, but with the IRA, and that he was under arrest.

Almost stunned in the realisation of the incredible mistake he had made, the man's confidence vanished, leaving him in a state of near collapse. Terror-stricken, he begged for mercy, and the fear of summary justice showed plainly on his face. The officers were disturbed by a basic uneasiness as they thought of the tenuous bog surface of uncertainty which the Republican Army had often thought to be firm land. Here it was opening up hidden depths. In any locality this quagmire could confront unsuspecting men and to the listening officers it proved what a chimera their supposed security could be. Even here, this ex-soldier, if not kept as a prisoner, could and might give word to the RIC at either of the neighbouring posts. The officers took him away to the rick of straw behind the barn. They decided to shoot him, but deferred his execution until the police would be ambushed since they feared the sound of shooting might give away their position to the enemy. Besides, they would have more time to deal with him afterwards, and the delay would give him a better chance to prepare for his end.

At times there was reluctance to shoot spies, but they had no pity for this informer who had so casually and cheerfully implicated men with the Column that morning. Nor was it intended to refer his case to Dublin. At that time, evidence given at the court-martial of a spy, and the sentence imposed, had to be forwarded to General Headquarters in Dublin where the evidence would be re-examined and the sentence confirmed or remitted. In the meantime, a convicted spy had to be kept under close guard, which entailed strain and constant alertness on the part of his captors. A daring spy, having sensed his fate, would be the more ready to chance a break for freedom. His guards ran the additional risk of identification if surprised by an enemy raiding party. In this case the officers decided that the men should not be exposed to the dangers attendant on keeping him alive and in custody, pending a directive about him from Dublin.

When evidence was doubtful, a report would have to be sent on to GHQ, who would advise as to how the suspect should be dealt with. He might be instructed to leave the neighbourhood, or he could be ordered to leave the country at once. As a suspect had to be kept a prisoner while a GHQ decision was awaited, he would be brought to what was called 'an unknown destination', which usually for the safety of neighbours meant an empty house or an isolated outhouse or bog shelter. Every brigade had a few such 'prisons' in which were confined persons who had broken the civil law and were awaiting a Dáil district court. Suspect prisoners had to be guarded day and night by armed men and this was considered a great waste of effort. Then there was always the danger that a prisoner's guards would become friendly in a human way, for being free men they served their State not as servants but as helpers. This attitude would lead to chances of escape, or the British might stumble on him and his guardians in a chance raid or round-up. In case of a raid the armed guards would be involved in immediate danger if their prisoner was determined to abet his rescuers in summary punishment, and if caught in arms in the Martial Law Area the guards would be liable to the death sentence if the case was pressed.

The men kept as quiet as they could in the short grass as the sun moved over them and warmed their stiffness from the strong darts of a dewy ground. They listened to rustling noises in the hedges and the shrill warning from thrushes who unexpectedly discovered them. The wind blew the sweet scent of hawthorn blossoms across the fields to them. The long wait imposed a strain. Long inaction tended to make men careless or inattentive, especially when they were in scattered groups. Frequently in such a situation the most incongruous thoughts would jumble together and a dry or blatant sense of humour would throw out a series of laughter ripples which had to be stifled in the short grass. Sometimes men would be off guard at the very moment when they needed to be most alert.

There were not sufficient men to form outposts which could have included an all-round protective watch, and instead concentration was mainly directed from each separate position on to the roadway. From the rick of straw a ridge of the Slieve Bloom mountains could be glimpsed, its massed heather a brilliant mauve in the distance. Nearer at hand the scented white blossoms and whitethorn branches shut off their view.

In the distance some of the hidden men heard the sound of motor-engines and before the noise could be properly located there was an excited movement from the observers close to the Borrisokane road.

At last Bill O'Dwyer passed on the word: 'Here they come.' The signaller turned and began to send his message towards the barn. Jack Collison watched the flailing arms of the signaller in some consternation, for he seemed to think he was threshing oats. He had begun slowly with 'U' for bicycles, but then he used 'R' and 'L' in frequent addition. Up and down his arms moved furiously, giving warning of an approach which Collison interpreted as 'two bicycles, two bicycles, two bicycles, a motor car, a motor car, two bicycles, two bicycles, a motor car, a motor car, two bicycles, a lorry.'

The enemy numbers crept up to finally mean twelve cyclists, four motor cars and a lorry. This meant that the Column, instead of having to face about thirteen or fourteen RIC men, would now have to contend with a force which might amount to between forty and forty-five trained men. Jack Collison looked at Sean Graynor. The problem was to choose whether they would attack a strength which outrifled them by three to one, or whether, like Brer Rabbit, they should lie low and let them pass on. The Brigadier was willing and he agreed with Collison that they should attack. Both of them knew that as well as their being outnumbered, some of the motor cars and the lorry would still be outside of the held position between the two bends when the attack commenced. That would throw into the unequal fight an additional danger: an outflanking party which could be used against their roadside positions from the onset. If the wall on the road beyond the first bend was manned at once by the RIC, they would have in their sights O'Brien's men behind the road bank. In the brief time which remained, Collison selected Tim Gleeson to go with him and they took up new positions by the whitethorn hedge north of the hayrick, where the two of them as marksmen could provide a flanking party of two to meet the possible threat of enfilade from the lorry or from some of the cars, and to keep the British from outflanking the men behind the low wall in front of the barn. That movement brought the regular Column Commander eventually at least three hundred yards away from anyone save the nearest rifleman on his flank.

Seán Gaynor rushed down quickly to O'Brien to tell him of the alarming increase in the number of their opponents, but found that he, too, was eager for the fight. The only change in the plan was to allow the cyclists in front to pass beyond their bend and to wait until the first car came abreast of them before opening fire.

The first three pairs of police on bicycles seemed to the waiting men to take a long time to round the bend. Then when the car was almost at the corner the Brigadier blew his whistle, the shotgun men let fly with a loud volley, and the car came to a halt with its dead and wounded. The stoppage of the first car would prevent other enemy transport from pushing past it. One of the RIC, a Tan by his accent, had been singing loudly as the car came round the bend

> *I'm for ever blowing bubbles,*
>   *pretty bubbles in the air.*
> *They fly so high, they reach the sky*
> *Then like my dreams they fade and die.*
> *Fortune's always hiding,*
> *I've searched everywhere.*
> *I'm for ever blowing bubbles . . .*

but a frothy blood closed his mouth before he finished the chorus.

Paddy O'Brien and his riflemen fired at the leading cyclists, and their volley was echoed by the six riflemen at the other bend. The vehicles halted, but the military lorry, alone of the convoy, had not entered the trap but had pulled up, and within a matter of seconds its complement of some twelve to sixteen soldiers was down on the roadside, jumping for shelter close in to the banks, then raking the IRA hedges with rifle fire, and a gunner began his kettle-drum rattle of machine-gun bursts. The lorry was turned round fast and with the accelerator pushed down hard, the driver urged it up the hill in a noisy roar of engine, on his way back to hurry up reinforcements. Once he reached Borrisokane calls for assistance would be telephoned to the military barracks in Birr, fourteen miles to the north-east, and to Nenagh, some eight miles away to the south-west with a smaller military barracks but a large concentration of RIC. In addition there were police barracks at Toomevara, Borrisokane, Cloughjordan and Roscrea, whose garrisons could soon converge on the ambush position.

The escape of the lorry helped to buttress the morale of the larger force, who were unaware of their opponents' true strength, for they were accustomed to multiple exaggeration which really only alarmed themselves. For them then it was a question almost of a rearguard action until reinforcements would arrive to outflank their attackers.

The Volunteers at the Borrisokane bend had accounted for the first six police on bicycles and the leading car. The police in it, who included two sergeants, had been killed or badly wounded. The District Inspector, who had no bad record, had been able to get underneath the car uninjured, but the driver had been flung right over the hedge close to Paddy Kennedy. The RIC man who had sent out information about contemplated British round-ups when the Column was in training near the Shannon, and who had subsequently saved men by his prompt information, now sprawled limply dead beside his bicycle.

Paddy Kennedy was very worried by the moans of the Tan

near to him. The driver who had suddenly leapfrogged over the hedge was crying, 'Mother, Mother'.

Kennedy wondered what he could do to help the unnerved man and several times he asked his section leader who was busy trying to get a target further up the road. At last O'Brien told him to bloody well look after himself and keep his eye on the armed enemy until the fight was over. Paddy Kennedy usually carried his rosary beads in his hands when on the march, and even when positioned to attack, the beads would dangle.

A few times British soldiers tried to advance towards the barn by way of the fields, but good shooting by Collison and another two riflemen from behind the thick hedge kept them at a distance. The long field was bare. It rose gently, with little cover until the whitethorn hedge itself, three hundred yards away from the road.

When the constabulary had become somewhat accustomed to being under fire, the soldiers attempted to flush the three riflemen out with rifle grenades, but the grenadiers' range was inaccurate and the metal splinters passed harmlessly over the laneway behind the barn. The bursts made the Column men tense; they were an outflanking threat to strike against both the riflemen behind the hawthorn hedge and those along the road bank. Military now moved along a fence which ran obliquely beyond the position held by the six IRA men at the first road bend and threatened to outflank them by continuing alongside a bank. The six-man section, led by Glennon, fell back a little to the north-east, towards a barn, but from their new position they could not any longer control a section of road between the two bends, and this meant that RIC or military on the roadway had more concentrated fire power. Collison's isolated section, however, still kept some of the military away from the road and drew their fire.

The machine-gun had luckily been quieted; whether this was due to a mechanical stoppage, a direct hit, or the killing of the gunner could not be known, but its lapse from activity decreased the numerous odds which were now less heavy against the Column.

The remainder of the Column did not know of the withdrawal

of Glennon's section as there had been no communication possible between the group and the main body on the opposite side of the road since the beginning of the attack. Only one man, Dinny Whelan, now remained in an opposite position to prevent outflanking movements.

Excited cursing from soldiers and RIC spread up the road, together with intensification of fire agsinst the barn. The British were shouting encouragement to each other. 'Come on now, we've got the bastards,' they were yelling. 'Fix your bloody bayonets.' But in spite of the shouts and the ominous click of bayonets being shoved home on to rifle-bosses, there was no serious attempt to charge up the road.

The two Bouchiers had a difficult corner to hold. It faced up the straight length of road from the second bend and would now have been a good site for riflemen, as the enemy across the lane exposed themselves unduly when firing from their right shoulders. Any attempt now to use a shotgun over the bank in their corner was met by concentrated fire which cut into the bank. O'Brien and his riflemen section fired at any movement up the road, but the four motor cars which had stopped at varying angles cut off the field of sight. A policeman sheltering behind a telegraph pole exposed his hind quarters which were quickly punctured; another had sixteen bullets in him, it was later found, but he did not die.

Seán Gaynor talked to Jack Collison out on the flank. Then he came down along by the whitethorn hedge to speak to Paddy O'Brien. There was no chance now of closing in on the straight length of road between the bends. British reinforcements could soon be expected either in front of, or behind their positions, and as there had been no attack on enemy transport up to this in the battalion area, converging lorries would not be inclined to slacken their speeds in caution. Roads had not been trenched or blocked in any direction by the IRA, nor had telegraph wires been cut, as quick results had been expected from this ambush. There had been a few demands from the Column for their opponents to surrender, but the replies were well packed with curses.

The Brigadier ordered a withdrawal. Rifles and ammunition

had been gathered up already by Joe Mangan from the Tans and RIC who lay stretched beyond the southern bend. The retreat was carried out unknown to the mixed enemy force who at first continued to fire on the hedges and along the roadbanks, while the IRA men slipped away in groups.

The Brigadier went with some of them in the Nenagh direction as if it was their intention to continue towards the west, but having gone a short distance they doubled back on their tracks, crossed the Cloughjordan road and made for Ballingarry. As they hurried across Killeraune bog they caught up with O'Brien and other Column men, and turf-workers using their slanes told them that a number of riflemen had passed that way close on half an hour ago. Undoubtedly these were the section of riflemen that had not been accounted for and that information relieved their minds about them, for they thought they might either have been captured or forced to draw away with any wounded. Some time later, when they were a field removed from the road, the heard the noise of heavy engines and quickly dropped down out of sight. An observer from behind a plantation hedge saw a number of lorries coming from Birr barracks and raising dust as they hurried towards Modreeny.

As was customary then, actual British casualties were not given in full, but it was later learned by the IRA that four of the enemy had been killed and fourteen wounded. The British admitted four killed and five wounded. They lost four rifles and a few bicycles which had been concealed by Joe Mangan and his men. The District Inspector of police who had hidden beneath the first car had escaped uninjured.

Five miles away from the ambush bends, close to Knockshegouna hill, the complete Column met up again. Luckily, they had no casualties that day. They waited patiently for dusk which would not come until ten o'clock or later, intending then to cross country in the direction of the hills towards Gortagarry, close to the Devil's Bit to the south beyond Moneygall. The brow of the hill on which they lay was over six hundred feet in height and from it they could watch the country all around them. The men were full of talk of what they had seen during the engagement and about what had been done, all except Pat Nolan, who was older than any of them and was thinking of an incident in the fight that concerned his brother Jimmy whose repeating shotgun had jammed suddenly. Jimmy had tried hard to eject the defective cartridge, but the swollen case would not be budged and in his excitement he stood up from behind cover. Pat suddenly saw a Tan turn the muzzle of his rifle on his brother but had fired himself before the Tan could sight. Pat's silence was noticed by his comrades.

'Did you hit a peeler, Pat,' he was asked. 'I don't know about that,' Pat said in his slow way, 'but anyway he fell.'

The men were hungry, now that the excitement of the fight and their watchfulness along their way to the height had ceased, but as they had not brought any food with them in the morning, feeling that the action would be brief and they could get something to eat as they retired, hunger had to be dismissed. Intense searching of the countryside was continued by the military and sections of RIC until dusk, but when the darkness drew down the Column men could wander where they wished, with guides to lead them across country, making their way beyond Moneygall towards the mountains which ended in the short gap of the Devil's Bit. At night the British might hold a crossroads in strength, but roads in the darkness they were afraid of. They did not exactly believe in ghosts, but they were afraid of the freedom of the countryside and the only security was the solace of their strongholds.

In the excitement of the fight, the ex-soldier had been forgotten by the three officers who had questioned him and by a man who was to have kept watch on him. Although not knowing the exact position of the Column's flankguards, he had guessed that while the Column men were not immediately concerned with him, any movement on his part might induce a rifleshot. He pulled down straw from the rick and covered himself under it. He emerged when all the firing had ceased and soldiers were about to set fire to the barn as the start of punitive expeditions during which they fired the barn and six houses as well, amongst them those of some of the local men who had been in the ambush. His reception by his true friends was hardly what he might have expected. As soon as they caught sight of him, soldiers rushed at him with fixed bayonets, roaring from excitement, and with the sharp points pressing against his stomach he was in poor shape to put his story across. The soldiers were more inclined to run their bayonets through him than listen to what they regarded as another Irish fairy tale, but luckily for him he was saved by some of the RIC who knew who he was. Whatever about his intentions to oblige the enemy, he must have doubted his personal safety in his own neighbourhood when remembering what he had said to the IRA officers. Both the RIC and British officers would expect him to identify prisoners whom they might catch in their unwieldy net as they swept the country for participants. Now he must have recognised himself as wanted by the IRA, and as they controlled the countryside around, the only secure local place would be a barracks. In the event, the British brought him to Dublin Castle where he was kept for a while, perhaps in the hope that he might be of assistance to them. Then, like many another in those days, he was taken across to England which some regarded as security.

CHAPTER NINE

THE HARD ROAD TO CARROWKENNEDY

MAY–JUNE 1921

IRA morale would depend on previous fights in which either officers or men had taken part, or on any resoluteness or determination gained over the past years during the routine training of a Volunteer company in combating enemy aggression. Gaol experience, with its resultant combination of ingenuity, improvisation and discipline, could also make an important contribution. Indeed these three factors were a natural foundation on which a column could be built. Gaol, in addition, brought men into arduous contact with others who were regarded as leaders, or with those who afterwards evolved in control. Gaol was a testing ground in which qualities were severely tried in a vacuum, to fruit or to wither.

Discipline in the service of a cause is very different from parade discipline, and weapon assurance based on thorough and efficient use which creates its own reliability and dependence, was lacking in many IRA column men. A personal discipline growing from independence of mind could develop a degree of self-reliance and a sense of responsibility. Each IRA section had to depend utterly on itself. There was rarely a chance of a unit in action being reinforced as there were no fixed points from which help could be summoned. Each section of a column was its own base, dependent on its fighting qualities and its knowledge of ground. That extra quality, intimate knowledge of land, could and did give assurance and certitude. It was almost an instinct which could free the mind for other problems. A friendly people, who in sound areas observed every enemy movement and covertly were aware of suspects, helped to create a sense of security and protection which could be of use to armed men.

Officers or men seldom drank and the greatest punishment for a column Volunteer was that of being summarily returned to

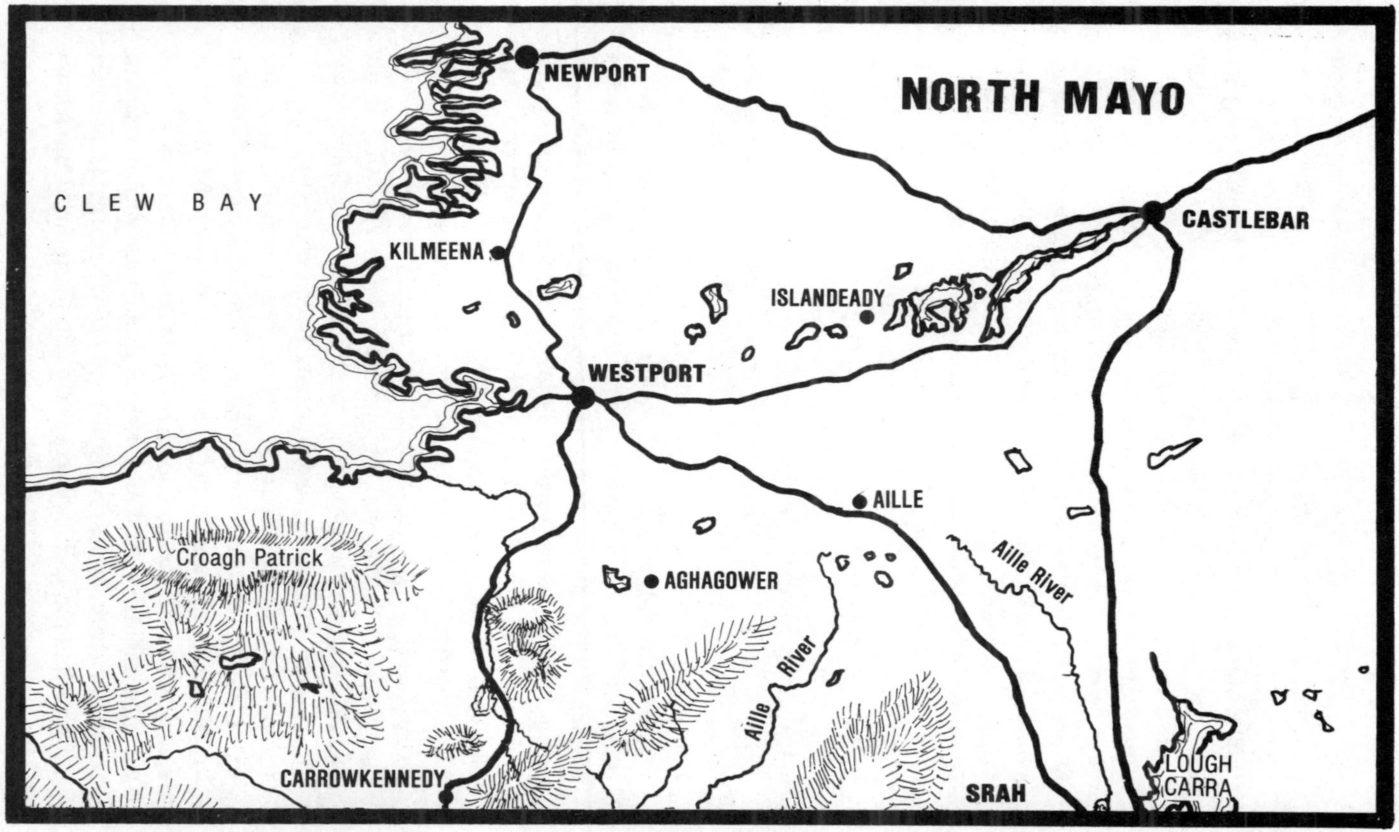
NORTH MAYO
CLEW BAY
NEWPORT
CASTLEBAR
KILMEENA
ISLANDEADY
WESTPORT
AILLE
Croagh Patrick
AGHAGOWER
Aille River
Aille River
CARROWKENNEDY
SRAH
LOUGH CARRA

his battalion. There would be no chance of a section getting out of hand, or of carrying out reprisals because some of their number had been killed or wounded. In this respect a column, wandering in the country, was very different from Auxiliaries, Tans, RIC and military who were kept in guarded barracks and whose every action could be controlled. The IRA stood over their activities. If a civilian was shot as a spy, he had previously been court-martialled, and a label placed on his body stated that he had been executed by the IRA. If a house was visited for arms, the occupants were made aware that the IRA had carried out the raid. When a house which the British had intended to occupy was burned, the owners were informed of the reason for its destruction. Forces of the Crown, when they carried out burnings, shootings or maltreatment, were not acknowledged to be responsible for such deeds by their spokesmen in the House of Commons, not until evidence in January of 1921 began to track them down.

In every IRA battalion area there were people who had been traditional enemies of the Irish and whose loyalty was to the British authorities. During the period from 1918 onwards many loyalists had changed. They objected to the punitive methods of the British and on occasions they had been manhandled. The houses of obdurate loyalists were easy targets for the IRA, more particularly in districts where there had been much destruction of houses and other property by the British military and RIC. Not until June of 1921 was an order issued by IRA General Headquarters that houses could be burned in any area where the British were destroying houses or property: 'For purposes of such reprisal no one shall be regarded as an enemy of Ireland, whether they may be described locally as Unionist, Orangeman, etc., except they are actively anti-Irish in their actions.'

Some brigades were scantily armed, but when columns began to be formed the need for weapons became more pressing. General Headquarters was able to import a small quantity of arms, ammunition and explosives. There were a few hand grenade factories in Dublin, but none was working in the country except in Cork early in 1921. When the IRA swore allegiance to the Dáil, grants were given to the Army but money was not forwarded to brigades. Each brigade paid for whatever warlike equipment it received from the Quartermaster-General. Headquarters officers and attached staffs, men of the Intelligence Squad and in the Dublin Active Service Unit were paid organisers, and I think a column in Cork city was paid, but in the rest of the country, Volunteers, column men and officers served freely. Brigades raised money to clothe their columns and the Cumann na mBan provided them with medical equipment and cigarettes. Country people, many of whom had helped to over-subscribe the Dáil Loan, fed columns, men on the run and an increasing number of full-time battalion officers.

The disconcerting point about a flying column was that there had been no precedent for its organisation and use ever since the days of the Tories and Rapparees whose area of action had been wider, perhaps because distrustful elements in the population broadened its range. Nor could a General Headquarters in Dublin give guidance in the use of such a body of men. There was no stereotyped standard of training or efficiency, and with very few exceptions men who had been trained in the British Army and who had been through active service were not put in charge of IRA active service units. Example in other counties was a stimulus and incentive, but individual experience in the employment of the new unit had to be learned in every brigade. In each battalion, by the autumn of 1920, there were men who were being raided for by the British. Raids meant a condition of alertness at home while a man carried out his normal work, but as raids increased men had to leave their homes which had become too obvious a target. Their time could now be given to Army work, and as they moved through the country they learned adequately how to protect themselves; should they be officers, local companies were given experience of guard duties. Officers and men were by this time inclined to carry arms or side-arms with them and such familiarity ensured respect and a regard for their care.

At times in good districts the countryside was on the alert from the moment the hum of a lorry was heard in the distance. A column then was able to avail itself of men who had a training in security, of a company system of alertness to protect wanted men, and it profited by the awareness of friendly people who acted as voluntary scouts.

The West Mayo Column was not formed until the spring of 1921. It comprised what had been independent battalion columns based on Castlebar, Westport and Newport, the three principal towns in the Brigade area. For some months before the amalgamation these units had been in the field, anxious for an opportunity to test their strength against the British. Such columns, coming late into the fight, had to meet an enemy now on the alert and inclined to take few chances. By degrees the military and RIC had become better equipped, and their transport, communications and intelligence had been re-organised. In one sense soldiers who are fighting each other mature automatically in the ways of war. One project is countered with another and in this fashion their military education develops. Now, Mayo columns had to plunge into the full current of ruthlessness without that gradual build-up of knowledge and competence. Lessons had to be learned quickly and mistakes were more obvious and produced a swifter nemesis than they would have done in 1920.

After the three independent columns had coalesced in the hills at Aille, south-west of Westport, to form the Brigade Column, Michael Kilroy, the Column Commander, found it far from easy to locate suitable enemy elements to attack. The Column had lain in ambush frequently but without avail, largely because of difficulty in getting information about the hour when convoys travelled. IRA groups had gone into Castlebar, Westport and Newport to attack police or military patrols, but they had failed to make contact. Then, during a subsequent incursion into Newport, an RIC sergeant was killed and a constable wounded. The sergeant had been sniped at across the river from some four hundred yards as he worked his way through the intricate maze of barbed wire which guarded the front of the barracks.

That same night the Castlebar Column, under Paddy Jordan, had made its way as far as the village of Ballinacarrigan among the lakes between the three towns and moved quietly into the scattered houses, unaware that the Newport Column had arrived at the neighbouring houses that evening and was already in bed. This was a safe area where the people were friendly and evidently careful of their talk, as the district had never been raided, either when a column was there or when it had temporarily left its shelter. Paddy Jordan soon met Michael Kilroy and as they talked news came in about the killing of the Newport sergeant. Kilroy knew that as a result of the shooting there would be much enemy activity that night and the following day. Indeed his own house had already flamed to the sky, with another for company, and a British punitive patrol might be expected any time on the hill road between Newport and Castlebar, or on the road between Westport and Newport. He decided to turn out the Westport men and bring them at once to a good position at Kilmeena, which he thought they could occupy that morning with reasonable prospects of engaging the enemy. The men were impatient to get in a really good crack at the British, and this new move born of the events in Newport seemed more certain of positive result than the random operations that had so far been carried out by the Brigade and battalion columns.

Dawn brought a cold wind which ruffled the scent of hawthorn across the line of march, and bird-song made a cheerful prelude for some of the tired men. By first light the Column, having eaten on the way, was at the crossroads close to the Knocknaboly bridge. Men lay down to rest while some of the officers walked the ground and examined positions to hold against alternative British approaches. At first, they had occupied a site commanding the road bridge over the railway line. There was a right-angle bend at either approach to the bridge and that meant a slowing down of lorries and an almost certain collision if a driver was injured at that point. Although a good position for shotgun men to hold, it was decided against remaining there as one flank would be exposed. The earth-work protection necessary to render the site safe as shelter from rifle fire would take time to build up, and these preparations might also attract attention.

The main ambush position was eventually chosen to the south, below Knocknaboly crossroads and about forty yards in from the road. A rough blockade was placed a little distance down the road which the men had come along that morning, to prevent lorries from suddenly turning the flank of the ambush position. Behind a bank the men waited, while across the road at another bank Dr. John Madden and a comrade acted as flankers. Beyond the brow of the hill to the south of the position and in the Newport direction, an outpost of four men could dominate the Newport road from a ridge about a hundred feet above road level. On a hill to the north about eight hundred yards away towards Westport, there was an observer who would signal a British approach by firing his automatic pistol. If, however, there were two lorries he could not use this signal until the second lorry had reached his position. In that event the ambush section would have very little time to ready themselves for the first lorry. This was an unusual method of signalling information. The sharp crack of an automatic could be heard by the men in ambush but it would be more audible to the approaching British.

Men lay down behind the bank. There was a fair number of shotguns sprinkled among the riflemen. The effectiveness of the first volley might well depend on the support that could be given by the shotguns if the lorry drivers were not either killed or wounded by the riflemen and the transport brought to a standstill inside the field of fire. The men were alert at the beginning but as the morning hours became monotonously long their attention was diverted by time and fatigue. In front and around them circled the low hills of Kilmeena, called Drumlins. They had been formed from glacial clay on the edges of ice sheets, and duplicated shapes when continued out to sea had become the islands in Clew Bay. The rounded hills pushed up in gentle even curves, embodying something of the sea as if whales had surfaced at intervals. Beyond the ridge of land the blue mountain height of Clare Island marked off the entrance to the Bay, closing it to the outside sea swell. The Rock topped the intervening hills to the south in a steep blue-white pyramid of granite which exaggerated the impression of bulk and height. To the north and north-east was the half-circle of mountains from Corraun that ends in the isolated granite cone of Nephin.

The day was heady in the drowsy warmth of May and that again contributed to relax tired muscles and to weaken concentration.

A local house-owner was aware of the Column in his vicinity. He had been striding up and down the road in protest, thinking that if he persisted in front of the held position he would either drive the men away from this ambush or prevent them from firing on the British. He was anxious about his 'weak' family, as a large young family in the West was called. The result of any attack on a convoy might mean for him later the burned wreck of a house and a crowd of RIC and Tans taking their indiscriminate revenge on him and his family. He had to be peremptorily ordered off the road.

There was a time during the long wait when fingers lay tensely on triggers as two cars came over the bridge from Newport, but before any shot was fired what had looked in the distance as RIC uniforms had changed into the black mantles of nuns who were on a day's outing connected with a celebration in their order. A murmur of relief went up after they had passed, for one random shot could easily have led to others. The men had been a long time in their places and it was approaching noon. The Commander was now thinking of moving them away. In the nearby Cummins's house Tim Kelly from the Column was supervising the cooking of eight fowl in the kitchen, assisted by hungry helpers from the banks outside.

There was always a danger in remaining hidden for hours in a countryside. Where there were houses nearby, someone would notice that men were concealed. If the position was to be held for a long period the men would have to get food prepared for them. In a long occupation there was a risk that Volunteers would not continue on the alert indefinitely, and unless they had a good signalling system to give ample warning they might be unprepared to fire quickly and accurately when the necessity arose. Also there would be uncertainty as to whether their presence had been observed by a casual passer-by. Always there was danger from a travelling tinker, tramp or beggar, although local company men would at once recognise a stranger, be able to estimate his possible risk and then, if necessary, put him under temporary arrest. A more immediate danger might come

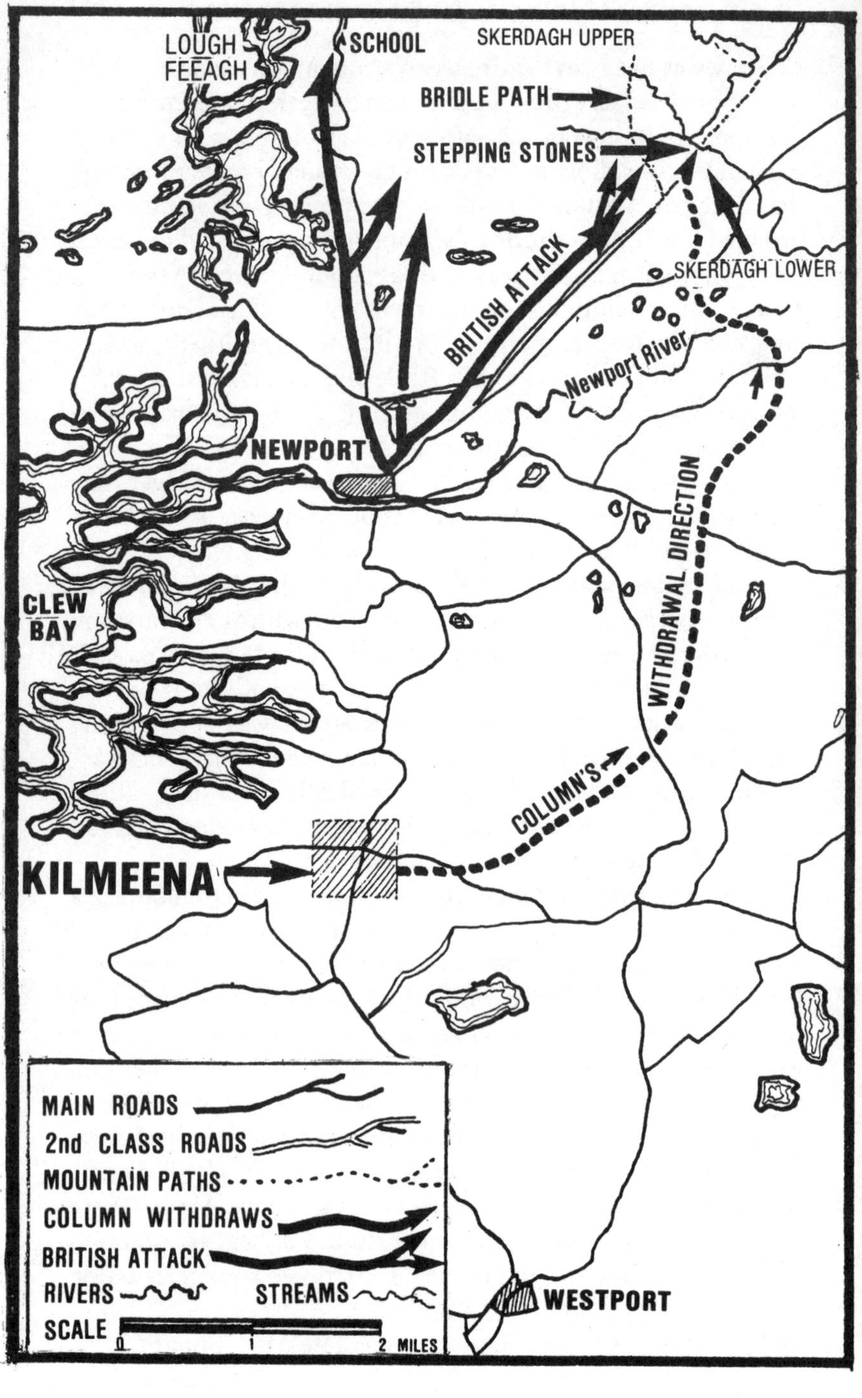
LOUGH FEEAGH
SCHOOL
SKERDAGH UPPER
BRIDLE PATH
STEPPING STONES
BRITISH ATTACK
SKERDAGH LOWER
Newport River
NEWPORT
WITHDRAWAL DIRECTION
CLEW BAY
COLUMN'S
KILMEENA
MAIN ROADS
2nd CLASS ROADS
MOUNTAIN PATHS
COLUMN WITHDRAWS
BRITISH ATTACK
RIVERS
STREAMS
SCALE
0
1
2 MILES
WESTPORT

THE HARD ROAD TO CARROWKENNEDY 165

from information let slip to a pensioned RIC man

Kilroy had not decided whether or not to withdraw, when the enemy's arrival was suddenly signalled by two shots from the scout on the Westport side. Some of the men were asleep and were awakened by the firing. Others were able to get in a shot at the lorry as the driver pressed hard on the accelerator, making the vehicle sway uneasily as it took the curves to and from the bridge in a blaze of dust. Then it disappeared from sight, after about two hundred and fifty yards. Rifle shots from the outpost position on the hill towards the north indicated that the speeding lorry had run into further fire.

Above at the bridge on the Westport road, near the parish priest's house, a second police lorry and a motor car had been halted when the firing was heard. Inside in the priest's house a clerical conference was taking place and the Canon's car was parked outside on the road. RIC men got down from the lorry and grouped in stereotyped musketry fashion on the road, with knees bent and right arms at right angles in the correct manual positions, but a few shots in their direction made them scatter hurriedly across the road to take up a posture more determined by the contours of a bank than by a sergeant major's lesson in musketry instruction.

Soon a police Lewis gun was drumming an arc of bullets from a distance of over seven hundred yards. They spattered the hill beyond Tailor Flynn's and may have worried the further IRA outpost position, for fire from that observation post soon ceased. The men there had withdrawn though the Column men near the road were unaware of that development; however, they soon knew they were being fired on from the railway bridge beyond the tailor's. This site was quickly made uncomfortable for the police, for at some two hundred and fifty yards range a police cap and the head inside it perched nicely in relief above the straight parapet of the bridge. Lewis gunfire from the bridge then covered the police as they moved into a new position behind the tailor's house, one more dangerous to the Column. The hedge behind the house was continued by a small bohereen sheltered by a new sod fence which permitted flanking fire to be directed against the bank held by the IRA.

Michael Kilroy ordered his men to fall back to the bank behind them. Madden's position now became untenable and as he went further down into the small valley a Tan leapt forward over a bank to the east of the tailor's house to get a better aim at him. As the Tan steadied his rifle he was shot by Kilroy. The doctor reached the road, crossed it under sniping fire and came up the slope where the main body of the Column was withdrawing. His face was covered with blood on either cheek and it was thought he had been seriously wounded until his own reassurance convinced the others that splinters of gravel from a richochet bullet had been spattered against his face.

Along the spine of the second bank, to which Kilroy had withdrawn his men, another bank ran at right angles to the main road. From both sides of it banks stemmed at intervals, going downhill. There were gaps in this bank, sometimes as wide as fifty yards, where the IRA men were exposed to the RIC positioned beside the priest's house as well as to those who lay snugly behind the bank along the little bohereen beyond the tailor's house. Tailor Flynn heard the English accent of the Tans among the police as they shouted and cursed in excitement, but the Irish brogue of the RIC played as strongly a part. 'Creegan, keep well over here,' he could hear an English voice exclaim. 'You're a good shot.'

Creegan, a Westport RIC man who had recently been made a sergeant, did not long survive this fight. A Tan was shot through the eye at the back of the tailor's house and an RIC man was wounded nearby.

The RIC had an open valley between them and the Column's line of retreat, broken at intervals by banks, but no police seemed anxious to advance on the flank under cover and cut off this path of withdrawal. They lay down in the seemingly secure positions from which they could fire at ease. Perhaps a few casualties had made them more cautious, but they could with safety have continued along their ridge for over a mile.

John Staunton and James MacEvilly of the Column were fatally wounded at the second bank. MacEvilly probably bled to death there. Paddy Jordan suddenly rolled under some briars, but came out when called upon by his senior officer and lay

THE HARD ROAD TO CARROWKENNEDY

beside him quietly. Kilroy did not know then that Jordan was so badly wounded as he later discovered him to be, and he moved back with him towards the next bank. Paddy Mulloy of Newport was wounded on the way back as the IRA slowly retired. About three hundred yards further away a slight rise of ground above the diagonal bank hid the men from the view of the RIC near Father Conway's house, and also gave protection to the Column men from the Tans and constabulary in the bohereen at the back of the tailor's house, where esconsed men were watching for movement along the banks to the east.

At the third bank and lower down towards the valley, Kilroy found Paddy O'Malley whose shin had been shattered by a bullet. O'Malley was able to advise him on what part of the next bank police rifles were sighted, for he had observed the effect of their fire on men who had crossed in front of him. Tom Nolan, who lay nearby, had been wounded in the leg, and an unwounded Westport Column man named Pierce insisted on remaining behind with him. Jordan, though dazed, moved slowly onwards but he seemed to have the concentrated detachment of a sleepwalker. Kilroy took O'Malley's rifle, the foresight of which was to one side. Its owner had learned to use it accurately by allowing for the distortion, but in the suddenness of action the handicap might sometimes prevail. Kilroy tested the rifle a few times until he was satisfied with it. He could hear the police calling to each other as they came nearer, but he remained with the wounded as long as possible, firing whenever a target offered. Eventually he had to leave them behind, together with Pierce, for it was impossible for him to move them. When he was some distance away he heard the excited shouts of the RIC. Like hounds baying a quarry they had come across the wounded. They fired at Mulloy as he lay on the ground and they put a number of bullets through the soft tissues of his leg. Luckily for him they hit no bones. Whether Pierce suffered from a sudden shock which upset his judgment cannot be clear. He was never again seen by those who knew him and his fate has remained unknown. He had volunteered his services to the Westport Column when it was neither safe nor opportune for a man to belong to such a unit. Afflicted with a sudden mental breakdown he may have been racked by indecision, although to his Column Commander he seemed to be normal enough when he had last spoken to him.

When the Tans came up to the bank where Paddy O'Malley lay he heard them discuss himself and Nolan from a state of semi-consciousness. At first it was intended to shoot him where he lay but they decided that he and another of the wounded would die anyhow, and that ammunition could be saved. Tans and RIC pulled him down by the arms across fields and over banks while pain from the shattered bones shook his ebbing strength. When they reached the lorry they threw him in on top of the dead and wounded. They hauled Jordan by the legs and hoisted him in among his comrades like a sack of potatoes. In all, the RIC had collected four Column dead — James Mac Evilly and Tom O'Donnell of Castlebar, John Staunton of Kilmeena and Seán Collins of Westport — and five wounded, all of whom lay together in the lorry until the RIC were ready to return to Westport.

At the tailor's house the police demanded hot water for their wounded, and they took a blanket from his bed into which they swung their dead Tan. Prior to this a Tan had pointed a revolver at the tailor, ready to shoot, but another Tan struck up the levelled Colt and Flynn was ransomed by nothing worse than the wallop of a gun barrel on his head. The Tan who had saved him picked up a scapular which he wrapped around his wrist. 'Mother,' he said to the woman of the house, 'this may save me.'

The Column men counted their own losses as they moved away into the narrow valley approaches of Clogher. Two of the wounded, Michael Hughes and James Swift, both of Castlebar, were put to bed. Swift had been shot through the foot and he had been linked out of action. Nurse Joyce, home on holidays, tended the wounded under the direction of Dr. Madden. Kilroy had a talk with Madden. They both felt that they would be followed up in daylight and that they had best get outside of the triangle formed by Castlebar, Westport and Newport. The men were too tired and their morale too shaken for the long tramp to Aghagower which was in the hills, away from enemy posts and well isolated by bad surrounding roads. So Skerdagh, on the outskirts of the Nephin Beg range, was decided on as their place of refuge. It was a sound area, isolated at the butt of the mountains and backed by a waste of hills and difficult hill country devoid of roads. The wounded were placed on horseback and the Column moved away towards Derryloughan at one o'clock in the morning. They crossed the stepping stones over the Newport river, and when they reached Skerdagh the wounded went to a house in the upper village and Column men were biletted throughout Lower Skerdagh.

The officers were worried over the Column's losses, and the dead men's comrades ached at their memory. The death of a man would be reflected in his own townland. To his companions in arms and to his neighbours it would seem as if a portion of a hill they were familiar with from boyhood had suddenly disappeared from their remembered landscape. Success could sometimes be bought too dearly at the cost of a few Volunteers. IRA planning was based on avoiding casualties as far as it was possible to do so, and even in action this liability often had an influence on operations. This fear of loss and a reluctance to attack in the open were two factors which affected the Irish when competing with stereotyped soldiers.

Rumours of the treatment of the prisoners had come in from Westport. The wounded bodies and the sandwiched dead had been thrown down on the street outside the police barracks for a considerable time. Then the bodies were dragged inside. This indifference to dead and injured was probably meant to overawe the townspeople and to stress how incontrovertible was police authority. It may, however, have been contempt acidulated by victory. Even people friendly to the British in the town and neighbourhood were shocked rather than pleased or awed. Westport and Castlebar had been strongly held since Stuart times. The presence of Sligos and Lucans on confiscated Irish lands had meant an accumulation of relatives, adherents and servitors, and in all settled garrison towns possession and an element of snobbery bound together dominance and its underlings. The Marquis of Sligo had gone into the barracks to protest against the disregard for wounded prisoners.

Auxiliaries, Tans, RIC and military, in that order, ignored or neglected IRA wounded. It was perhaps unusual for police, soldiers or civilians to pay attention to the fallen, as uninstructed men are hesitant about handling the injured. Unless an army medical officer was present, wounds had to depend on the clotting ability of blood for protection. Column men, however, had nearly always looked after the wounded as soon as a fight was over, and whether a man was a former enemy or a friend seemed to make no difference in the care they received.

The people among whom the Column was billeted were equally solicitous and there the men felt secure, knowing that they were well posted against the broad extent and steep reaches of the mountains behind them. Yet they were thoroughly on the alert as each man had learned what protection implied from the bitter memories of their recent experiences.

Dr. Madden had returned from a Liverpool hospital earlier that year. He had reported to Dr. MacBride, an old Fenian, in Castlebar. Despite MacBride's protests about foolishness, this shooting behind hedges (with remarks parroted from the British and their adherents), and the moral guilt of ambush which he reiterated from the denouncements of practically all bishops and many priests, his assistant surgeon borrowed his bicycle and disappeared. It was natural enough for a senior surgeon to be irritated when a junior threw his prepared future away and acted summarily on his own authority, but it was most unusual for a professional man to be attached to a column, either as a doctor or engineer. Towns in Mayo had not been continuously shaken by the British through burnings, shooting of men in bed, or through killings of prisoners said to have tried to escape. The ingrained garrison adherence yet had some strength, although the countryside would quickly respond to a more remote allegiance associated with any attempt for freedom. John Madden joined in a fighting capacity and he proved his worth, but his technical skill gave great heart to the men. To a column commander who had many unusual responsibilities the immediate lack of care of the wounded bit at his nerves. Now this worry could be transferred. Madden was an additional asset as he was able to advise and help the people amongst whom he moved. Some immediate return could therefore be made for the many kindnesses given to the Column by the country people.

James Swift, who had limped out of action with a bullet through his foot, was operated on by Madden in Upper Skerdagh. The kitchen was cleared of the family. On a recently well-washed deal table, with Michael Kilroy as his untutored anaesthetist and assistant, two toes were removed.

The men rested for three days among the scattered cottages in the mountains. From their security of height they could watch the lower ground. A village in the mountain district, as in most parts of hilly Mayo, was not a collection of homesteads side by side, but a scattering of thatched cottages and slated houses over an area of a mile maybe. Sometimes a few families might build together and use the same yard, but the unusual separation of houses from one another entailed a wide distribution of the Column that made its protection more difficult.

Two of the Tirnir men with the Column, Jim Moran and John Connolly, had gone home on leave to see their families, as rumour had it that they had been killed. Late on Sunday night they returned to meet Michael Kilroy whom they knew to be then to the north-east of Newport. All three then started off in the darkness for the mountains, hoping to arrive unnoticed at the Column's retreat, before the dawn. It was shortly after three o'clock in the morning when they reached Upper Skerdagh. They had crossed the soft ground before it by the stepping-stones which served instead of a road, and followed up what had been an old bridle path between the mountains. They sat down at the back of MacDonnell's house where the wounded were kept, without making a noise as they did not wish to awaken the people so early in the morning. The next house, Dyra's, opened on to the same yard and there Madden and Kilroy were billeted. In the stillness beneath the dawn sky, the three men were quietly discussing the good line of retreat up by the bed of the stream behind them when, at about four o'clock, they heard rifle shots below, and the crack of rifle fire continued for a while. They did not know that an IRA sentry had started firing on police whom he had observed close to his post. The shots, however, meant immediate danger and the sound roughly announced the direction. Kilroy sent Jim Moran to Dyra's house to warn him and help Madden to remove the wounded by way of the river bed behind the house. Both Connolly and Moran had been billeted in Lower Skerdagh, and Moran had left his rifle behind there when he set out to visit his people. That lack of a rifle was a great loss now, for Moran, a fine natural shot, was the best marksman in the Column. Kilroy and Connolly started for the lower village, about three quarters of a mile away, and as they hurried down the hollow of the river bed, grey light, undershot by swarthy clouds, was in the sky.

Suddenly Kilroy saw capped figures about a hundred and fifty or two hundred yards away, but on higher ground. They must be police, he thought, as he signalled to Connolly who was in the rear. As an RIC man took aim, Kilroy threw himself to the ground, his rifle beside him, but the shot passed over him. He fired back at once and the two of them got in a few rounds apiece before other dark uniformed figures disappeared from their view. 'Wasn't that a good shot so early in the morning?' he heard an English voice say. Evidently Kilroy's sudden drop out of sight had been reckoned as a casualty by the Tans. Seconds later, the same voice exclaimed with surprise and urgency: 'What was that? It struck the peak of my cap.' A reply came back on the quiet air in a thicker burr of slower English speech. 'Take cover, take cover; you should always take cover in a case like that.'

Meanwhile in the lower village the Column men took up positions on the ground outside the houses in which they were billeted. There was some confusion until groups in the separate houses had made contact with one another, aware now of the immediate menace but unaware of the direction. Tom Kitterick and Paddy O'Connor heard rifle shots above them and, having decided that the upper village was surrounded and under attack, they thought they had best try at once to relieve it. Careful scouting uncovered the positions over which the RIC were spread out, but they were a Janus figure there, protecting themselves from the opposition in Upper Skerdagh and from the fire which had been kept up on them from the lower village. The main body of the Column, which had been billeted in the

THE HARD ROAD TO CARROWKENNEDY

lower village, skirted the police positions but could not engage the enemy because the range was too long for the shotgun men and because the riflemen had been issued with high velocity ammunition which was unsuitable for the Martini-Enfields with which most of them were armed.

A group of the Column men, only one of whom had a rifle, suddenly dashed out of the houses in which they had been sleeping and edged away hurriedly from the RIC. They had very nearly been surprised in their beds. Brown of Kilmeena was wounded in the stomach. He ran for a short distance and then fell. He could not be removed without covering fire and there he lay. Tom Kitterick, Cannon, Jack MacDonnell and Johnny Gibbons protected the main body as it made its cautious way towards the upper village. By that time Madden had arranged the moving of the wounded up the valley, but he was now anxious about Kilroy and Connolly. He came further down towards their position but he could not see them. He could hear bullet noises overhead as he went over the hillside above their position. A low artificial mound gave him cover when he lay behind it and tried to search the ground below him for hidden men. This was an elevation on which hawks were inclined to settle as they surveyed the ground for quarry and on such places a trap would be set for them in shooting country. His voice could be heard: 'Michael, where are you, Michael?' But Kilroy could not give away his position by an answering call. Connolly and he were in the open, firing at police movement. After some hours of careful crawling, the two men went backwards uphill, taking aim to protect each other. They were joined by Madden and by Kitterick, Cannon, MacDonnell and Gibbons who had successfully protected their own withdrawal and that of the main body. They were able to guess at the number of police below them, but it was long afterwards when it was found that there were twenty-four of them. The police had come out on foot from Newport before dawn, having left but one of their number behind to hold the barracks. Whether or not they were acting on information was never established by the IRA, but Newport was a town of dubious loyalty to Republicans and the RIC had active friends there.

On the previous Sunday some Column men had gone to a local wake. That focus of random talk and gossip over drink, carrying on the pre-historic tradition of funeral games, where every male from the neighbourhood attended for from three to five hours, may have been the source of leakage. To Column men it would have been a heaven's gift to talk about their wanderings and doings, for though the men kept a close guard on their tongues, a combination of friendly praise, their increased status in the eyes of stay-at-homes and the hospitality of the wake house could loosen talk in a mixture of imagination and reality which would amply satisfy. In addition to this there was the significance which the police might have given the coffin that had been brought out from Newport for the wake. The RIC were on the lookout for wounded who had escaped them at Kilmeena and this news of local death may have been translated by them into the burial of a Column man. It may have been this opinion which brought them out on the hills, although their strength and the fact that they had been making for Upper Skerdagh where the wounded were kept would suggest that they had an important objective and knew where to locate it. In the process of doing so they had got themselves into a tight corner. It was noon and they were pinned to ground from which they could neither advance nor retreat. Already they had sent one of their constables to attempt a break-through for help.

An old tradition handed down locally as 'Brian Roche's prophecy' foretold a fight that would take place in Skerdagh between the Irish and their enemies. It had been often talked about at the firesides in the long winter evenings and it was well known in Skerdagh and to other older people. In the middle of the contest a red-haired man named MacMenamin was to jump on a horse to bring help to the invaders, otherwise they would all be killed. There are people named MacMenamin in nearby glens and it is possible that they came down from the North when the O'Donnells with Gallaghers, Kanes, Dohertys, Sweeneys and other Northerners came into Connacht in the early 17th century, although there seems to be a spoken record that people of that name were already in the glen at that time. The fact is that the constable did break through to get help for the police trapped at Skerdagh, that he was a red-haired MacMenamin, a native of Donegal, and that he got hold of a horse on which he galloped away in the direction of Newport. Any of the older country people who had seen the red-haired peeler dash across country, crouched bare-back on his mount, might have thought of Brian Roche's prophecy and, as the Skerdagh countryside was both hospitable and friendly to the Column, would have hoped that the rider would fail in his appeal for help.

When the seven Column men who had fought the rearguard action joined forces, Kilroy and Connolly had fired close on a hundred rounds. Ammunition was at once pooled and divided up equally amongst the seven and as there was little standard .303 left, they were faced with the question of whether to use dum-dum ammunition which they had captured from the police in a raid beyond Burrishoole. This problem was debated seriously, as they were short in supply, and what decided them in favour of using it was the memory of the whip-cracking sound made by bullets that had passed over the Column positions at Kilmeena. The bullets which went over them had crackled like the lash of a strong whip and there the men attributed that piercing sound to the use of dum-dum ammunition by the police. Having divided all the ammunition they extended over a considerable distance in order to outflank the RIC. Every now and again the police, who were about five hundred yards away, put up a piece of clothing or a rifle butt to test the vigilance of the men above them. Later, from their position close to a few houses, the IRA observed a line of lorries coming along the road from Newport. These halted near Skerdagh school on the Crossmolina road and military began to move up the slopes.

The IRA rearguard had no choice but to pull out quietly, one by one, without attracting the attention of the police below them. The seven began to climb up by the bridle path to the west of Glenlara. Long before, a small trench had been cut to one side of the path for the purpose of drainage. It had been filled in with earth and was now overgrown with grass of a darker shade of green than that of the growth on either side. Kilroy ordered his men to move over the dark strip as they would be less likely to be observed from below. They crossed to the far side of the stream where they were given some cake and a can of buttermilk at Chambers' house, but when they emerged with rations they saw police climbing towards the positions they had just vacated, to the west of the small valley.

As they went up the side of Birreenomagh, bursts of machine-gun fire swept the slopes, but in a way which suggested that the police were merely probing the mountainside with the object of flushing the Column out of cover. Police on the Buckoogh side also fired their rifles into likely places of cover, and louder explosions heard at intervals indicated that they were using rifle or hand grenades for the same purpose. The rearguard's line of withdrawal lay through a hollow in the mountainside caused by an extensive landslide. The hollow was overgrown by moss and rushes, and in it the seven men lay down long enough to drink the buttermilk from the can, which one of them threw carelessly to one side when they finished with it. After that they resumed the ascent, all the while watching for events below them. Suddenly they dropped and flattened against the earth. A blue-green RIC man passed up close to the discarded can which glinted on the heather below them, as if it was tapping out warning messages to their enemies. It was the last man in an enemy line, stretched in extended order across from the heights of Buckoogh and moving up the valley. There were moments of intense strain while the IRA men lay still, gripping their weapons, their eyes fixed on every movement by the police. It seemed inevitable that the empty can must be noticed and its significance appreciated, and that two exposed Column men on the flank of the enemy line could not escape observation. The men waited tensely for the excited shouts and warning shots that would mark the discovery of their positions, but to their surprise and relief the police moved on without noticing anything.

The seven continued to climb until they had reached a peak where in places the bog was washed clear away to the underlying gravel below. The surface was bone-dry for there had been no rain for close on a month. Here they had cover and they could remain on guard at ease. It was pleasant to lie close to the heather on a warm May day. A slight wind blew the strength of the sun from their faces. Every now and then a man could have a peep at the world below or watch the bridle path which went below Mount Eagle on to Shrahmore. They had a telescope which had been taken in a raid on Burrishoole.

The sound of rifle shots came from the distance, deepened by machine-gun bursts as the mountains further back were being searched for the main body of the Column. The military had gone up towards Shrahmore to the west by the side of Lough Feeagh and the police followed round the bridle path leading across to Shrahmore Lodge. An ambulance could be seen near to the school below and the IRA counted what appeared to be bodies carried into it. Enemy casualties were always a subject for rumour. Bodies, according to later accounts, were said to have been brought off to Foxford in lorries, and in another local version there was an export of dead in bacon boxes to England from Ballina. The British admitted a head constable killed and a constable wounded, but the DI, Munroe, was also wounded that day. He had a decent reputation in the Newport area and he was said to have prevented the police from burning houses in Skerdagh once reinforcements had made them so sure of themselves that they felt safe to attack the defenceless villagers.

From their vantage point on the peak, the seven IRA men were able to identify the islands in Clew Bay which gave the impression of being clustered together when seen from such a height. Beyond, on the south side, the Reek pushed up its cone, and echelloned behind were the sharper outlines of the Sheffry mountains and the triple peak of Mullrea further west on that sea edge. Away towards the east the lakes glinted, Beltra nearby, Mask a wide stretch, with the narrow strip of land between it and Lough Cullin at Pontoon. Below them, glistening in the reflected light, as far as they could see, was the whole history of the district. Some of them could supply memoried fragments which in a folklore territory went back to medieval times.

Time there brought past, present and future together. The British would solve a problem as if time were a matter of temporary expediency, but it would be difficult for them to relate the past and present and future in an indivisable unit. The seven talked about the next enemy move and how to circumvent it. Previously they had been anxious to keep outside the triangle formed by the three towns of Castlebar, Westport and Newport. Now it was felt that this search might be the beginning of a mountain round-up. The British would either place picquets on the ground they had covered this day, surround the area between Lough Feeagh and Ballycroy where there was hardly a house, or move northwards to Nephin Beg and sweep across eastwards towards the isolated brow of Nephin.

It seemed best for the seven to cross the triangle and make for the hills near Aghagower. It was dusk when they came down to Jack MacDonnell's house where now a dead body was lying: the corpse of a pig shot by the RIC. The police had fired on the houses on their way up, before they searched them.

Hungrily the seven IRA ate boiled salmon, drank large mugs of welcome tea. Their hill hosts were glad that their poaching proclivity was appreciated. The neighbours came in to listen to the story of the rearguard and the day-long endurance of the village, that episodic drift of Irish resistance and quiescence. Suddenly in the weavings of these happenings the seven thought of the men farther to the north in the hills, and became silent. When they left the house they carried with them a reserve of salmon in jars, while the dogs in Skerdagh barked an unappreciated accompaniment to their hurried journey towards the Crossmolina road. They were anxious to get as far away as possible from the mountain approaches, and expected the British might already be in position or would be moving up troops under cover of darkness. They crossed the Newport river by a small bridge near Divers. It was midnight before they were on the far side, and in the distance, across Beltra lake, they saw beams of light moving in their direction. That meant the British had begun their round-up, and that the IRA rearguard seven were in danger of being cut off unless they got beyond the Crossmolina road before the lorries came up. As hard as they could leg it they ran towards the road, their rifles hard to control as they jostled and swung. They were fit, hardy men, but after their long and arduous day and the night march that preceded it, that last mile across country tested their endurance as they ran for their lives. They had just crossed the road, taking a wide bog drain in a wild jump, when the enemy lorries came close and stopped near where they had flattened down behind clamps of turf. Soldiers got down on the road. Officers shone flash lamps on maps or examined them under the headlights of their lorries. They peered at the topography and mispronounced local place-names so that the men behind the ricks of turf found it difficult to hold back laughter. Those voices, difficult to understand through their accents, suddenly enlightened the Column men as to how insoluble both they and their place-names were to these probing forigners.

One man with no cause for humour was John Madden, lying at the bottom of a drain into which he had fallen through miscalculating his jump. It was a deep drain, and his companions' urge to laughter drew added stimulus from the thought of Madden swearing inwardly as he lay in the muck; they knew that his command of invective was equal to all demands.

Following deliberations amongst British officers, a detail of soldiers was sent to hold the bridge near Divers, over which the IRA had crossed a short time previously, and the convoy then moved slowly forward in the warm May night.

During that day — and while the rearguard held up the advance of Newport constabulary — the remainder of the Column had climbed the mountain path which skirted the steep reaches of Buckoogh. The wounded Swift was put on horseback and held securely by a man astraddle behind him, but Hughes was now able to walk. A message had already been sent on to Skerdagh to John Chambers, a lieutenant of the mountain company, who lived in the first house to the northward beyond Buckoogh, near by the lakes in Derrybrock. 'Green' Chambers, as he was known to distinguish him locally from others of the name, quickly crossed beneath the mountains until at about eight o'clock he met the Column winding up the narrow valley. None of the men knew the mountains and to him they were too slow moving, for there was possible danger ahead of them. But he was a hillman whose leg muscles had been made limber by hill heights, and the mountains instead of being obstacles were an easy security.

Moane had hoped to bring the wounded to the caves

underneath the cliff edges of Curreen which stretches its narrow spine below Nephin Beg to the west of the Altaconey river. There he felt they could best lie in safety as the few houses in the hills would most certainly be searched by British troops. Chambers, however, knew that British reinforcements could pass up by road alongside Lough Feeagh to Shramore and cut them off before the Column could reach the hills to the north. He suggested that they cross quickly by the ridge between Mount Eagle and Bireencorragh, toward Leamadartaun to the north-east. When they were beyond the ridge they could rest and then decide about their further climbing.

Troops from Castlebar or from Ballina could bring their transport into the hills as far as Bunaveela which lay further to the east. To avoid encirclement from that direction, the Column men would have to move northwards some distance. Before they reached Leam, as it was locally called, an aeroplane engine was heard in the distance. The men lay close to the slit of a black dyke in the lighter rise of bog. The chestnut pony was freed so as not to attract attention and he kicked up his heels in delight as he raced away over the dry bog surface. When the aeroplane, which circled round a few times, had moved slowly westward, the men spread out. Swift was now carried in turns across a man's back until Leam was reached. There, the thirsty men drank tea, while a scout was sent up to a height from where he could watch the surrounding valleys. He heard rifle shots in the distance towards Shramore Lodge but could not discover any advance of khaki or the bottle-green RIC.

Swift was put astride another pony and the Column moved on among low rises until they halted on the steep hillside which ran down into Bunaveela Lake. They lay deep in the comforting heather while waiting for further news of a round-up. Messengers soon came up from Shrahmore Lodge with the latest information. The RIC had been in 'Green' Chamber's house beside the small lake. They had demanded food, then they had gone on to the Lodge. Through their field glasses the police had seen a straggled line of Column men cross a ridge over two miles away, but by now RIC legs were traitors to RIC desires. They were too tired by their wanderings in the hills to walk any

THE HARD ROAD TO CARROWKENNEDY

further and despite the efforts made by their district inspectors and by other officers to persuade them to follow over the hills, they sat down at their ease. An officer said they would advance in the early morning, if not at midnight, and as soon as they had rested in Newport they would go up by Shramore towards Glendavoolagh.

The depleted Column remained on the hillside until seven in the evening. They could now climb into the mountains which loomed away in a series of bastioned cliff edges, or to the northwest towards Bangor Erris, or they could wind their way among lakes scattered like currants in a cake to the north-east. Most of the Column intended to remain close to Letterdesh beside the lake until they would be informed by mountain men of the approach of British troops guided by constabulary. Their scout would be 'Lame Willie' Chambers, who knew the hills from searching winter drifts for hidden flocks, or by following up the tedious wanderings of almond-eyed mountainy sheep. That intimate knowledge could serve him even in a dark night.

Castlebar men, however, were anxious to bring the wounded back to their own battalion which would likely be outside of any convergence of troops. By nine o'clock they had set off by the lake side, guided by 'Green' Chambers, who was to bring them across the slopes of Bullaunmore towards the roadway from the east which ended at Glendavoolagh Lodge. Close to Keenagh the wounded were given women's clothing from a small village of Hegarty's. The slimmest boy was dressed as a young girl, while the most elderly became an old lady with a dancing bonnet of spangles. If they were halted they were to be a wedding party on their way towards Glenisland, a safe retreat for the Castlebar Column. Their driver had been an RIC man up to a few months ago before resigning. When they came close to Boghadoon, scouts told them that already soldiers of the Border Regiment from Castlebar had held up a crossroads to the south on the way to Glenisland and the road to it was now unsafe. Hurriedly the driver turned to the east under the long shadow of Nephin. 'Green' Chambers then left them. He was anxious about the men who were behind him, near Bunaveela. When he came to the village beyond the lake side at Letterdesh he was told that the Column had gone away to the west, intending to get across to the valley of Glendahurk. Chambers made his way in the darkness through the hills to Derrybrock, but as he was close to his own house he heard voices, English voices, and he threw himself down quickly in the grass. He saw dim figures pass below him with rifles slung on their shoulders. When he came to his house he was told that English soldiers had been there, unsure of their direction, and they were on their way to Keenagh.

Meanwhile the Westport Column had heard about the Kilmeena fight from one of their men who had been present and who had subsequently made his way to them across country. That same night two men who had been at work in England, Willie Malone and Joe Walsh, came home to join the Column. They got off the train at Islandeady station and were brought to the Column during the night. The night following the encounter at Skerdagh, word reached this Column that the wounded IRA men in Westport were to be brought away under guard by train next day. In the morning, at Cushin, the train was held up while the Westport Column waited near the railway line to make a rescue bid; but neither escort nor wounded were aboard. In order to have something to show for the morning's work, however, mails were taken off the train and censored. It was hoped, too, that this operation, showing that a column was busy in another direction, would cause the British to withdraw troops from the mountain round-up which was endangering Kilroy and his men. This round-up with its staff basis of map planning was just another of a series of operations carried out through many counties during the dry weather which held from the end of April onwards. A rapidly increasing strength of khaki and police searched hills and mountains, treating all whom they met with as hostile. All men between seventeen and seventy were moved back under a strong guard to an isolated farmhouse or to schoolrooms. There they were sharply questioned by intelligence officers, while one of the big moustaches from the RIC peered through a curtained slit in a window at successive batches of prisoners, using his memoried eye. British regular officers and RIC inspectors, irritated at the conscious stupidity (and lack of understanding) of some of the men they questioned, often used their fists and revolver handles, or handed their sources of upset over to the ready rifle butts and boots of their subordinates. People, though frightened by the theatrical grimness of the inquisition, were determined to guard what little information they had. Most of the detained men were freed at nightfall, but any suspects were sent on to the nearest barracks for a further scrutiny and a variation of the methods for extracting information.

In this round-up of Nephin and its neighbourhood no IRA man was captured and the Column, so far as the British were concerned, had vanished into the mountain mists. The British reports referred to large rebel concentrations in the tree-bare mountains. A conception of the rival nations which holds good for propaganda and general purposes seemed to have been reversed. The heightened imagination of British reports as forwarded to their gullible superiors, when compared with the Irish version to their General Headquarters of this simple, but effective, rearguard action is curious. The Irish report is conservative and factual, but British Headquarters again inflated their own field version of concentrations of cornered rebels to an enlarged distortion. Evidently whatever large movement the British undertook had to be justified in result from minor to major ranks until at length it could be triumphantly read by the British Cabinet in London. What a pleasure it would be to have overheard how place-names known as wandering ground to wild geese, duck and the slim fox were now so emphasized.

Less than a week after Skerdagh, the Brigade Column was billeted in the straggly village of Clady to the south-east of the road from Westport to Leenane, under the sharp shoulders of the Partry mountains. To the south of the scattered houses on the ridge, bogland stretched in a level breadth to the main road. Further west the sharp crests of the Sheffry hills mount towards Doolough Pass which is backed by the steep sides of Mweelrea. An odd grove of stunted trees broke the tawny-green land surface where there was shelter, but higher there was nothing but smooth mountain curves to lead the eye from one shapely form to another. Strong sunshine and a mass succession of moving cloud sharpened and shaded out-thrust and valley, until every projection and recession had been softly sculptured with light and shade and coloured subtly. To the north a few isolated hills lay in the distance below the sharp flanks of Croagh Patrick on whose southern side the pilgrims' road swung in a sudden white curve as it led upwards. The landscape in colour and bog, hill and mountain, was a crystallisation of western scenery and economic difficulty. As well, it was a symbol of the Column's historic background and an indication of their roots.

The recent rearguard action had heightened the spirit of the Column which now comprised a strong Westport section, with men from the Newport battalion and from Louisburg. The previous night some of the men had burned the empty RIC barracks at Drummin below the Reeks. It had recently been evacuated following a brush between a patrol and some of the Column. The men had carefully examined the barracks before they entered it as it had been discovered that the police were leaving booby-trap mines behind them in deserted posts. One of the Column men found a hand grenade attached to the inside of the front door so that it would explode when the door was opened. The grenade was disconnected and examined. It helped to increase the Brigade armament. The grenades carried by the Column were of steel piping cut to section grooves, but they were not as effective as other models from Dublin factories based on the Mills pattern.

On the evening of June 3rd a scout brought in word to Clady that two lorries and a motor car of RIC had halted some distance down the Leenane road where a filled-in trench had been opened afresh by the local Volunteers. He reported that men who had been working in the nearby bogs were rounded up by police and compelled, under the menace of fixed bayonets and a careless handling of revolvers, to empty their cartloads of turf into the gap. While the fuel was filling up the trench, police jibed at the unwilling workers and boasted about their victory at Kilmeena.

THE HARD ROAD TO CARROWKENNEDY

The end house of Clady was close on a mile and a half from the main road, so before the Column was mobilised time had ticked away and the police had moved on. Kilroy knew that they would probably have to return by the same road, for the bridge at Delphin, which ordinarily would allow a car to pass through to Louisburg, had been destroyed. That gap would also prevent the RIC from turning at Doolough up the rutty road which ran through Glennumera by the Red Gap back to the Westport road, some three miles beyond to the east. Kilroy instructed Brodie Malone, Vice-Commandant of the Westport battalion, to put his men in temporary positions with sections placed at such distances as would allow them to deal individually with the three enemy vehicles which he expected would be well spaced out on the return journey. Tom Kitterick, the Brigade's inimitable Quartermaster, who could be expected to borrow a sword from the Archangel Gabriel and then question its return, was with the group to take on the second lorry. Kilroy, Madden and Joe Ring went down the Westport road to inspect another more suitable site, beyond a curve some six hundred yards away.

Malone placed his first section on a rise of ground about a hundred and fifty yards from the road. There was a flat stretch behind for a short distance. In front there was a wall of boulders running from knee to breast height. Beyond, towards Leenane, was scrub and a stone wall, under cover of which communications could be maintained with the second section about a hundred and fifty yards away. Some fifty yards below Malone's men was a cottage, its gable facing the road. There were a few outhouses alongside it, and a narrow passageway shut off on either side by loose stone walls wound upwards from the roadside.

The second position was on the site of an old police hut which Johnny Duffy, captain of Aghagower company, had burned down in the Easter of 1920. Paddy Duffy, his young brother, was now making a loophole up in the first position. He was a good shot and he sighted his rifle on the topmost edges of wall and bank along the roadside. The police hut had been built during the Land War to keep the Widow Salmon, whose house was on this small holding of land, in order. She still lived in her house about fifty yards behind the site. She had fought hard to avoid eviction, and was known locally as 'William O'Brien's widow', for O'Brien, who was then living in Mallow Cottage beyond Westport, had looked after her interests and had provided for her, admiring her staunch fighting qualities, but which, with the vehemence of land bitterness, had nearly driven her crazy. Peter Skahill had grabbed her small holding but he did not get any ease of life along with it. The only occasion the widow turned 'grabber' herself was when she caught a grip of Skahill by the whiskers in the chapel at Cushlough and the priest had all he could do to part the two of them.

Tom Kitterick and Ned Moane spoke of the widow as they explored their position. Between them and the first position was a rise of ground which contained scattered boulders, scrub and a grove of young oak trees. A passage that served as a laneway led down to the main road, but it was more like the rough, dried-up bed of a mountain torrent. A stone wall on its flank gave cover for moving men if they went cautiously. Kitterick and Moane had a view of the Leenane road for a short distance beyond the cottage of the Widow Salmon, but that road then swung abruptly in a curve. They could deal with the second lorry provided it came about two hundred yards or more behind the first one. The success of the action would depend upon the distances between the three vehicles when fire was first opened. If the motor car was in the lead, the patrol might extend over four to five hundred yards of the road, in which case the two rear sections would have to engage the two lorries at the outset. The other section which held the most secure and best position would be confronted only with a Ford car, though in that event the car could be quickly accounted for and the men could then link up with the nearest section.

On the slope of a hill about one hundred feet high to the rear of the McGrale cottage, and almost at right angles to the main road, were the ten men of the third section. This position had a few good banks which screened it from the road and a small grove of trees permitted movement. The men had a good view of the Westport road for about eight hundred yards. They could fire down at any vehicle which might suddenly turn into the

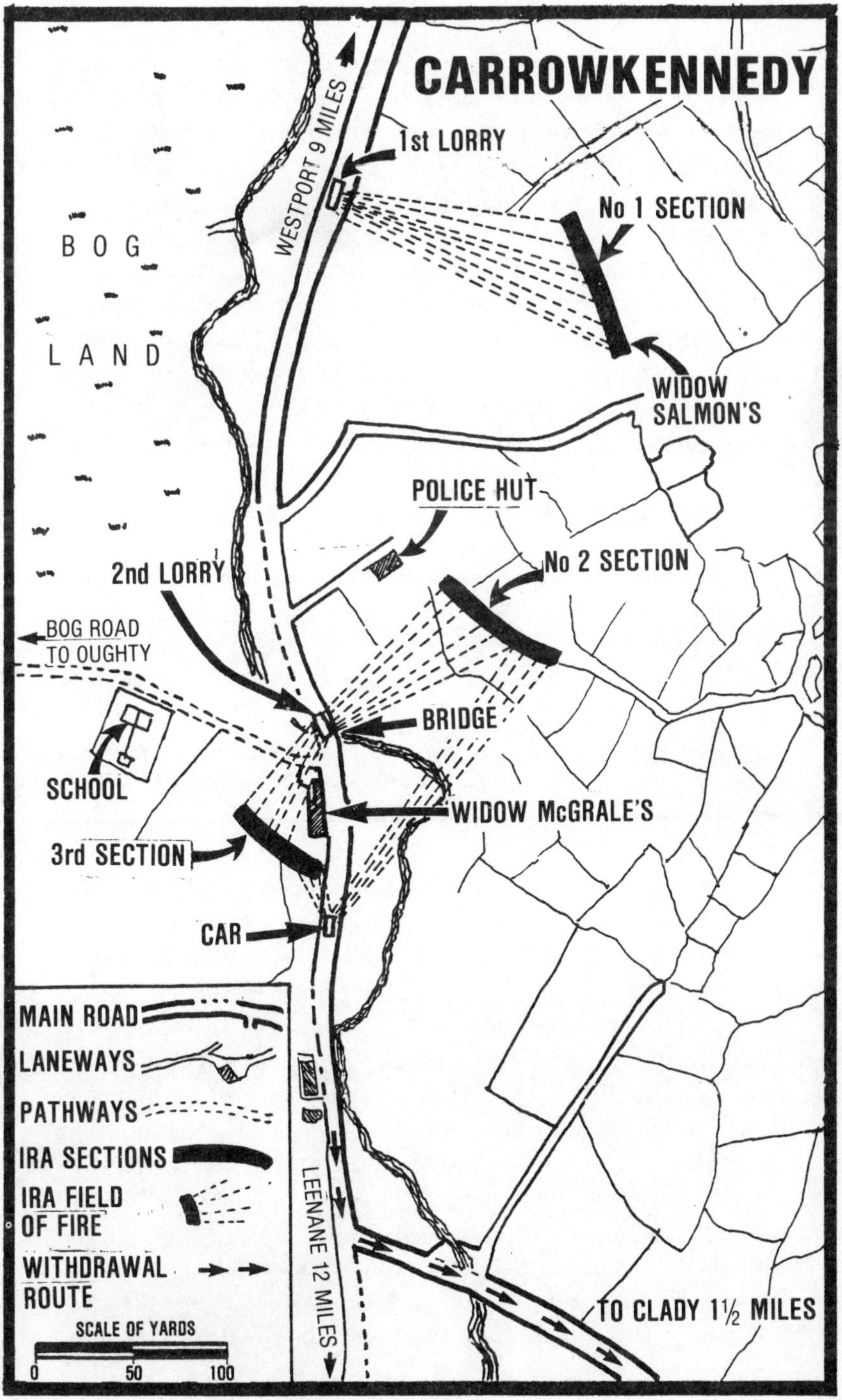
CARROWKENNEDY
WESTPORT 9 MILES
1st LORRY
No 1 SECTION
WIDOW SALMON'S
BOG
LAND
POLICE HUT
No 2 SECTION
2nd LORRY
BOG ROAD TO OUGHTY
BRIDGE
SCHOOL
WIDOW McGRALE'S
3rd SECTION
CAR
MAIN ROAD
LANEWAYS
PATHWAYS
IRA SECTIONS
IRA FIELD OF FIRE
WITHDRAWAL ROUTE
SCALE OF YARDS
0
50
100
LEENANE 12 MILES
TO CLADY 1½ MILES

raised bog road leading to Oughty, for there had been insufficient time even to throw boulders or stones on the road surface to slow up a lorry which might swing off the main road in an attempt to avoid the ambush.

While Kilroy with Madden and Ring walked towards the road bend, the men of the three sections were testing alternative positions until each felt he was satisfied that he had a good one for sighting his rifle on to the roadway or his shotgun on to intervening ground. The section behind McGrale's were judging distance and endeavouring to remember landmarks which would help them to adjust their sights to the required range when needed. Malone's section had an easier task. They were one hundred and fifty yards from the road and their longest range would be between two hundred and three hundred yards, provided the RIC kept to the roadway. To the west beyond the road was a dun-covered softness that was exposed to their fire. They were occupying a natural bastion. Even the boulders had ready-made loopholes for use.

One of the men pointed out Owen O'Malley's house some little distance away, or rather what was left of it, and then the charred ruins of Pat Cox's home. Other men tried to pick out towards Drummin a further two houses of their friends, which had been burned one night in March.

The Column had been in Clady on a moonlight night when Joe Ring, Brodie Malone and Michael Kilroy walked the road to Derrynakillew looking for ambush positions. They were wearing gaberdine trench coats and leggings, regulation column outfit, which could be identified at a distance. As one of them, Malone, turned, he saw four police on bicycles at a curve of the road behind them. The RIC were nosing around as usual, listening for random talk and in search of information. The three IRA officers, who carried automatics, wheeled round as the police dismounted. One policeman rushed past them, and a moonlight gun battle began, with the sharp crack of Peter and Parabellum against the duller thud of the Webley. There could be no 'shooting from behind hedges' now for it was a raised, unfenced road, but there were ditches in which the RIC took shelter. All four of them were wounded, one fatally, and four revolvers were captured. This sudden patrol encounter had been the first success of the Column. Two nights later, on March 24th, the RIC broke loose in Westport. They held the town for five hours from midnight, during which they burned one house, wrecked the contents of shops, then used heavy bombs on buildings and removed furniture to the middle of the street where it was set on fire. They threatened Tom Kitterick's parents with revolvers and burned their furniture; then bullied the women in Brodie Malone's house. They were very specific about what would happen to Kitterick and Malone when they fell into their hands.

On the night following the bombing of a Westport patrol at Red Bridge, a Tan District Inspector from Newport, with a crowd of Tans and RIC roared through the streets of the town looking for fight. Fudge, the District Inspector, had developed a distorted sense of humour which hunted men in their shirts out into the night cold, or made them sit astride bullocks which were then lashed to a buckjumping frenzy. Another joke, unappreciated by the women, was to spread their hens' tribute on the floor and force men and boys of the household to walk in bare feet across the eggs.

The Tans harnessed Ned Horan and Malone's father to an outside car and some whipped the elderly men around the streets while others sat at ease on the side seats. They fed their 'horses' as they called them with raw salt ling, and when they reached Horan's shop they poured down his throat, through a tundish, a gargantuan quantity of his own porter. Malone managed to escape while the Tans halted to pull other men out of their beds, but Horan paid for the missing man through kicks and the heavy thuds of revolver butts. When they came again to Malone's house, they threatened to shoot his daughter when she told them she did not know where her father had gone to. They added a man called O'Reilly, whom they had first beaten crooked, to the car harness. He was also made to paint red, white and blue the fountain on the fair green which had been erected to Doctor Johnson. Men whom they laid hands on later they painted with green, white and orange to show how impartially they were guided by unpaid-for drink.

Then the RIC and Tans, having exhausted the possibilities for such entertainment in the town, wandered into the country. In the kitchen of Owen O'Malley's house they found a sick cow that had been brought in for treatment. Creegan, the Westport sergeant, poured a tin of petrol over the sick animal and sacrificed it in a ceremonial flame that also consumed the house. Owney, son of the house, whose misfortune it was to have been at home when the visitation took place, had his jaw broken by the Tans who, with their RIC comrades, danced about the flames like a war party of Red Indians. In between their extravagant humours they beat people with rifle-butts and kicked them with studded boots. Sergeant Hallinan and a Tan named French particularly distinguished themselves that night and on other occasions. By this time the Tans had been well instructed by the regular RIC on what families were to be manhandled and what houses were to suffer wanton destruction in raids.

This destruction in Westport was the first unofficial reprisal in Ireland for which the British in their House of Commons had made themselves responsible. In reply to a question in the House, Denis Henry, the Attorney-General, stated:

The house of one person and the contents of the houses of certain other persons were systematically destroyed by members of the Crown forces, acting under orders from their superior officer. The persons whose property was destroyed were known to the police to be actually engaged in the rebel conspiracy.

The decision to destroy the property was taken by the responsible police officer on the spot, acting on his own discretion. I am satisfied that the officer concerned acted according to the best of his judgement, believing that immediate action of a drastic character was called for if future outrages were to be adverted.

Lord Robert Cecil asked if it were left entirely to the discretion of the local officer, necessarily not of very high rank, whether this destruction was carried out or not. In reply, Mr. Henry said: 'There are occasions when it is necessary to act rapidly and it must be left to the officer in charge.'

This strange answer came after six months of continuous questioning in the Commons as members tried to make government representatives state that their troops or police had been responsible for reprisals.

Indeed, both Brodie Malone and Tom Kitterick, as they awaited the return of the police on that June evening in 1921, had letters from home in their pockets, telling them of recent armed threats, made by Hallinan, French and others, to their women-folk during frequent and aimless raids on their houses.

Now, for the threads of those nights' work to be woven to a proper satisfaction, there came a shout from the nearest section: 'They're coming! They've just left Darby's! Get ready!' Darby Hastings' pub, which had suffered on the night of the constabulary burnings, was a little over a mile down the road, so the patrol should be inside the ambush position in a few minutes. The men were excited and tense as they sighted their rifles and kept close to the cover of their boulders.

The usual formation of a light patrol consisted of two tenders or lorries and a motor car. The lighter vehicle was often used as a scout on narrow roads and it could be sent some distance ahead to carefully observe the road in front and the surrounding countryside. When the road surface was blocked by a trench, loose stones or fallen trees, the light car could be manhandled past these obstacles. In case of attack, the car might be sent for assistance.

A short time before the patrol was signalled, an old man below the bastion had been using a spade along a potato ridge. Suddenly he saw above him seven men who were shifting stones to improvise loopholes. He saw them, as he thought, poking at stones, and he swelled with rage at the thought of another onslaught on his walls by playboys looking for rabbits. 'Get to the devil out of here,' he shouted, as he waved his spade in anger. 'You did enough damage last Sunday, you and your rabbiting.' Malone, anxious for the old man's safety as he heard the lorries burring on their way, attempted to placate him. But he continued: 'Making bruss of my fine walls. Go on away out of that.' As he straddled a wall to get closer to them, the wall collapsed under him. At this moment the signal came from the second section and the men laughed at the old man's confusion as they settled down with their weapons.

Rifle fire was opened on the leading lorry which wavered and then halted close to the bank, a little beyond the passageway leading down to the cottage below the IRA position. Police tumbled out quickly and got down behind the bank which gave them some cover but not protection. Two did not move. One was a District Inspector named Stevenson. The patrol convoy had gone as far as the bridge at Glenacullew which was partly demolished, and had then turned back. At Darby Hastings' pub Stevenson had taken the wheel from the driver. When opposite the laneway, he turned his head as if he had noticed something and at that moment he received a bullet through the forehead. The other driver was also killed instantly.

'They're throwing out the machine-gun', Tom Heavey shouted, and a metal object landed on the road out of sight of the section. The muzzle was swung towards the third section on the west of the road which had this lorry and the lorry behind it under their sights. A short burst of fire came from the Lewis gun, then another, and then the gunner lay dead beside his gun.

Paddy Duffy, Johnny, his brother, and Kane, who were all good shots, were watching from above for any movement near the gun. Kane was a natural shot, as was Jim Moran who was close to the burnt-out police hut. It was said of Moran that he could cut a telegraph wire at a distance with his Mauser rifle. Kilroy had insisted that his Column men should practise with the disc, which had improved their use of sights, and they had had ample trigger practise as well. That training had produced good results, but no rifle would give prolonged service without an armourer's adjustment. Too well men knew that the best rifle was a recently captured rifle.

A second gunner fired a burst of eight or nine shots from the Lewis in the direction of the third section; then he swung the muzzle in the air to protect himself from the riflemen above, but enough of his body was still showing and he, too, fell dead beneath the gun.

Rifles were projected over the sides of the first lorry and an occasional shot was fired, but the second section, who could observe but little of this action, could see a pair of legs exposed near the open tail of the lorry and some of them fired the odd shot in that direction.

The second lorry had rounded the bend beyond the bridge and passed the road to Oughty which led through Derrynakillew. It was stopped by rifle fire from both sides of the road as soon as the reports of shots were heard from the direction of the first tender. This lorry had been commandeered that morning in Westport and it was driven by a civilian. The RIC in it made for rough cover above the road and by degrees they got as far as the stream bridge, under which some of them sheltered. The driver lay down behind a lorry wheel and flattened himself down on the roadside. After a while the constabulary ran towards McGrales' thatched cottage facing on to the road. Here they prepared the house for resistance until reinforcements could reach them. They poked rifles out through the windows in front and through a window high up in the gable which controlled a view down the Westport road. After making continuous noise with their rifles, as if the din was a solution for their difficulty, they found they had been too lavish in their attack on the threatening scenery. Their spare supply of ammunition had been left behind in the lorry. They endeavoured to make the Widow McGrale go out to the lorry and, when she refused them, they tried to induce her young son to venture out. He would not be fired on, either going out or coming back, they assured him, for certainly the men outside would not injure him.

'Go out and get it yourself,' the Widow said, 'and leave the boy alone; it's your ammunition.' Her shouts of 'Give it to them! Fire away, lads!' could be heard up the hillside, her words addressed to the IRA in defiance of her unwanted visitors.

The motor car was some distance behind the second lorry and it halted beyond the cottage. Three police jumped off the exposed side and two remained on the sheltered edge of the road which had a thicket beside it close to the cottage. Out on the extreme flank of the ambush sections was Jimmy Flaherty who, as he had been billeted in the farthest house, was the last man to reach the position. He had served nine years in the 1st battalion of the Connaught Rangers. Now as he waited until the RIC would come closer, only one of them continued to advance; the other two retreated to the far side of the road. These two were under Flaherty's rifle but he did not fire. The other man had disappeared into the broken ground which was sprinkled with outcrops of rock, hollows and small clumps of thorn bushes.

Flaherty knew the man was advancing by the shouts he heard. 'Come on, the Shinners are retreating, come on.' Then after an interval his animus was directed to his comrades. 'Come on, you effers! The rebels are beaten.' Suddenly he reappeared as he crossed a wall over a hundred yards away. Flaherty fired but the policeman suddenly vanished again. Perhaps he was trying to move up further towards the noise of the firing coming from the first tender, the ex-Ranger thought. Then he saw him once more, about seventy yards away, and he fired again. After a long pause he saw a policeman moving slowly up on to the road and by his movements he knew that he was badly wounded. Then he saw the blue-green uniform suddenly fall near to the bridge.

It was now two hours since the first shot was fired. Batty Coyne had been steadily shooting at what he said was a policeman's head beside the lorry wheel, but when a few others had a careful look they found he was shooting at the sun-god. The sunlight was reflected from off the wheel-hub and this shimmering circle he had mistaken for a face.

Michael Kilroy was worried as he watched the progress of the fight. Unless the surrender of the first lorry was forced quickly, the Column might not have time to concentrate on the police in the McGrale cottage. Enemy reinforcements could arrive at any moment from Castlebar, Westport and Ballinrobe, either by road or over the hills on their eastern flank. As he went towards the redoubt he met Joe Baker who had a few men with him, and he talked over his difficulties. Baker with his men would move down the stony concealed passageway to the south, while a few others would work their way round to the north of the police to bomb the lorry. The police had been firing grenades from the lorry for some time. These exploded ten or fifteen yards below the stony wall of the redoubt and made a great deal of noise, but the men above were secure from the flying splinters. During a lull in the grenade throwing, fire was observed coming from a hill about four hundred and fifty yards away. It was quickly silenced by a few shots. Afterwards it was found that it was Joe Ring who had been firing on the lorry from that point. He had moved well out to one flank to get a better target.

Kilroy now spoke to Malone and arranged that a fresh assault on the lorry would be made by Johnny Duffy, his brother Paddy, and by Kane. Paddy was the youngest lad in the Column, only seventeen years of age, but in his determination he had plagued his officers until he was allowed to join the Westport section. Johnny had a bayonet which he could fix on the rifle boss, as had Tommy Heavey who was close to Baker's group and was a little older than Paddy. The bayonets were to be used for the final charge. Their principle use up to this attack was for cutting up Bendigo and cut plug tobacco, for which purpose they were admirably suited. The three were given grenades to throw when they got close to the lorry. As they began to move down behind stone walls, Johnny Duffy was held up by rifle fire and he signalled to the other two behind him to move further on to his flank.

Down a water-rutted lane to the south, Joe Baker, Jack Mac Donnell and Tommy Heavey pushed on toward the road. Heavey used his rifle from the left shoulder so as to expose his body less to the police fire from the gable of the Widow McGrale's house. As they advanced, a rifle grenade that was being hurled by one of the police fell back into the lorry and exploded. It never became known whether the man with the missile was first hit by a bullet or not; the explosion killed him instantly and fatally wounded other police beside him. At once a handkerchief was hoisted on top of a rifle as a token of surrender. The taking of a surrender was always a dubious procedure. The RIC had been notified from their headquarters that they should at all times carry a revolver inside their tunics. After a tentative series of halts, Column men advanced to the lorry.

Only one of the police was unwounded. He had dug himself into the bank beside the road and had not fired any cartridges from his rifle magazine nor had he used the ammunition from his sling. Leaning against a wall, as though resting, was an elderly sergeant who was to have retired on pension next day. He was dead and fell on his face when touched. He had been compelled to go on patrol by the Tans in the party. Sergeant Creegan, who had been wounded in the lorry, was again severely injured when the grenade exploded. Splinters from his rifle butt were driven into his stomach and groin.

When Malone came down the rough ground by the Salmon house he saw the front door was open and he wondered what had happened to the Widow, as intermingled fire from rifles, Lewis gun and rifle grenades had crossed the roof and sides of her house during the action. Inside, settled at the turf fire, was the Widow Salmon. She blew a good puff of smoke from her pipe as she turned her head. 'Did ye kill all the black bastards?' she asked. A door borrowed from her house was carried down to be used as a stretcher for the badly-wounded Creegan. When the wounded Sergeant was lifted on to it, he saw Tom Kitterick near him. 'Is this what you did to me, Tommy?' he asked, 'after I saved you that day I saw you in the workhouse?'

Some time previously the Westport workhouse had been raided and Kitterick and Tom Gavin were inside, in the hospital. They had managed to get out of the building, but evidently some of the raiders had seen them.

When Creegan and another constable were carried up to the cottage, the Widow Salmon at first refused to allow them to be brought inside her door. She was, perhaps, remembering the bitter land war and the resistance displayed on the land beside her home. 'No peeler will darken my door', she said stubbornly, but relented after some persuasion and prepared a drink for the two wounded who remained outside in the open under the warm sun. She sent a pillow for Creegan and a rug to keep him warm. The Column men helped to bandage the wounded and as they lighted cigarettes a spate of talk soon relieved the tension of the uneasy constabulary. Suddenly Heavy and Ring, who had come back across the bog, noticed that the second policeman, Cullen, was tearing up a piece of paper. When questioned, he asserted that the paper was a private letter, but when it was examined it was found to contain a list of Westport men who might have been concerned in the ambush at Kilmeena.

THE HARD ROAD TO CARROWKENNEDY

Column men clustered around the lorry, examining the armoured plates with interest. This protection, they thought, was better for their opponents than if they had been 'firing from behind hedges'. Yet the hedge had proved to be stronger than the steel which at near distance did not effectively resist rifle bullets. Kilroy, who had an experimental mind where material was concerned, fired a few bullets into the steel to satisfy himself about resistance or otherwise. The men handled captured rifles with as much care as if they had been gold ornaments from the National Museum. The Lewis gun was approached with hushed voices. Here was a source of power which had given strength to the enemy and was now to be their concentrated protection, even if only on occasions when ammunition could be afforded.

The other wounded police were carried up from the roadside. 'You chaps weren't at Kilmeena', said a Tan, 'for here you couldn't stick up a bloody finger but it would be shot off.'

John Madden brought the Lewis gun to Flaherty who had been a number one gunner in France. It was a good gun, he found, and was in perfect order. He examined some of the drums, then moved the Lewis into a covered position closer to the McGrale cottage. The unwounded constable from the tender was sent under a flag of truce to the cottage, but the RIC refused to come out and kept the police constable inside. He had been told to tell them that if any of the people in the house were injured as a result of the subsequent attack, they would be held responsible and they would pay dearly for it. The RIC were also told that if they refused to surrender the prisoners held outside might be shot. They were asked to allow the woman and her children to come out under a white flag, but there was no answer to this request.

Kilroy was talking to Madden about the problem of the McGrale house, saying he would have to move up more men under cover until they got above it on the hill, when the conversation was suddenly interrupted. Flaherty sprayed a few bursts of bullets across and back the thatched roof until the dried thatch flaked off as if it was being thudded by MacBirna's flail. Then he rattled bullets on the small windows until the glass disintegrated and the door was made a sieve. There came an excited cheer from the Column men when they realised that the enemy's main strength, the Lewis which had supported the police at Kilmeena, was now being used against them. A rifle with a dish cloth attached was slung out a window.

The police were slow to make up their minds. 'Come on out, quick' was shouted to them. There was a long silence. The RIC were uneasy about facing the men outside, and their recent histories stirred at the bottom of uneasy stomachs. 'Are you going to come out?' Then they walked out with their hands above their heads.

The Widow had a great welcome for her rescuers who came inside to gather up the police rifles. She made little of the damage done to her house. 'Oh, the door will do,' she said to some of the men who were examining the many holes in it. 'Sure, it'll make the kitchen fine and airy.'

The constabulary were not at all sure of themselves, it could be seen. Some must have felt their records put them beyond the pale of mercy, and the Tans probably expected to be shot, since there had been an order in the autumn of 1920 from General Headquarters to shoot Tans on sight. Brodie Malone went up to Sergeant Hallinan who stood uneasy by the roadside.

'I have you now, Hallinan,' said Malone.

'I know you have, Brodie,' replied the Sergeant. 'I know that well.'

When they were prisoners, with death as an expected corollary, some of the Royal Irish were anxious to show their desire to please, and eager to make use of the softening effect of the Christian name which in the easy intimacy of the West brought people closer.

Kitterick came running down the road and Hallinan saw the 'Peter' in his hand. 'Can I have a priest, Tommy,' he asked in uncertain voice.

'I'll priest you', said Kitterick determinedly, coming closer, as if he was ready to give the coup de grace to a salmon. Then he and Malone laughed. Their laughter, provoked by the Sergeant's fright, now eased his fear and he felt more hopeful.

A short time previously Malone had said to Kilroy: 'I suppose we'll shoot them, Michael,' as if he had expected an order. There was a pause. Then Kilroy spoke in his slow serious way.

'No, Brodie, we can't do it; our nature is not hard enough.'

The police stood to attention on the roadside. Then Kilroy noticed that blood from a Tan's boot was raddling the dry dust. 'Why didn't you tell me he was wounded,' he asked the head constable. The wounded Tan sat down and was shortly joined by his companions. Cigarettes were shared by the Column men who chatted with their prisoners. The police became reassured almost against their will, although they had already been told as they paraded that nothing would happen to them.

French, a notoriously aggressive Tan, was lying on the roadside near the bridge, but when he was moved he moaned. A man dipped his handkerchief into a stream so as to squeeze the water into the wounded man's mouth, but the Tan turned his head aside. 'I never took a drink from an Irishman in my life,' he said.

French it was who had faced up the rough ground to outflank the position, thinking that the Kilmeena weakness was being repeated. Now, when his pockets were searched by the roadside, a letter was found from his wife in England who had been anxious about him. She had dreamt that he was in trouble, rifles were lying around, and she saw him lying dead. The letter ended: 'So look after yourself, John.'

There was now respect for the cross-grained man who had spent his short bitterness in Westport, for in trying to help the other police he had met with that inexorable enemy, death. He had carried a pet jackdaw around the town with him, and when he dozed off in a pub the bird would peck at him. Whenever a stranger entered the bar where he was drinking with friendly civilians, the jackdaw gave him warning taps.

By this time rifles, revolvers, ammunition, boxes of grenades and machine-gun drums were piled together. The Column men now had good service rifles to carry with them and as they loaded themselves the weight increased. They had twenty-two extra rifles to bring with them, eight drums for the Lewis gun, several boxes of grenades, twenty-one revolvers and about six thousand rounds of rifle ammunition. The Lewis gun had been christened 'Mrs. Murphy' and the loaded ammunition drums became her 'wardrobe' which bore heavily on her retinue. This extra weight when distributed among the twenty-four column officers and men, twenty-one of whom were from the Westport battalion, made them a less limber fighting force. If they happened to meet British reinforcements in strength each man, except the machine-gun crew of two, would have two rifles to use in action. In case of retirement, if outpressed, their difficulties would be serious by reason of the excess of their virtues in armament. A small revolver which DI Stevenson had carried had an inscription on the gold-mounted handle. It was given by Sir Edward Carson to the DI's father when the elder Stevenson had been Head Constable of Glasgow. DI Stevenson had served in Erris, but immediately after Kilmeena he was transferred as an additional officer to Westport to keep the police more aware of danger.

Petrol was shaken from tins over the two lorries and the car. Flames spurted and roared; further petrol added to the furious blaze. A Tan named Upton suddenly doffed his tunic. 'That's the fifth rifle I've surrendered since I came to this bloody country,' he said, 'and I've enough of it now. So here goes.' He hurled the uniform tunic into the blazing lorry. 'Now I've finished with them, those RIC bastards,' he added.

Then Kilroy spoke to the police. He warned them that reprisals on houses would mean that RIC houses would be burnt first and that others would follow. If there was any shooting of IRA or civilians as a result of this encounter, the captured police would be held responsible, and if IRA wounded were not respected in future it would be hard on any further police captured. Some of the Column had abused the villagers within constabulary hearing, knowing well that the information, when passed on, would help their friends. A policeman had been released to carry information to Westport about the wounded men, who had been attended by John Madden, but who now needed a doctor and a priest. The constable was given a bicycle but when he tried to ride it he fell off when he had gone a few yards. The excitement had been too much for his straight guidance. Column men straightened out the damaged rim into shape and he mounted more surely the second time. When he came to the barracks in Westport the barracks orderly, O'Brien, would not allow him in, but when he shouted 'They're all killed and captured at Carrowkennedy', the door was opened and the messenger fell in on top of him. O'Brien, who was an elderly man, had been ordered out that morning on patrol, but an English Tan said, 'You're too old. I'll go instead of you for I want to get a crack at these damn Shinners.' That Tan who had relieved him was killed in the second lorry. Six police were killed and four wounded, of whom two were to die during the night.

The belligerent RIC garrison of Westport kept indoors that evening as soon as the firing was heard in the faint distance and they remained in until morning. The military from Castlebar, warned of Column movement from Westport, branched off the main Westport road towards Aghagower but they must have felt their way cautiously or have waited until daylight to move on a little further. Reinforcements which came on through Westport were careful. A priest was sent ahead and behind him troops and constabulary were closely interested in certain aspects of scenery. The captured Lewis gun, which had been made such good use of by a Column man the previous evening, was now a concentrated threat to the convoy. Their slow approach paid tribute to the expected use of the weapon.

The Column marched off jauntily along the bohereen to Clady. They told the people on the way not to mention the direction in which they moved. Then when they arrived at Peter O'Malley's at the end of the village, Kilroy had a talk with him while the men drank from milk-cans and ate home-made cake and butter rather than wait for the welcome tea which would have delayed them. Peter would tell the invading British that the Column had gone on towards the east, which would throw them off their immediate track. The RIC had also noticed the direction in which the Column had gone and they would naturally acquaint reinforcements. Had the men continued on as they purported to move, they could have been found near Aille and Castlebar, or towards Aghagower among the hills, but they turned back after a short distance when out of sight of the village, crossed the Leenane road below Cuslough, walked west and then north towards Durless below the Reek, which they reached at the dawning. Weapons and ammunition weighted them down as they went on, but the pleasure of victory straightened them up.

Here in Durless were the two houses of the Joyces — Black Pat's and Red Pat's. They were bachelors and the Column men had an easy freedom in their houses to which they always looked forward. These houses for them were 'No Woman's Land' and some of them knew that both the Black and the Red kept a welcoming sup in a bottle. Soon two wethers were skinned and a serious massacre of duck took place. Men dozed off under cover while smells of home-cured bacon mingled with bubbling scents from iron pots, as the Joyce brothers listened to the growing epic of Carrowkennedy from a succession of narrators and concerted speech. Their hosts were as anxious to listen as the hungry men were to eat. The meal itself was a gloss on the interpolated stories, and not until the last bone was carefully sucked did stomach pang and curiosity subside.

In the morning aeroplanes were busy. There was a landing field near Castlebar and another outside of Galway. From the air the entire mountain district was slowly searched. Auxiliaries came from Galway, as well as troops and RIC, and they added to nearby garrisons, swarming like bees over the fighting ground. Divisional Commissioner Cruise was in charge of the counties of Mayo and Galway. His work was to co-ordinate constabulary and military effectiveness and being himself a County Inspector of police he could use their espionage propensities to the full for the military benefit.

Divisional Commissioner Cruise questioned the Clady people closely but no one had much information to give him, except for Peter O'Malley. Peter's careful, precise and descriptive English had now a simple scope. The Commissioner was impressed and congratulated him. As a consequence an aeroplane overhead was signalled to in morse and it flew back to Castlebar with the Commissioner's important news, adding misinformation to the additional troops there. Meanwhile the objects of the British quest were savouring the hospitality of the Joyces on the bare ridge at Durless.

AFTERWORD
APRIL 1952

The men are now scattered. Many have found a livelihood in foreign lands, and some are already in their graves. The Cause for which they fought and were willing to give their lives, lives on, and it may be that those of us who still remain will yet witness its fulfilment and share in the complete freedom of all our country from foreign rule. If that privilege is not to be ours, we can but hand down the traditional love of freedom that has ever animated our race, to those who come after us, and pass on to join our departed comrades, thanking God to have lived in a generation that succeeded, at least, in driving the British invader out of twenty-six of our thirty-two counties.

— Peter J. McDonnell,
OC West Connemara Brigade IRA,
Commander West Connemara Brigade
Flying Column,

ERNIE O'MALLEY was born in Castlebar, County Mayo, on 26 May 1898. When he was eight, the family moved to Dublin where Ernie went to O'Connell Schools, later winning a scholarship to University College which he entered in the autumn of 1915.

During the Easter Rising of 1916, he became caught up in the cause of Irish nationalism, and joined the Irish Volunteers. By 1918 he could no longer live at home, as his parents were unsympathetic. He left medical school and became a full-time organiser for the Volunteers (IRA from 1919). From 1918 to 1921, travelling under difficult conditions, he was active in organising battalion and company units in some fourteen counties, reporting directly to Michael Collins, Director of Intelligence, or to Richard Mulcahy, Chief of Staff.

In the winter of 1920 he was captured at Inistioge, tortured, and sent to Kilmainham Gaol from which he escaped in February 1921. He returned to take command of the newly formed Second Southern Division, and until the Truce in July that year he was officer commanding five brigades. Republicans like O'Malley would not accept the Treaty with Britain, signed in December 1921, and his Second Southern broke away from GHQ the following April. On the outbreak of the Civil War at the end of June he became Assistant Chief of Staff of the Republican army, and was also OC of Leinster and Ulster. Badly wounded and captured in November 1922, he was held in prison until July 1924, the last Republican to be released.

Feeling there was no place for him in this new Ireland, O'Malley went first to Europe, then to America, to 'take up the threads of inscrutable destiny'. There he wrote *On Another Man's Wound,* his memoir of the war against the British, which has become the classic account of that struggle. He died in 1957. His memoir of the Civil War, *The Singing Flame,* was published posthumously.

INDEX

Adams, Private, 86
Allis, Dan, 41

Baker, Joe, 194, 195
Baxter, Captain, 98
Boland, ___, 34
Bouchiers, 142, 152
Bourke, ___, 127
Breen, Dan, 29, 42, 52, 53, 56, 65
Brennan, Michael, 29
Britt, Paddy, 32
Brown, ___, 173
Brugha, Cathal, 10
Bunting, Private, 86
Burke, Seán, 74

Cannon, ___, 173
Carew, ___, 45
Carson, Sir Edward, 200
Carty, 'The Yank', 41, 52
Cecil, Lord Robert, 190
Chambers, ___, 176
Chambers, John, 179, 180, 181-182
Chambers, Willie, 181
Churchill, Winston, 93
Clune, Archbishop of Perth, 94
Clune, Conor, 94
Clune, John, 72
Cohalan, Dr. (Bishop of Cork), 96
Cole, District-Inspector, 111
Collins, Micky, 112
Collins, Seán, 168
Collison, Jack, 135, 136, 138, 139, 140, 142, 143, 144, 145, 148, 149, 151, 152
Conlon, Dr., 34, 37, 39
Connole, Tom, 78
Connolly, John, 171-172, 173, 175
Connolly, Seán, 98, 100-101, 107

Conway, Father, 165, 167
Cooney, ___, 112
Costello, ___, 124
Cox, Pat, 187
Coyne, Batty, 194
Creegan, Sergeant, 166, 190, 196
Cromwell, Oliver, 94
Cronin, Felix, 136-137
Crowley, Timothy, 91
Cruise, Divisional Commissioner, 202
Cullen, ___, 196
Cummings, H. B., Brigadier-General, 92
Cummins, ___, 163
Curtain, Michael, 76

Dalton, Canon, 132
Daly, Paddy, 142
Davins, 29
de Valera, Eamon, 98
Devitt, Maureen, 77
Dohertys, 174
Doherty, Commandant, 51
Donovan, Tommy, 28, 31, 40
Duffy, Johnny, 185, 192, 195
Duffy, Luke, 104, 106-107, 109
Duffy, Paddy, 185, 192, 195
Duffy, Seán, 101, 107
Dwyers, 42
Dwyer, Bill, 33, 34, 46, 135, 148
Dyra, ___, 171, 172

Evans, ___, 112

Fallon, Martin, 114
Feeney, Padráic, 120, 129, 132
Finnegan, Dr. (Bishop of Kilmore), 96, 97

Flaherty, Jimmy, 193-194, 197
Flanagan, Tom, 78
Flannery, ———, 50, 57, 59, 62-63, 65
Flannigan, Susan, 79
Flynn, ———, 165, 166, 168
Foley, Jack, 37
French, John, 190, 191, 199
French, Lord, 91
Fudge, District-Inspector, 189

Gallaghers, 174
Gallagher, Steve, 73
Gavin, Tom, 196
Gaynor, Seán, (see also Brigadier), 136-137, 138, 139, 140, 142, 143, 144, 148, 149, 152, 153
Gibbons, Johnny, 173
Gilmartin, Dr. (Archbishop of Tuam), 97
Gleeson, ———, 46
Gleeson, Tim, 149
Glennon, Seán, 142, 151, 152
Gorman, Jim, 15, 16, 18-19, 20, 21, 26, 42, 46, 57-58, 59, 60-61, 63
Greenwood, Sir Hamar, 84, 87

Hallinan, Sergeant, 190, 191, 198
Hampson, Sergeant, 84, 85, 86
Hanlys, 31
Hanly, ———, 34, 37
Hannon, Canon, 85
Hastings, Darby, 191, 192
Hayden, George, 31
Heavey, Tom, 192, 195, 196
Henderson, Arthur, 87
Hennessey, Patrick, 85, 86
Hennessey, Séamus, 68, 70, 73-74, 75
Henry, Denis, 190
Hoare, Rev. Dr. (Bishop of Armagh), 97
Honan, ———, 77
Horan, Ned, 189
Hughes, 'Cushy', 104, 111
Hughes, Michael, 168, 179

Ibberson, Lieutenant, 125
Igoe, Eugene, 46

Johnson, Dr. Samuel, 189
Jordan, Paddy, 160-161, 166-167, 168
Joyce, 'Black Pat', 202
Joyce, Nurse, 168
Joyce, 'Red Pat', 202

Kanes, 174
Kane, ———, 192, 195
Keane, ———, 77
Keenan, Constable, 86
Kelly, Tim, 163
Kennedy, Paddy, 142, 150-151
Kennelly, Dan, 73, 74, 75
Kenny, Seán, 145
Kilgon, Private, 86
Kilroy, Michael, 128, 160, 161, 165, 166, 167, 168, 171-172, 173, 175, 182, 185, 188, 192, 194, 195, 197, 198-199, 200, 201
King, ———, 38
Kinnane, Paddy, 42, 46, 57, 58, 60, 61
Kitterick, Tom, 172, 173, 185, 186, 189, 191, 196, 198

Lally, ———, 127, 129
Leavy, Seán, 101
Lehane, Dan, 77, 80
Lehane, Pake, 79
Lehane, Pat, 74
Lendrum, Captain, 82-83
Linane, P. J., 78
Lloyd George, David, 94
Lucans, 169
Lynch, Liam, 99

MacBride, Dr., 170
MacCormack, Captain, 134
MacCurtain, Tomás (Lord Mayor of Cork), 46
McDonnell, Constable, 85
MacDonnell, Jack, 171, 173, 178, 195
McDonnell, Peter J., 203
MacEvilly, James, 166, 168
McEwan, Private, 86
McGrale, Widow, 186, 193, 195, 197, 198
McLeod, Lance-Corporal, 86

INDEX

McLoughlin, Private, 86
MacMahon, ___, 81
MacMenamins, 174
MacMenamin, ___, 174–175
MacNamara, Michael, 83–84
Madden, Dr. John, 162, 166, 168, 170–171, 172, 173, 179, 185, 188, 197, 200
Madden, Pat, 102, 104, 106, 107–108, 109, 111
Magner, Canon, 91
Maguire, Tom, 118, 120, 121–122, 124–125, 127, 128, 129, 130
Maher, ___, 145
Malone, ___, 189
Malone, Brodie, 185, 188–189, 191, 195, 196, 198
Malone, Willie, 182
Mangan, Joe, 143, 153
May, Paddy, 118–119, 120
Meehan, Jack, 63
Middleton, Lord, 106
Moane, Ned, 179–180, 186
Moran, Jim, 171–172, 192
Moroney, ___, 69
Mullooly, Michael, 111–112
Mullooly, Pat, 111
Mulloy, Paddy, 167
Munroe, District-Inspector, 177
Murphy, Dr., 27
Murphy, Dr., 129
Murphy, Rev. J., 96–97
Murphy, Patsy, 33
Murray, Lt.-Colonel, 85

Nangle, Brian, 111
Neylon, John Joe, 72, 74
Nolan, Jimmy, 142, 154
Nolan, Paddy (Pat), 142, 154
Nolan, Tom, 167, 168

O'Brien, ___, 200–201
O'Brien, Michael, 118, 120, 121, 124–125, 132
O'Brien, Paddy, 142, 143, 144, 145, 148, 149, 150, 151, 152, 153
O'Brien, William, 186
O'Connor, Constable, 86
O'Connor, Paddy, 172
O'Connor, T. P., 84
O'Donnells, 174
O'Donnell, Tom, 168
O'Dwyer, Bill, 148
O'Dwyer, Michael, 72, 74, 75
O Flanagan, Father Michael, 94
O'Gorman, ___, 77
O'Leary, Thomas, 85, 86
O'Loughlin, John, 85, 86, 87
O'Malley, Owen, 187, 190
O'Malley, Owney, 190
O'Malley, Paddy, 167, 168
O'Malley, Peter, 201, 202
O'Neill, Ignatius, 67, 69, 70, 72, 74, 75, 76–77
O'Reilly, ___, 189

Peeke, Captain Sir Alfred, 106, 110
Pierce, ___, 167–168
Plunkett, Lord (Bishop of Tuam), 117

Quigley, ___, 51

Redmond, John, 101
Reilly, Ned, 11, 16, 18, 31, 32, 33, 34, 36, 37, 39, 42, 53, 63, 65
Ring, Joe, 185, 188, 195, 196
Robinson, Séamus, 11, 13, 18, 19–21, 23–25, 26, 27, 29, 30, 35, 38, 40
Ryan, Jack, 11, 16, 18, 31–32, 35, 42, 46, 65
Ryan, Martin, 53, 55–56
Ryan Lacken, Paddy, 43, 50, 52, 55, 58, 60, 62

Salmon, Widow, 185–186, 196
Sammon, ___, 79, 80
Shanahan, Phil, 13, 14, 16, 17, 31
Shanahan, William, 83–84
Simons, Frank, 104, 109
Skahill, Peter, 186
Sligo, Marquis of, 169
Stapleton, Jim, 42, 46, 57, 60
Staunton, John, 166, 168
Stevenson, District-Inspector, 192, 200

Sweeneys, 174
Sweetman, ____, 94
Swift, James, 168, 171, 179, 180

Treacy, Seán, 11, 13, 16, 18, 21, 25, 26, 27, 29, 31, 32, 33, 34, 35, 40, 42, 51, 52, 53, 56, 60, 62, 63, 65
Tudor, General, 93

Upton, ____, 200

Vaughan, Mick, 79
Vaughan, Peter, 70, 75

Walsh, Joe, 182
Walsh, Paddy, 15
Whelan, Dinny, 143, 152
Williams, Major, 134
Wilson, Sir Henry, 93
Wrynne, Séamus, 98